Inside Cover of book:

Lobbying, the legal bribery of politicians, is the most egregious example of how the U.S. Congress is corrupt to the core. Every American should be disgusted that central bankers own Congress and that lobbyists often write most of the legislation that is always against the best interests of the average American citizen. The plutocrats, the oligarchs, and the corporate elites do not wish to end poverty or cure diseases. They want to suck the life out of the economy, pay slave wages, and live in luxury.

The plutocrats have polluted the air we breathe, contaminated the water we drink, polluted our oceans with oil that makes fish unsafe to consume, destroyed the middle class, and used stolen money to bail out their greed. They made us slaves to their corporations, they own our property, and they shipped away most high-paying middle-class jobs. The only reason the fiat system hasn't already collapsed is the made in the U.S. system that forces nations such as China, Venezuela, Mexico, India, Russia, Argentina, Iran and many others to acquire dollars, which keeps dollar demand high. When the system unravels and the fiat system crashes, our paper money will be worth less than toilet paper. It is time to demand many things from the plutocrats Americans have allowed to control them since the Fed took over in 1913.

By Sheldon & Associates.

How the Plutocrats Turned Our Republic into an Oligarchy began more than four years ago when a few friends and I exchanged ideas. We wanted to alert all citizens to the corrupt laws being made while we watch silently and do nothing.

I would like to thank the following people for helping to put together this informative book.

Joyce H. Winfield, Ph.D, Writing Resources, Chief Editor
Shakhizada Suleimenova, L.N Gumilyov Eurasian National University
Joy Louison, R.N
Vicki L. Weatherman, Realtor and Time Share Specialist
Cristina Salcedo Co, R.N, B.S.N
Liehventz Jean Gilles, Insurance Consultant
Ashok G. Patel, Serial Entrepreneur and Life insurance Consultant
Peter Hines, Author

I would also like to thank Terry Bocas, Owner of Breed Art Work, for designing the cover art.

Copyright © 2018 Sheldon & Associates. All rights reserved. No part of this publication may be reproduced, distributed, or transmitted in any form or by any means, including photocopying, recording, or other electronic or mechanical methods, without the prior written permission of the publisher, except in the case of brief quotations embodied in critical reviews. For permission requests, please write to the publisher Sheldon Andre, 1560 Firethorn Drive, Wellington, FL 33414.

How the Plutocrats Turned Our Republic Into an Oligarchy

1 Introduction

2 Big Tobacco: The Most Corrupt Corporations in America

3 Big Pharma

4 Unsafe Water and Toxic Processed Food

5 Corruption on the High Seas

6 Conclusion: Is There Hope for a Better World?

I used to be a china doll
Who sat against a paneled wall
The world outside, I'd hear and see.
But nobody saw me.
I thought that I was very weak
But with glass eyes I could not weep
I had no fear
I did not care
I planned to stay asleep.
I thought that as a china doll
I would be crushed by one bad fall
But I was wrong
I'm very strong
Despite pain, I endure all.
They hit me and I did not cry
They poisoned me, I did not die
My tears flow freely when I weep
I do not have much time to sleep
So much corruption to expose
Takes all my strength as I compose
This book about the evil men
Who will pretend to be your friend.
Do not be fooled by plutocrats
They'll smile then stab you in the back
Their power must come to an end
Because they'll never be your friend.
Because of God, I have no fear
He'll help me get from here to there
The plutocrats control us all

The human world will someday fall
But without weapons I'll be saved
'Cause I refused to be enslaved
By men who forced their rules on me
I broke them all and now I'm free.

Introduction

"The money power preys upon the nation in time of peace and conspires against it in times of adversity. It is more despotic than monarchy, more insolent than autocracy, more selfish than bureaucracy. I see in the near future a crisis approaching that unnerves me, and causes me to tremble for the safety of our country. Corporations have been enthroned, an era of corruption will follow, and the money power of the country will endeavor to prolong its reign by working upon the prejudices of the people, until the wealth is aggregated in a few hands, and the republic is destroyed."

President Abraham Lincoln

"History records that the money changers have used every form of abuse, intrigue, deceit, and violent means possible to maintain their control over governments by controlling money and its issuance."

President James Madison

Both Abraham Lincoln and James Madison knew that greed might destroy America's republic if bankers began to control money and its issuance. The main purpose of central banks is to manage the currency, money supply, and interest rates. All of this is now done through central planning. Instead of leaving money and banking to markets–which would likely select the most workable money, instruments, and banking practices–America is stuck with a fiat currency controlled and manipulated by an organization that permits fractional reserve lending.

Fractional reserve banking is fraudulent because it entails lending money depositors have not authorized the bank to lend. The reason they can do this is because those working for the Federal Reserve System declare this to be legal and guarantee to print money to restore reserves if necessary. If this risk were privatized, they would have to be far more careful and be explicit with depositors as to what funds they will use to lend to borrowers.

The Bank of England, and later the Federal Reserve, completely divorced currency from money, resulting in a totally fiat, centrally planned monetary system. Today, central banks are able to print currency and buy debt instruments, effectively subsidizing debt. Under today's global fiat money monopoly, we don't see real competition that would alert us to problems with the market. The primary consequence of this is that central banks can now subsidize debt and suppress interest rates. This sends bad signals to lenders, savers and investors, encouraging present consumption unwarranted by real economic conditions that eventually must be corrected. For example, a real estate developer might think it a good idea to build an office building given a 13 percent interest rate. However, because that rate doesn't actually represent real goods, labor and resources spared through savings. As the project chugs along, the real estate developer will find the cost of inputs increasing until it becomes clear that the project won't be as profitable as initial prices and the interest rate had suggested. He defaults. If this happens throughout the economy, it makes clear how devastating central banking has been to sustainable economic development.

The fractional reserve banking system is the reason America has become an oligarchy because it is a banking system in which only a fraction of bank deposits are backed by actual cash on hand and are available for withdrawal. This is done to expand the economy by freeing up capital that can be loaned out to other parties. Many U.S.

banks were forced to shut down during the 1930s because too many people attempted to withdraw assets at the same time. That could easily happen again as long as the government spends money it does not have and then the economy and stock markets crash. The people who play games with our money–hedge fund managers, central bankers, and Wall Street crooks–control the future of our children. The plutocrats turned the republic we used to have prior to 1913 into an oligarchy, very similar to feudalism.

Socialism usually fails because most people are willing to make sacrifices to improve their family's quality of life. To save their spouse, child, or a close friend, people will often sell all they own. People have an instinct for self-preservation. They also have an instinct for their community and wanting to help family, friends, and countrymen. In a socialist system, there are many resources and a few people will be charged with managing these resources. This is a lot of work and responsibility. It is also a losing proposition. There will be times when the person in charge will have to turn down requests from his or her best friends in favor of someone needier. Most people who care about others find this job emotionally and psychologically exhausting.

Charismatic sociopaths want this kind of power and it always leads to corruption.

Fractional reserve banking makes a few people very rich, and it leaves everyone else constantly in debt (even if you are personally out of debt, the taxes you pay are your interest payments on an unpayable public debt). Fractional reserve banking creates compounding, unpayable public and private debt, which causes the cost of living to constantly go up for all Americans. How can U.S. citizens stop the central bankers who insist we continue to pay interest on an unpayable public debt that was created without their consent?

The people who work at the Fed are supposed to "pump and prime the well" when money needs to be expanded during times of deflation, and shrink the money supply during times of inflation. Their job is to maximize periods of economic growth in our country and minimize periods of recession by manipulating the money supply through the uses of interest rates. The reason they can't do the right thing is that outside pressure from the wealthy does not allow them to do that job. All politicians depend on the plutocrats for campaign contributions and this significantly impacts public policy and legislation. The New Deal was fought tooth and nail by America's elite and would never have passed if the citizens had not realized the only alternative was another civil war.

The continuing escalation of corporate interests managing the U.S. legislative process is transitioning the free market economy with an artificially overpriced market for most basic goods and services. That makes most products and services unaffordable to the majority of citizens. We already have that problem with private medical services, education, financial services, and medicine. If things do not change in the near future, the U.S. will suffer economic chaos.

There is only one mechanism for getting to the correct interest rates: a market of savers and borrowers. Savings constitute the supply and borrowing constitutes demand; the resulting price is the real rate average. When the Fed covers banks that lend more dollars than they have in savings, these banks can lend at much lower rates than if they were privately liable. This allows increased present consumption as well as debt-funded investments, which would not be permitted by market forces in the absence of a centrally planned monetary system.

The central bank has the power to authorize printing currency and issuing electronic currency. Debt buying suppresses interest rates far more than fractional reserve banking, because it expands the monetary base upon which fractional reserve lending can occur. The result is the business cycle. Because interest rates are necessarily targeted arbitrarily and according to political interests, they do not accurately coordinate the desire for future consumption with that for present consumption.

When the government creates a bond for a million dollars, it can be sold to a bank or other investors. In turn, it can be sold to the Fed for 1.02 million new dollars, and then the government is expected to pay the Fed the principle and interest. Because the dollars the Fed uses to buy this debt are not savings from people earning a living by producing goods and services, they don't represent real resources available. Nevertheless, they can still be lent to buy real things. An increase in the currency available to lend (supply) reduces the price of borrowing (interest rates). Interest rates went way down after the crash of 2008. This was allowed to happen because of quantitative easing, a program of creating money to buy debt to keep interest rates down.

Quantitative easing is an unconventional monetary policy in which a central bank purchases government securities or other securities from the market in order to lower interest rates and increase the money supply. Quantitative easing increases the money supply by flooding financial institutions with capital in an effort to promote increased lending and liquidity. It is considered when short-term interest rates are at or approaching zero, and does not involve the printing of new bank notes. A bank note is a negotiable promissory note, which a bank can issue. A banknote is payable to the bearer on demand, and the amount payable is apparent on the face of the note. Banknotes are considered legal tender; along with coins, they make up the bearer forms of all modern money. A bearer form is a security not registered in the issuing corporation's books, but which is payable to its bearer, that is, the person possessing it.

Unlike normal registered instruments, no record is kept of who owns bearer instruments or of transactions involving transfer of ownership. We can continue consuming and investing in the present regardless of the strain on real, scarce resources. Government intervention takes buying power away from consumers and weakens the power of demand. People are more than able to impact the market by the ability to choose who gets their business. Image is important when you have to compete. Large-scale boycotts for unacceptable behavior can tarnish names and hurt businesses.

Nations borrow from the International Monetary Fund (IMF) in order to pay interest on their mounting debts. Then, the IMF charges more interest. This does not alleviate poverty or further any development. It just creates a steady flow of wealth from borrowing nations to the money changers who now control the IMF and the World Bank. The permanent debt of Third World countries is constantly being increased to provide temporary relief from the poverty being caused by previous borrowing. These repayments already exceed the amount of new loans. A noble attempt to repay these loans is unsuccessful. World resources continue to be sucked into this vortex of greed because of the behavior of the central bankers around the world.

The result is a shortage of real savings (goods and services spared from present consumption for purposes of present investment in anticipation of future consumption). What this means is that investors will look at prices of inputs like building materials, labor, and the artificially low interest rate and conclude that they've found a profitable opportunity. As the project proceeds, the excess of present consumption and investment causes prices of inputs to rise to account for the subsidized interest rates, eventually revealing that the project is not as profitable as it once looked. Because this is an economy-wide phenomenon, many projects are sometimes abandoned in concert, causing a decline in employment and a crash in the value of financial instruments backing the projects. The crash actually stops the massive waste and allows investors to reallocate resources in more genuinely profitable ways.

Lobbying, the legal bribery of politicians, is the most egregious example of how the U.S. Congress is corrupt to the core. Every American should be disgusted that central bankers own Congress and that lobbyists often write most of the legislation that is always against the best interests of the average American citizen. The plutocrats, the oligarchs, and the corporate elites do not wish to end poverty or cure diseases. They want to suck the life out of the economy, pay slave wages, and live in luxury.

The plutocrats have polluted the air we breathe, contaminated the water we drink, polluted our oceans with oil that makes fish unsafe to consume, destroyed the middle class, and used stolen money to bail out their greed. They made us slaves to their corporations, they own our property, and they shipped away most high-paying middle-class jobs. The only reason the fiat system hasn't already collapsed is the made in the U.S. system that forces nations such as China, Venezuela, Mexico, India, Russia, Argentina, Iran, and many others to acquire dollars, which keeps dollar demand high. When the system unravels and the fiat system crashes, our paper money will be worth less than toilet paper.

The Supreme Court, in its *Citizens United* case, enshrined the right of corporations to buy government by removing limitations on campaign spending. However, money is not speech, corporations are not people, and America is no longer a republic like it once was. To get our republic back, we must make campaign contributions illegal and give the country back to "we the people." To do that, we need taxpayer-funded, single-payer campaign financing, which the plutocrats will never allow because they like the oligarchy. I hope that exposing the truth about the corruption will make people want to band together and fight back.

Many large corrupt corporations pay the politicians for voting their way, and it is legal for them to do so because of Citizens United legislation. It is not possible for corporations to have the same rights as individual human beings, while remaining immune to the laws that affect human beings. The biggest problem with this is that people have a soul and are capable of moral reasoning, whereas corporations have one goal only: profit. The Citizens United decision enabled the plutocrats to buy the candidates and legislators and control the U.S., and their goal is definitely not to live in an egalitarian society. The crony capitalism in this country is organized, systematized, legalized theft. It can only happen because the richest people control the legislative process and create laws that guarantee extreme inequality.

Many conservatives believe that government programs that seek to provide services and opportunities for the poor actually encourage dependence and reduce self-reliance. This is true to some extent, because the welfare system encourages single women who do not want to work to reproduce and get a bigger check with each baby they have. If welfare pays women more than the minimum wage jobs they qualify for, they won't have any incentive to work. Self-reliance gives people dignity and layoffs strip people of their pride. They don't need welfare. They need healthcare and education and they will be able to work and provide for themselves.

Conservatives who insist government is a necessary evil abhor the idea of redistributing income to assist poor people who are suffering. They think that people who earn a lot of money through hard work should not be forced by the government to pay taxes to make the country better for everyone. Social conservatives believe that private voluntary charitable organizations (especially faith-based charities) are responsible for helping the poor, *not* the government. The problem with this theory is that there are numerous legal but immoral ways to make money. It does not always take hard work. Hedge fund managers risk other people's money and suffer no losses if they make a mistake. That does not sound like hard work compared to building a house, trimming trees, mowing lawns, or standing up all day behind a cash register dealing with rude impatient people. Do these people work so hard that they deserve to make $200 million a year when most people make less than $50,000? Of course not.

When I sit at my desk in my air-conditioned office, I look out the window and see immigrants doing construction work in the 90 degree heat. Who is working the hardest? Me, the educated person with a laptop while I sip my Starbucks iced latte or those guys out there with the shovels? Conservatives do not like to acknowledge that not all people who are poor are lazy. Some of them work very hard and earn very little because they are exploited by the owners of many unethical corporations, as the next four chapters will demonstrate.

Governments are supposed to care about the quality of life of their citizens. Companies care only about profit and will never care about anything else. According to the International Labor Organization, Americans work far more hours than workers in Japan, Britain, and France. Conservatives are wrong when they say that most poor people are lazy. Most people prefer the dignity of work to collecting unemployment checks. Arthur Brooks, president of the American Enterprise Institute, views poor people not as liabilities to be managed by government, but rather, as human beings with tremendous untapped potential. This might be true for healthy poor people who can work hard, learn, and become successful, but it is certainly not true for everyone in society. The people in nursing homes have no untapped potential. They are completely reliant on either their family, their church, or their government.

Conservatives say that poor Americans benefit most from "free" markets, but that is a lie. The poor do not benefit from capitalism as much as the people at the top because even if they work very hard, they are rarely rewarded for it with a raise. The poor would be much better off in a country where their needs are met even if they cannot work based on their circumstances. We are all one major illness or accident away from losing our self-reliance.

According to Professor Joseph Stiglitz, a professor at Columbia University, "Lax enforcement of antitrust laws, especially during Republican administrations, has been a godsend for the top 1 percent. Much of today's inequality is due to rules that have been bought and paid for by the financial industry itself—one of its best investments ever. . . . When you look at the sheer volume of wealth controlled by the top 1 percent in the country, it's tempting to see our growing inequality as a quintessentially American achievement--we started way behind the pack, but now we're doing inequality on a world-class level. And it looks as if we'll be building on this achievement for years to come because what made it possible is self-reinforcing. Wealth begets power, which begets more wealth."[1] Professor Stiglitz is a former senior vice president and chief economist of the World Bank and is well known for his support of Georgist public finance theory and for his critical view of the management of globalization, of laissez-faire economists (whom he often refers to as free market fundamentalists). Georgism is an economic philosophy holding that, while people should own the value they produce themselves, economic value derived from land (including natural resources) should belong equally to all members of society. Developed from the writings of the economist and social reformer Henry George, the Georgist paradigm seeks solutions to social and ecological problems, based on principles of land rights and public finance which attempt to integrate economic efficiency and social justice.

Unless corrupt industries are properly regulated and workers are paid a decent wage and treated well, the poor will remain trapped at the bottom of the ladder. Future political candidates' every statement is gauged by whether or not they think their wealthy sponsors will approve. The big donors with wealth in the top .01 percent (they know who they are) tell those we elect—these are our requirements, and we have all the financing and PR apparatus set up ready for you to run a campaign. It is clear to me that the plutocrats have turned our republic into an oligarchy and it all began in 1913 when the Federal Reserve was created.

Ronald Reagan told us that government is the problem, not the solution. This line seems like a proposal about governing, but it is just the opposite: it's an admonition not to think, not to engage, not to govern. It is as if a scientist would say "The scientific method is the problem." To declare "government" the enemy is not to advance any political position, let alone any solution; it's to block the function of government so those whose power is constrained by it can do whatever they please. This is the opposite of politics. It's stealing the ball, killing the referee, and stopping the game.

The Republicans hate food stamp recipients, but they seem to have no problem with lazy rich children who inherit money and live on their interest income for the rest of their lives. Are trust-fund babies entitled to be lazy just because their parents were successful? Conservatives also seem to have no problem with corporate welfare, bribery, and elections being controlled by the richest people in the country. The Republicans' ceaseless tirade against "big government" is empty rhetoric intended to appeal to voters who haven't figured out who the real enemy is. Republican politicians are happy to see government's reach expand in the service of favored interests, provided they get something in return. Since the majority of corporate campaign contributions go to Republicans, they'd be depriving themselves of the chief source of their electoral success and the driving reason behind the hammerlock they now have on many state capitals if Citizens United were overturned. Far from showing any interest in curtailing the influence of big money, the Republicans are working very hard to tear down the few remaining barriers to total corporate control of our country.

According to Victor Fleischer, a law professor at the University of San Diego who studies the intersection of tax policy and inequality, "We have two different tax systems, one for normal wage-earners and another for those who can afford sophisticated tax advice. He adds, "At the very top of the income distribution, the effective rate of tax goes down, contrary to the principles of a progressive income tax system."[2]

After NAFTA was passed, Mitt Romney and his firm, Bain Capital, bought companies and moved them, lock, stock, and barrel, to places like China, India, and the Philippines to continue making the same products while cutting labor costs down to pennies on the dollar. The difference was pocketed as profit. Romney benefitted from tax policy that essentially allowed him to pay nothing to the U.S. government. This isn't trade–it is typical for big companies. The problem isn't trade policy, keeping a balance between exports or imports or any of the other economic factors in trade. The problem is when your own corporate citizens undermine the national economy to squeeze out more profit.

The feudal society to which the ruling class aspires is currently being created in East Hampton, Connecticut. The nobility arrive at their palaces on weekends in private helicopters with an army of staff and assistants in tow. There is a small merchant class running the infrastructure–shops and small businesses catering to their ever-changing whims. There is also a vast army of serfs and peasants, mostly foreign born, doing backbreaking labor, such as landscaping, masonry, housecleaning, and changing diapers for minimum wage. Due to the lack of affordable housing, they generally live in squalid conditions—mattresses on the floor where they collapse after 14-hour days for substandard wages.[3]

It is clear to most intelligent people that it is not the immigrants who are screwing the working class. It is the ruling class, the plutocrats, the powerful leaders of our oligarchy who are screwing the majority of Americans and those being screwed the most are our bravest men and women—our veterans. Those in the military are the real heroes and their children often live on food stamps because of their low pay. It is time to stand up for our troops, not for the corrupt politicians who ask them to risk their lives for their country. Blame the international bankers and stop letting them get away with redistributing income upward while the wives and children of our troops struggle to pay for enough food to eat.

Congressmen get paid well and the troops who risk their lives get paid little because the Fed has cheated the government of the U.S. and the people of the U.S. out of enough money to pay the nation's debt. This evil institution has impoverished many of the citizens of the U.S., has bankrupted itself, and has practically bankrupted our government. It has done this through the defects of the law under which it operates, through the maladministration of that law by the Fed, and through the corrupt practices of the rich vultures who control it.

Some people think that the Federal Reserve Banks are U.S. government institutions, but they are actually private monopolies that prey upon the people of the U.S. for the benefit of themselves and their foreign customers, foreign and domestic speculators and swindlers, and rich predatory money lenders. These financial pirates deceive us into granting of new concessions, which will permit them to cover up their past misdeeds and set again in motion their train of crime. These private credit monopolies were deceitfully and disloyally foisted upon this country by the bankers who came here from Europe undermined American institutions.

The bankers stole American money to finance Japan in a war against Russia. They created a reign of terror in Russia with our money and they instigated the separate peace between Germany and Russia, driving a wedge between the Allies. They financed Trotsky's passage from New York to Russia so he could assist in the destruction of the Russian Empire. They instigated the Russian

Revolution in 1917, and placed a large fund of American dollars at Trotsky's disposal in one of their branch banks in Sweden, so through him, Russian homes might be thoroughly broken up.

The National Monetary Association, under the chairmanship of the late Senator Nelson W. Aldrich in 1912, presented a vicious bill called the National Reserve Association bill. This bill is usually spoken of as the Aldrich bill, even though Senator Aldrich did not write it. He was merely the tool of the European bankers who had been scheming to set up a central bank in this country for nearly 20 years. In 1912, these bankers spent vast sums of money to accomplish their goal.

Many were opposed to the Aldrich bill for a central bank. The men who ruled the Democratic Party promised the people if they were returned to power, there would be no central bank established while they held the reigns of government. Thirteen months later that promise was broken and the Wilson administration, under the tutelage of sinister Wall Street figures, began the destruction of our republic.

The Federal Reserve Bank destroyed our way of doing business and forced upon us the tyranny from which the framers of the Constitution tried to save us. A half a million dollars was spent on propaganda organized by these bankers for the purpose of misleading public opinion. Congress also got the impression there was an overwhelming popular demand for the federal reserve and the kind of currency that goes with it, namely, an asset currency based on human debts and obligations.

Dr. H. Parker Willis appropriated the text of the Aldrich bill. The Federal Reserve Act was tainted with corruption from the start. Unlike government property, physical property is held under private deeds, and is subject only to local taxation. Some citizens do not realize that the Federal Reserve Bank is *not* part of the Federal government. It is a private corporation with a legislated monopoly on currency and credit that has allowed it to buy its paper currency for nothing more than the cost of the paper, ink, and labor, from the Bureau of Printing and Engraving (U.S. Treasury). Why are private unelected individuals controlling the American currency system and virtually running the entire country, the stock market, the banks, the lending rates, nearly everything? Where is any of this in the Constitution?

Because of this system, America has no permanent money supply like it used to have with gold and silver coins that never disappeared from the accounting books. American citizens are now enslaved to the repayment of debts for the loans from the banks. The entire nation is beholden to the bankers for its viability and solvency because there is no permanent money supply in existence. Thomas Jefferson warned us long ago that the issuing power must be taken from the banks and returned to the people where it rightfully belongs. If only people had listened to him, there would be no Federal Reserve and the government could print its own money interest free! Perhaps there is nothing we can do to stop sociopaths from rising up and attempting to control the world, but I'm not giving up without a fight and you shouldn't either.

Because of this so-called banking system (that is really not a banking system at all, but a sophisticated system of debt service), all of our national politics are directed by the bankers, not the government. The system is failing due to the Federal Reserve and the fractional reserve banking system that controls the government and the global markets. The market cannot perform as intended when there are those who can influence it to the extent the banks and governments can.

When the Nobel Prize-winning economist and professor at Columbia University, Joseph Stiglitz wrote the 2011 Vanity Fair magazine article entitled "Of the 1 percent, by the 1 percent, for the 1," the content supported Stiglitz's claim that the U.S. is increasingly ruled by the wealthiest 1 percent.[4] Some researchers have said that the U.S. may be drifting toward a form of oligarchy, as individual citizens have less impact than the ruling class and organized interest groups on public policy. In my opinion, America has already become an oligarchy. It began in the 1980s and we've been going down the wrong path ever since Reagan took office.

The Federal Reserve banking system was the worst thing that ever happened to America. Instead of Congress creating and controlling our money supply, it was forfeited into the hands of private greedy bankers' families in 1913. Many believe President Wilson was bribed but nobody has any definite proof. The term "Federal Reserve" is a misnomer. It is not federal and there is no reserve! It's all fiat money with nothing of true value backing it. The Federal Reserve System has plundered America into massive debt. How can the Federal Depositors Insurance Corp. guarantee that my $250,000 is safe in my online bank account if the Federal Reserve private bankers control the government? The Fed's power will someday end and it will likely cause a global depression as the fiat system collapses.

The Federal Reserve has played a large role in turbocharging the rise of billionaires worldwide. To boost growth following the global financial crisis of 2008, the Fed pumped record amounts of money into the U.S. economy through multiple rounds of quantitative easing—buying bonds on the public markets. The U.S. has since experienced its strong recovery of the postwar era, coupled with an unprecedented period of financial speculation. Most of the easy money was diverted into purchases of stocks, luxury homes, and other financial assets, as well as into financial engineering such as share buybacks designed to further increase the price of those assets.

When the world went off the gold standard in 1971, the global economy no longer was a capitalist enterprise, and instead it morphed into a purely credit one. This is why central banks have had to continuously create new money backed by nothing simply to be able to roll over outstanding debts, and formulate bubbles that make economies look like they are growing. Unfortunately, the world is now on a collision course for debt implosion, making it very difficult to bring the global economy back to equilibrium.

When you send money to the IRS to pay your taxes, the money does not go into the Treasury. It goes straight to the Federal Reserve Bank to service the debts owed to them. Wealthy bankers have usurped control and made us their financial slaves. What right do they have to control and manipulate our currency through their ownership of this bank, and then use their power to manipulate the policies of our government?

Our political system makes it impossible for decent human beings to get elected. To get on the ballot, candidates must convince many wealthy donors that an investment in their campaign would provide sufficient return. A mensch probably could not deal with that due to his moral values. Therefore, any candidate with a serious chance of winning will likely have a character that is amenable to prostitution. That candidate will have no trouble selling his or her soul to the donors who fully expect to receive privileges that are not available to ordinary citizens.

Once the candidates take office, they will have to devote most of their time to ensuring the continual satisfaction of donors, while soliciting additional donors to fund the next (even more costly) campaign. Money creates a "one dollar, one vote" perversion of democracy that excludes candidates and politicians who are decent human beings with compassion while selecting those who can best attract and retain donors. Unfettered capitalism combined with an unregulated financial sector will lead to extreme inequality.

In my opinion, the highest-paid employee should not make more than 50 times as much as the lowest-paid employee. The current 350:1 CEO/worker ratio is absurd. The banks got bailed out and the people got sold out, and Wall Street executives would do it again if they could. What gives them the right to gamble with other people's money and take no risks? Hedge fund managers legally risk other people's money and they lose nothing if they make a mistake. This is because they write the laws with loopholes so that what they do is unethical but not illegal. Every Organization of Economic Cooperation and Development (OECD) country gives their citizens healthcare whether they have a job or not. American politicians say America First and call America exceptional and it is -- exceptionally cruel to those who can't afford food, medicine, and shelter. The owners of the giant banks and giant corporations are motivated by profit and often don't care about human suffering as long as it happens elsewhere.

Some people believe the myth that the big corporations are job creators. When corporations have more profit than they expected, they give the money to the shareholders. The best solution to this problem would be putting an end to open-market stock buybacks. Rule 10B-18 is a Securities and Exchange Commission (SEC) rule that provides a "safe harbor" for companies and their affiliated purchasers when the company or affiliates repurchase the company's shares of common stock. In a 2003 update to Rule 10b-18, the SEC explained: "It is not appropriate for the safe harbor to be available when the issuer has a heightened incentive to manipulate its share price." In practice, though, the stock-based pay of the executives who decide to do repurchases provides this "heightened incentive." To correct this glaring problem, the SEC should rescind the safe harbor. The practice of tying executive pay to the stock price is undermining the formation of physical and human capital. It is very important that we rein in stock-based pay.

Many studies have shown that large companies tend to use the same set of consultants to benchmark executive compensation, and that each consultant recommends that the client pay its CEO well above average. As a result, compensation inevitably ratchets up over time. Studies also show that even declines in stock price increase executive pay. When a company's stock price falls, the board stuffs even more options and stock awards into top executives' packages, claiming that it must ensure that they won't jump ship and will do whatever is necessary to get the stock price back up.[5]

Because corporations aren't required to disclose daily buyback activity, it gives executives the opportunity to trade on inside information about when buybacks are being done. I think the SEC should stop allowing executives to sell stock immediately after options are exercised. Companies have been allowed to repurchase their shares on the open market with virtually no regulatory limits since 1982, when the SEC instituted Rule 10b-18 of the Securities Exchange Act. Under the rule, a corporation's board of directors can authorize senior executives to repurchase up to a certain dollar amount of stock over a specified or open-ended period of time, and the company must publicly announce the buyback program.

After that, management can buy a large number of the company's shares on any given business day without fear that the SEC will charge it with stock-price manipulation—provided, among other things, that the amount does not exceed a "safe harbor" of 25 percent of the previous four weeks' average daily trading volume. The SEC requires companies to report total quarterly repurchases but not daily ones, meaning that it cannot determine whether a company has breached the 25 percent limit without a special investigation. There is no rule preventing stock market manipulation through open-market repurchases.[6] The people conservatives believe are job creators are actually just manipulating the market with their stock buybacks, while wages stagnate and the middle class keeps shrinking.

Some inequality is necessary to reward talent, skills, and a willingness to innovate and take entrepreneurial risk. However, today's extremes of economic inequality undermine growth and progress and fail to invest in the potential of hundreds of millions of people. The rich get richer while the poor suffer. We should end tax and secrecy havens, offer equal access to vital services including health and education, and break the vicious spiral of wealth and power by which the rich manipulate our politics to enrich them even further. The increasing concentration of wealth in the hands of very few has deepened both ecological and economic crises, which in turn has led to an escalation of violence everywhere. The wealthiest use their financial power to bend laws and policy choices in their favor, further reinforcing their positions.

Inequality is not inevitable. Extreme inequality corrupts politics, hinders economic growth, and stifles social mobility. It is the result of policy choices. It fuels crime and even violent conflict. It squanders talent, thwarts potential, and undermines the foundations of society.

Lobbying, the legal bribery of politicians, is the most egregious example of how the U.S. Congress and large corporations are corrupt to the core. Every American should be disgusted that central bankers own Congress. Lobbyists often write most of the legislation that is passed, legislation that is always against the best interests of the average American citizen. The plutocrats do not care about ending poverty or curing diseases.

Human lives in America have been destroyed for the agenda of empire expansion, and for me, that makes it hard to be proud to be an American. Our politicians call America exceptional and it is -- exceptionally cruel to people who can't afford medical care, medicine, or shelter. The owners of the giant banks and giant corporations are motivated by profit and often don't care about human suffering as long as it happens elsewhere. There is only one meaningful public policy issue left in America, and that is whether public policy should be privatized as it is today through lobbyists and bribery. . .or whether public policy should be public through publicly, taxpayer-funded campaign financing. Legislators are nothing but fundraising chairmen.

The Federal Reserve Act signed by President Wilson funded the first world war and created the bubbles that burst in 1920 and 1929. Prices were allowed to readjust after the crash of 1920, ending it in only 18 months. After the crash of 1929, however, prices unfortunately were kept artificially high by further money printing, price controls, and purchasing of goods by the government. This turned a correction into a depression that lasted more than a decade. Keeping prices high by printing more money, aka quantitative easing, causes more problems than it solves.

President Richard Nixon took us off the gold standard in 1971 and he positioned the U.S. dollar as the de facto backing of every major world currency. With this new power, the central bank proceeded to subsidize debt heavily throughout the 70s, inflation rose, along with misallocations of capital, until the crash in the early 80s. Our money was completely replaced with fiat money distributed by the unconstitutional and privately owned Federal Reserve Bank. President Wilson's decision destroyed our republic. What our forefathers feared came true when this private banking cartel began to control the issuance of money. Fractional reserve banking creates compounding, unpayable public and private debt, which causes the cost of living to constantly go up for all Americans.[7]

On August 29, 2016, the Wall Street Journal had an article in the opinion section called "The Federal Reserve's Politicians." Every year the bankers meet in Jackson Hole, Wyoming. According to the Wall Street Journal's editorial board, "The Fed these days has more power than Congress. . . . Fed policies that raise asset prices have favored affluent stock owners over middle-class savers. . . no bank CEO can dare to disagree with the Fed on policy without fear of being destroyed."[8] The Fed has tremendous power over our lives. Changing that is necessary and it will not be easy, but we must all try.

Our forefathers were revolutionary to some extent, yet they still had a worldview limited to knowledge and technology that was not available in 1776. The idea that human beings have not and cannot evolve beyond what they were hundreds of years ago is nonsense. Judging from the wording in the Declaration of Independence and Constitution, the founding fathers clearly realized that the world would change as time passed. Because our founding fathers were afraid of a banking cartel, they clearly stated that if a government outlived its usefulness and inhibited liberty, it should be replaced or abolished. They knew long before 1913 what could happen, and they were correct.

When America was a much smaller country in the early 1800s, there were fewer people, who mostly made a living in agriculture and lived in rural, small towns. At that time, our government did not need to be huge. A banking system didn't need to be complex in the good old days. As cities formed, as America moved from an agrarian society to an industrial one, as the population exploded and all the problems inherent in an urban society evolved, government had to grow, new systems in financing and taxation had to develop. Unfortunately, these new systems led to far more corruption.

Many point at Venezuela and say this will happen in the U.S. if the government expands its safety net for the poor. Venezuela is an example of predatory lending that the IMF forced it into. Venezuela took on foreign debt instead of debt in its own currency. Its economy was dependent on one product—oil— and when the supply of oil started failing the economy suffered tremendously. This is not likely to happen in the U.S. in the near future because it is not in debt in a foreign currency. Unlike Venezuela, the U.S. does not depend on one product. The U.S. could support itself without foreign trade and Trump knows that or he would not have started a trade war. He does not care about the welfare of other countries because, as he has stated many times, America comes first.

Most people don't realize how human nature is corrupted by crony capitalism because this system brings out the worst in people. Most presidents and prime ministers are the malignant tumors that inevitably grow from an economic system based on injustice. It will always exponentially increase inequality, stress, and conflict. Despite the survival instinct, human nature is not set in stone. It is malleable. Unfortunately, the current government is not the answer because it has become so corrupt that it is too difficult to fix. The debt vortex has no bottom. Whoever has the money and power, aka the ruling class, has the ultimate freedom. For the rest of us, freedom is a mere illusion. The plutocrats control the world. The wealthy are getting wealthier but the rest of society is not. How can the economy be fixed without fixing our increasing inequitable distribution of wealth? Most conservatives deny it, but this is the ultimate function of good governance—preventing the excessive concentration of wealth in fewer and fewer hands.

If you accept that the Fed cannot be abolished, then deficit spending during a recession makes sense. Most people cannot envision a world where quantitative easing is wrong, but I can. In my opinion, if we compete more than we cooperate, we are all doomed. If we must be warriors, we should fight our real enemies—the plutocrats who control us and their systems of control that oppress us.

Fighting other nations and fighting each other is pointless bloodshed. Eliminating the ruling class is necessary if Americans want to stop living as puppets with the most powerful sociopaths in the world pulling the strings.

Footnotes

[1] Stiglitz, Joseph. The Great Divide: Unequal Societies and What We Can Do About Them. *W.W. Norton & Company.* NY London Co. 2015

[2] Scheiber, Noam and Cohendec, Patricia. (Dec. 29, 2015) For the Wealthiest, a Private Tax System That Saves Them Billions. *New York Times.* (Retrieved from http://www.nytimes.com/2015/12/30/business/economy/for-the-wealthiest-private-tax-system-saves-them-billions.html?emc=edit_th_20151230&nl=todaysheadlines&nlid=71338060&_r=1)

[3] Kristof, Nicholas. (May 30, 2015) Our Water-Gounging Food Factory. *New York Times.* (Retrieved from (http://www.nytimes.com/2015/05/31/opinion/sunday/nicholas-kristof-our-water-guzzling-food-factory.html?_r=0

[4] Stiglitz Joseph E. "Of the 1%, by the 1%, for the 1%" *Vanity Fair*, May 2011.

[5] Lazonik, Willilam. Profit without Prosperity. (September 2014) *Harvard Business Review.* (Retrieved from https://hbr.org/2014/09/profits-without-prosperity).

[6] Lazonik, William. Profit without Prosperity. (September 2014) Harvard Business Review. (Retrieved from https://hbr.org/2014/09/profits-without-prosperity).

[7] Perkins, Darren The Root of Your Economic Problems. Retrieved from (http://www.apfn.org/Mind_Control/money/root.htm)

[8] The Federal Reserve's Politicians (August 29, 2016) Wall Street Journal Editorial Board.

Big Tobacco: The Most Corrupt Corporations in America

"The modern conservative is engaged in one of man's oldest exercises in moral philosophy; that is, the search for a superior moral justification for selfishness."

John Kenneth Galbraith

Big Tobacco includes Philip Morris International, British American Tobacco, Imperial Brands, Japan Tobacco International, and China Tobacco. Together they hold more than 60 percent of world market power/share. Since 2008, tobacco companies have spent millions on lobbying and have doled out millions to members of Congress. In 2009, the industry convinced Congress to prohibit the Food and Drug Administration (FDA) from ordering the removal of nicotine or banning cigarettes entirely.[1] Considering the FDA is supposed to prevent companies from trying to make us sick for profit, it is obvious that they are not doing a very good job of protecting citizens from carcinogens and other toxins.

In the 1950s and 1960s, tobacco companies did internal research showing tobacco to be very harmful and addictive. They mounted a public campaign that said otherwise and helped fund scientific research that was later shown to be dubious. The tobacco companies were found guilty of a massive scheme to defraud the public. Big Tobacco sells a known carcinogenic poison and people willingly buy it because it is so addictive that they can't quit. That is, in my opinion, as corrupt as it gets. The only reason the FDA allows this poison to be sold is because of how much revenue it brings in. When someone invented a vaping pipe that allows addicts to gradually lower their nicotine intake and quit, Big Tobacco executives convinced the FDA to ban vaping. The ban was eventually overturned after legal fights.

Cigarette manufacturer Philip Morris/Altria is the most unethical among cigarette companies because of its marketing strategies. The company targets children and exploits their vulnerability to addictive habits. The company has also employed underage girls to hand out free Marlboro cigarettes to children at clubs and concerts. In 1970, President Nixon signed the Cigarette Smoking Act, which required tobacco manufacturers to place warning labels on everything they sell and banned them from advertising on radio or television. Banned from the airwaves, tobacco companies turned to films for the next two decades, making a concerted effort to place their products in cinemas across the country and let 40-foot celebrities do the advertising for them. One company provided free cigarettes to actors and directors in hopes of convincing them to light up on screen. Starting in the '90s, public opinion turned toward smoking by actors shown on the big screen. Studies showed the pervasive influence smoking in movies had on teenagers.

With their advertising opportunities dwindling, cigarette companies turned to a tried and true strategy of all drug dealers. They intentionally began to make their products far more addictive. According to a 2004 study by the Massachusetts Department of Public Health, between 1998 and 2004 nicotine content in 92 out of the 116 brands of cigarettes was found to have risen about 10 percent. The tobacco industry made approximately $93.4 billion in 2016.[2] In 1994, the top executives of seven tobacco companies testified under oath that they did not believe nicotine is addictive, but documents were leaked showing they knew nicotine is addictive.[3] While there are many other corrupt corporations–including Big Pharma, Big Food, and Big Cruise Ships, Big

Tobacco is the most corrupt of them all, selling a known addictive carcinogen to people for profit.

In 1998, The Tobacco Master Settlement Agreement was enacted between Philip Morris Inc., R.J. Reynolds, Brown and Williamson, Lorillard and the attorney general of 46 states. The states settled their Medicaid lawsuits against the tobacco industry for recovery of their tobacco-related health-care costs; the companies were also exempted from private tort liability regarding harm caused by tobacco use. In exchange, the companies agreed to pay, in perpetuity, various annual payments to the states as compensation for some of the medical costs of caring for persons with smoking-related illnesses.

It is now well known that smoking causes many kinds of cancer, heart disease, and respiratory illnesses that are fatal for many patients. Nicotine is physiologically and psychologically addictive. The overwhelming majority of smokers are strongly dependent on nicotine and this is a substantial block to smokers' quitting. In addition, secondhand smoke is a serious public health hazard, including causing childhood diseases such as asthma and bronchitis, and is a cause of lung cancer and heart disease in adults.

By the late 80's, Philip Morris and lawyers acting on its behalf set up a covert program in Europe. Scientists were recruited to counter the negative publicity surrounding secondhand smoke because smoking generates enormous funds for government and its principal partners, the giant transnationals. To ban cigarette sales would be the economic equivalent of removing around 5 percent of national governmental income, which is not a practical proposition; it could plunge some states into bankruptcy, which is not acceptable to anyone. In the U.S., many states depend on smoking-generated funds to maintain their solvency. The tobacco tax revenues funds keep them afloat.

The FDA has declared war on vaping because it allows users to slowly reduce nicotine until they can quit. For manufacturers and sellers of vapor products in the U.S., this is a death sentence for their businesses. Vendors were given two years to file their pre-market tobacco applications. Each application for approval to sell "tobacco products" will probably cost over a million dollars, and there is no guarantee it will be accepted by the FDA.[4]

The requirements are extreme. Aside from exacting scientific studies, businesses have to prove that their product has a net benefit to the overall public health. It is an impossible standard to meet. Without several million dollars to gamble with, nobody can survive if these regulations go into effect. That's intentional on the FDA's part. They know vaping businesses can't live in the world of extreme and exacting tobacco regulations and compliance.[5]

While claiming to protect children from nicotine addiction, Mitch Zeller, Director of the Center for Tobacco products, have delivered a carefully crafted ban of all vapor products, except perhaps cigalikes (e-cigarettes) made by Big Tobacco. They justify this by quoting the National Youth Tobacco Survey (NYTS) that shows vaping among teenagers growing. They ignore the National Institute on Drug Abuse survey that showed only 20 percent of teens use nicotine in their e-cigs. The NYTS surveys don't even ask whether teens use nicotine — or if they're regular users or have just taken a single puff in the last 30 days. They also ignore that all surveys show teen smoking at its lowest level ever. It's not about smoking anymore; the objection is now to nicotine itself.

The FDA specifically says that nicotine in pharmaceutical products like patches and gum is not addictive or dangerous, but they ignore all evidence that the same may be true of nicotine in vapor products and couch their regulation in the lie that they're protecting kids. Cigarettes, the most dangerous consumer product in the history of the world, remain available and protected from competition.[6] Because many states will go bankrupt without the revenue generated by cigarette sales, and because Big Pharma will lose money if medical marijuana is used to replace many of their dangerous pills, the FDA is allowing poison to be used while banning all medicinal plants, especially cannabis, which treats numerous diseases, including the lung cancer caused by smoking cigarettes. How dare they sell us the poison and ban treatments?

Medical Marijuana

The U.S. government officially denies any therapeutic use of cannabis even though cannabinoids act as neuroprotectants that limit neurological damage following ischemic insults, such as stroke and trauma, or in the treatment of neurodegenerative diseases, such as Alzheimer's disease, Parkinson's disease and dementia. Cannabis can do the opposite, and can protect against age memory loss and dementia. Cannabis protects the brain by reducing inflammation, but the lie that it has no medical use remains for political reasons: many will lose money if medical marijuana replaces the need for many synthetic pills made by pharmaceutical companies.

Chronic inflammation is at the root of many illnesses, including Alzheimer's. Gary Wenk, PhD, professor of neuroscience, immunology, and medical genetics at Ohio State University, has studied how to combat brain inflammation for over 25 years. He said, "PET imaging studies of humans have shown that after age thirty the brain gradually displays increasing evidence of inflammation. With advancing age, brain inflammation continues to worsen leading to a decline in the production of new neurons, called neurogenesis, that are important for making new memories."[7]

He coined the phrase "one puff is enough" after suggesting that ingesting small amounts of cannabis over years can be enough to protect the brain against inflammation. Wenk said, "The evidence available from studies of humans and animal models of Alzheimer's disease do indicate that long-term, low-dose daily exposure, during mid-life, to the complex blend of compounds found in the marijuana plant can effectively slow the brain processes underlying Alzheimer's disease."[8]

Cannabis is also a powerful antioxidant, protecting against toxic build up in the brain. As well as patenting cannabinoids as neuroprotectants, U.S. government officials also named them antioxidants. An aging brain has a tendency to accumulate excessive levels of glutamate, a neurotransmitter that is involved with nerve cell signaling. This can lead to glutamate toxicity, an overstimulation of the cell and ultimately cell death. When glutamate causes cellular damage, it becomes an excitotoxin. Excitotoxicity is viewed as a potential cause of many neurodegenerative diseases of the central nervous system, as well as strokes and hearing loss.[9]

Cannabis also helps promote new brain cell growth, may slow the progression of some neurodegenerative diseases, and sometimes makes Alzheimer's patients less agitated. Cannabis protects the brain against serious brain trauma.

Traumatic brain injury (TBI) is caused by a severe blow to the head. Resulting symptoms can include cognitive problems such as headache, difficulty thinking, memory issues, attention deficits, mood swings, and frustration. TBI is also proving to be an exciting area of research for the potential therapeutic use of cannabinoids. Tetrahydrocannabinol (THC) in particular has been shown to protect the brain from long-term damage following a traumatic injury. Professor Yosef Sarne of Tel Aviv University's Adelson Center for the Biology of Addictive Diseases at the Sackler Faculty of Medicine found that very low doses of THC administered over a long period of time were found to protect the brain from long-term cognitive damage in the wake of injury from hypoxia (lack of oxygen), seizures, or toxic drugs. Not only did he find that THC minimized the damage to the brain following an injury, but if administered before the incident it could prevent brain injury from occurring in the first place.[10]

Cannabis can also limit brain damage resulting from strokes. Whereas a TBI is caused by an external force injuring the brain, a stroke occurs due to a thickening of the arteries. There is poor blood flow to the brain, resulting in cell death. Both Cannabidiol (CBD) and Tetrahydrocannabinol (THC) have the ability to block the neurotransmitter glutamate, produced when the brain is deprived of oxygen, once again come to the fore as a way to limit cell death following a stroke. Numerous studies show the potential benefits for protecting our aging brains against neurodegeneration and even injury from external forces.

The federal government's official position is that marijuana, as a Schedule 1 substance, has no medical value. Nothing could be further from the truth. Even many of the most ardent critics of medical marijuana do not agree with the Schedule 1 classification (drugs that supposedly have no medical use), because it has impeded the ability to conduct research on the plant's potential therapeutic uses. Every U.S. commission or federal judge who has studied the evidence has agreed that cannabis is a very safe drug. The U.S. holds a patent on medical marijuana, Patent No. 6630507, which explains how cannabinoids are neuroprotectants and can treat neurological damage following ischemic insults, such as stroke or trauma. Given that the U.S. holds this patent, the federal government's position that marijuana has no medical value is absurd.

The short-term effects of marijuana include immediate, temporary changes in thoughts, perceptions, and information processing. Marijuana can cause impaired reaction time and motor skills. It can also cause food cravings, so it is not helpful to obese people who want to lose weight. The cognitive process most clearly affected by marijuana is short-term memory. People under the influence of marijuana usually have no trouble remembering things they learned previously. However, they temporarily display diminished capacity to learn and recall new information. This diminishment only lasts for the duration of the intoxication. A large-scale, longitudinal study of adult marijuana users corroborates earlier findings that marijuana produces no long-term negative effects on cognitive skills in adults.

Young, developing brains are more susceptible to harm from marijuana than adult brains. Some recent studies suggest that regular use in teenage years leads to a permanent decrease in IQ. Many people believe if medical marijuana is legalized will make it easier for teenagers to buy. The opposite is true. Rates of marijuana use among young people has been shown to decrease when a state adopts medical marijuana. Access is decreased when marijuana moves from street drug dealers to inside licensed dispensaries, where a prescription is needed to buy marijuana.

While cannabis intoxication varies with psychological set and social setting, the most common response is a calm, mildly euphoric state in which time slows and sensitivity to sights, sounds, and touch is enhanced. A possible adverse reaction to marijuana may be a panic or anxiety attack. Many opponents of medical marijuana make much of the purported link between marijuana use and mental illness. However, there is no compelling evidence to support the claim that marijuana is a causal risk factor for developing a psychiatric disorder in healthy individuals.

CBD and THC are the principal cannabinoids found in cannabis. When ingested they have a synergistic effect, reducing inflammation, controlling spasms, and preventing neurological damage. Medical evidence clearly indicates that cannabis is the best overall treatment for all diseases where the neurological system of the body is disrupted, because this disruption is counteracted by the neuroprotective properties of cannabis. Cannabis helps young children with epileptic seizures without getting them high, and it helps adults live with chronic pain and enjoy life in greater dignity and comfort.

Cannabinoids are one of the best disease- and cancer-fighting treatments available. Cannabinoids refer to any of a group of related compounds that include cannabinol and the active constituents of cannabis. They activate cannabinoid receptors in the body. The body produces compounds called endocannabinoids and they play a role in many processes within the body that help to create a healthy environment. Cannabinoids also play a role in immune system generation and re-generation. Cannabinoids can also be found in cannabis and have been proven to reduce cancer cells as they have a major impact on the rebuilding of the immune system. While not every strain of cannabis has the same effect, more and more patients are seeing success in cancer reduction in a short period of time by using cannabis.[11]

It is possible that certain cannabinoids will slow cancer growth and reduce the spread of some forms of cancer, but we won't know until the federal ban is overturned and medical professionals can do further research. There have been a few early clinical trials of cannabinoids in treating cancer in human beings. Some doctors are skeptical because even if a substance can cure cancer in lab animals does not mean that it can cure cancer in human beings, but it is certainly worth a try. Many people believe that marijuana oil can cure their cancer and are blogging about it online, and no one knows for sure whether or not the conclusions they came to from their research are correct. The United States should begin to find out. The first step is to make medical marijuana legal in every state so researchers will be allowed to study it without fear of legal consequences. Big Pharma does not want that to happen because they would lose too much money if a cure for cancer were found.

According to a study conducted at Harvard University in 2016, cannabis has the ability to halt tumor growth. Researchers have shown that lung cancers that over-express epidermal growth factor receptor (EGFR) are usually highly aggressive and resistant to chemotherapy. THC that targets cannabinoid receptors CB1 and CB2 is similar in function to endocannabinoids, which are cannabinoids that are naturally produced in the body and activate these receptors. The researchers suggest that THC or other designer agents that activate these receptors might be used in a targeted fashion to treat lung cancer.[12]

Researchers found that when THC was administered to mice with implanted lung cancer tumors, these tumors shrunk in half after just three weeks. The researchers think that THC is beneficial for preventing tumor growth because of its ability to activate molecules that stop the cell's life cycle. There is also a possibility that THC interferes with vascularization and angiogenesis, two processes in the human body which contribute to the growth of cancer cells.

In 2016, a clinical trial testing THC as a treatment against cancer growth was oomplctcd in human glioblactoma (a malignant tumor affecting the brain or spine). For three weeks, researchers injected standard doses of THC into mice that had been implanted with human lung cancer cells. Tumors were reduced in size and weight by about 50 percent in treated animals compared to a control group. These researchers believe that THC may also interfere with angiogenesis and vascularization, which promotes cancer growth.[13]

European Study

In 2009, Spanish researchers found that THC is effective in killing brain cancer cells through a function called autophagy. The Spanish researchers found that when they gave THC to mice with implanted human tumors, autophagy was initiated and as a result the tumor growths were reduced. In addition, two human patients who were suffering from aggressive tumor growth in their brain also displayed signs of autophagy after they received THC through intracranial administration. The study, which was co-led by the University of Anglia in England, says they've found a way that THC could reduce tumors. According to Dr. Peter McCormick from the University of Anglia: "THC, the major active component of marijuana, has anti-cancer properties. This compound is known to act through a specific family of cell receptors called cannabinoid receptors." The team is still unsure of which receptor has played the most vital role in shrinking tumors.[14]

The National Cancer Institute (NCI) publicly features studies on cannabis and its ability to kill cancer cells. The National Institute on Drug Abuse (NIDA), a research agency that is also funded by the government, has also admitted that cannabis extracts can reduce cancer cells and even kill specific cancer cells. On its website, NIDA clearly states, "Evidence from one cell culture study suggests that purified extracts from whole-plant marijuana can slow the growth of cancer cells from one of the most serious types of brain tumors." NIDA's statement acknowledges the findings of a 2014 study published in Molecular Cancer Therapies. The study as conducted by researchers of St. George's University in London. According to study results, THC and CBD were able to cause "dramatic reductions" in glioma tumors in mice subjects. Glioma is responsible for 80 percent of malignant brain tumors in humans. It has been known since 1974 that cannabis can often kill cancer cells and save lives. In 1974, a study conducted by the Medical College of Virginia revealed that THC "slowed the growth of lung cancers, breast cancers and a virus-induced leukemia in laboratory mice, and prolonged their lives by as much as 36 percent."[15]

The FDA keeps out the medicines we need and lets in all the poison. Many people get rich and do not care how many others suffer. The only reason cannabis is not legal according to the federal government, but tobacco remains legal, is because of greed and corruption. Remember, many states would go bankrupt without the revenue from selling cigarettes. On average, a person dies every 19 minutes in this country from a legal prescription drug overdose, while it is virtually unheard of to die from a marijuana overdose.

The potential medicinal properties of marijuana and its components have been the subject of research and heated debate for decades. THC has proven medical benefits in particular formulations. The FDA has approved THC-based medications, including dronabinol (Marinol®) and nabilone (Cesamet®). They are prescribed in pill form for the treatment of nausea in patients undergoing cancer chemotherapy and to stimulate appetite in patients with wasting syndrome due to AIDS. If the synthetic version works, why not just let patients use real cannabis instead? The obvious answer is because it cannot be patented if in natural form and Big Pharma can't make any money on it.[16]

An NIDA-funded study done by the RAND Corporation in 2016 showed that legally protected access to medical marijuana dispensaries is associated with lower levels of opioid prescribing, lower self-report of non-medical prescription opioid use, lower treatment admissions for prescription opioid use disorders, and reduction in prescription opioid overdose deaths. The reduction in deaths was present only in states with dispensaries (not just medical marijuana laws) and was greater in states with active dispensaries.[17] NIDA is funding additional studies that will provide data relating to medical marijuana and opioids, including:

- effects of access to medical marijuana on substance use, including non-medical use of prescription opioids,

- mental and physical functioning of a cohort of pain patients seeking medical marijuana treatment, and

- the impact of medical marijuana policies on health outcomes.

Though none of these studies are definitive, they cumulatively suggest that medical marijuana products have a role in reducing the use of opioids needed to control pain. More research is needed to investigate this possibility, and cannabis needs to be removed from Schedule 1 for more research to be done.[18]

Unfortunately, the Justice Department under Attorney General Jeff Sessions has blocked the Drug Enforcement Administration (DEA) from taking action on numerous requests to grow marijuana to use in research. According to one senior DEA official, "The Justice Department has effectively shut down this program to increase research registrations."[19] Sessions has called medical marijuana "hyped, maybe too much" and signaled that he is skeptical about the benefits of smoking it.[20]

Cannabis is not the only plant that has medicinal properties, but it is the only one that is not addictive and safe for adult use. Another plant called kratom is a tropical deciduous tree (Mitragyna speciosa) native to Southeast Asia, with leaves that contain mitragynine, a psychoactive mind-altering opioid. Kratom is consumed for mood-lifting effects, pain relief, and as an aphrodisiac. It can cause sensitivity to sunburn, nausea, itching, sweating, dry mouth, constipation, increased urination, and loss of appetite. If used in a small amount, it can be a good thing for some people. It can cause increased energy, sociability, and increased alertness, much like sativa cannabis. However, unlike cannabis, in high doses kratom can cause sedation and euphoria because it is an opioid and it is addictive. Cannabis is not addictive and is far more medicinal than kratom. Unlike cannabis, kratom has withdrawal symptoms including muscle aches, insomnia, irritability, hostility, aggression, emotional changes, runny nose, and jerky movements. The only treatment option is to cut down slowly and quit.

Kratom is the most natural opioid to treat and relieve chronic pain and help addicts get off opioids, as long as they use small amounts during withdrawal and don't decide to use a large amount to get the euphoric effects. Any drug that can induce euphoria is dangerous in the hands of an addict. If there is a choice between kratom and the synthetic Suboxone/buprenorphine, I'd pick the natural opioid plant to reduce withdrawal symptoms. If you are not addicted to opioids and are not in pain, it is best to avoid them completely.

Given how useful cannabis is, why isn't more research being done on the drug? The first hurdle is getting it out of Schedule 1, which is for drugs with no medical use. The second hurdle is Attorney General Jeff Sessions who won't let scientists do the necessary research to prove it has medicinal value — for many horrific diseases. Sessions is a nightmare for medical marijuana, either because he is an idiot or because he is being bribed. More than two dozen federal applications to grow cannabis for research purposes have stalled as Sessions' Justice Department lets them languish. The bottleneck is frustrating researchers and doctors eager to learn more about the drug. In 2017, the DEA began accepting applications to grow cannabis for research, a move meant to improve the availability and quality of cannabis for use in scientific research. As part of the approval process, the DEA needs Sessions' sign-off and he refuses to help. A senior DEA official told the Washington Post that "the Justice Department has effectively shut down this program to increase research registrations."[21]

As a result of what's effectively become a DOJ roadblock, researchers are struggling to access cannabis to conduct experiments into the drug's health effects and clinical applications. There is currently only one place in the U.S. that has permission from the federal government to grow and distribute cannabis: the University of Mississippi. The cannabis that is grown there barely even looks like cannabis.[22] Why isn't this stuff being grown in the Emerald Triangle in California where they have high quality cannabis?

In a Post Traumatic Stress Disorder (PTSD) study in 2017, researchers at Johns Hopkins University were slated to help conduct the multi-year clinical trial. The nonprofit group Multidisciplinary Association for Psychedelic Studies, or MAPS was the sponsor. Soon after the researchers received the government-grown cannabis, Johns Hopkins pulled out of the study because the quality of cannabis produced at the University of Mississippi was too poor to study for medicinal benefits.[23]

Government officials do not want anyone to find a cancer cure or find a way to treat diseases without Big Pharma's pills. They appear willing to do anything to prevent people from using cannabis as medicine for anything.

Medical marijuana treats all of the following diseases:

Human Immunodeficiency Virus (HIV) and Acquired Immunodeficiency Syndrome (AIDS)

The human immunodeficiency virus is a retrovirus that invades cells in the human immune system, making it highly susceptible to infectious diseases. According to the World Health Organization, more than 500,000 Americans have died from HIV and AIDS. More than one million U.S. citizens are living with the disease. Cannabis is used by many people living with HIV/AIDS to treat symptoms of the disease, as well as the side effects of various antiretroviral medications. HIV/AIDS patients who inhale cannabis four times daily experience reduced HIV-associated neuropathy.

Alzheimer's Disease

Alzheimer's disease (AD) is a neurological disorder of unknown origin that is characterized by a progressive loss of memory and learned behavior. Patients with Alzheimer's are also likely to experience depression, agitation, and appetite loss. No approved treatments or medications are available to stop the progression of the disease. Cannabinoid therapy provides symptomatic relief to patients afflicted with AD and also moderates the progression of the disease, other than Namenda and Aricept, that can only slow it down but not cure it.

ALS (Lou Gehrig's Disease)

Amyotrophic lateral sclerosis (ALS) is a fatal neurodegenerative disorder that is characterized by the selective loss of motor neurons in the spinal cord, brain stem, and motor cortex. An estimated 30,000 Americans are living with ALS, which often arises spontaneously and afflicts otherwise healthy adults. There is no cure for this disease. More than half of ALS patients die within 2.5 years following the onset of symptoms. Cannabinoids delay ALS progression, moderate the disease's development, and alleviate some ALS-related symptoms such as pain, appetite loss, depression and drooling.

Antibiotic Cannabidiolic Acid Disinfectants

Young unbudded hemp plants provide extractions of cannabidiolic acids (CBDs). There are many antibiotic uses for the cannabidiols, including treatment for gonorrhea. The acid side of tetrahydrocannabinol cannabidiols occur inversely to the amount of the plant's THC and is therefore more acceptable to prohibitionists because it won't get a person high.

Cancer

Gliomas (tumors in the brain) are especially aggressive malignant forms of cancer, often resulting in the death of the patient within 1-2 years following diagnosis. There is no cure for gliomas and most available treatments provide only minor symptomatic relief. Studies demonstrate cannabinoids' ability to act as antineoplastic agents, particularly on glioma cell lines.

In addition to cannabinoids' ability to moderate glioma cells, separate studies demonstrate that cannabinoids and endocannabinoids can also inhibit the proliferation of other various cancer cell lines, including breast carcinoma, prostate carcinoma, colorectal carcinoma, gastric adenocarcinoma, skin carcinoma, leukemia cells, neuroblastoma, lung carcinoma, uterus carcinoma, thyroid epithelioma, pancreatic adenocarcinoma, cervical carcinoma, oral cancer, biliary tract cancer, and lymphoma. Some experts now believe that cannabinoids retard cancer growth.

Chronic Pain

Many Americans live with chronic pain. Some of these people suffer from neuropathic pain, a condition that is associated with numerous diseases, including diabetes, cancer, multiple sclerosis, and HIV. In most cases, the use of standard analgesic medications such as opiates and nsaids (non-steroidal anti-inflammatory drugs) is ineffective at relieving neuropathic pain. Further, long-term use of most conventional pain relievers, including acetaminophen, opioids, and nsaids, is associated with a host of potential adverse side effects, including stroke, heart attack, and death resulting from an accidental overdose. Marijuana is sometimes a better pain reliever than opioids.

Epilepsy

Epilepsy is a central nervous system disorder characterized by uncontrollable twitching of the arms or legs and/or seizures. Charlotte Figi is a child whose brain was locked in nearly nonstop seizure activity. She suffered from Dravet syndrome, a severe form of intractable epilepsy. Doctors tried seven different medications, stringent diets and high-dose supplements without success. For Dravet Syndrome, the American Epilepsy Society says that there are approximately one million people for whom existing therapies do not control their seizures. Information from the society said anecdotes about medical marijuana "give reason for hope" and said the society supports "well-controlled studies that will lead to a better understanding of the disease and the development of safe and effective treatments." One marijuana strain helps to ease painful symptoms of epilepsy and it has been named after one little girl who is getting her life back one day at a time. It's called Charlotte's Web, and it does not get children "high" because it is a strain of marijuana high in CBD and low in THC. GW Pharmaceuticals now offers a cannabinoid product called Epidiolex®. It is a liquid formulation of pure plant-derived cannabidiol, or CBD, which is in development for the treatment of a number of rare childhood-onset epilepsy disorders.

Fibromyalgia

Fibromyalgia (FM) is a chronic pain syndrome of unknown etiology. The disease is characterized by widespread musculoskeletal pain, fatigue, and multiple tender points in the neck, spine, shoulders, and hips. An estimated 3 to 6 million Americans are afflicted by fibromyalgia, which is often poorly controlled by standard pain medications.

Inhaled marijuana can significantly alleviate neuropathic pain. Preclinical data indicates that cannabinoids, when administered in concert with one another, are more effective at ameliorating neuropathic pain than the use of a single agent. The administration of single cannabinoids such as THC or CBD produce limited relief compared to the administration of plant extracts containing multiple cannabinoids, terpenes (oils), and flavonoids (pigments).

GI Disorders

Gastrointestinal (GI) disorders, including functional bowel diseases such as irritable bowel syndrome (IBS) and inflammatory bowel diseases such as Crohn's disease (CD) and colitis, afflict more than one in five Americans, particularly women. While some GI disorders may be controlled by diet and pharmaceutical medications, others are poorly moderated by conventional treatments. Symptoms of GI disorders often include cramping, abdominal pain, inflammation of the lining of the large and/or small intestine, chronic diarrhea, rectal bleeding, and weight loss.

Observational trial data reports that cannabis therapy use is associated with a reduction in Crohn's disease activity and disease-related hospitalizations. Researchers at the Meir Medical Center, Institute of Gastroenterology and Hepatology in Israel assessed disease activity, use of medication, need for surgery, and hospitalization before and after cannabis use in 30 patients with Crohn's disease. Authors reported, "All patients stated that consuming cannabis had a positive effect on their disease activity" and documented "significant improvement" in 21 subjects. Researchers found that subjects who used cannabis significantly reduced their need for other medications.

Glaucoma

Fourteen percent of all blindness in America is caused by glaucoma, a progressive loss of vision. Cannabis smoking would benefit 90 percent of our 2.5 million glaucoma victims, and it is two to three times as effective as any current medicines for reducing ocular pressure. Cannabis use has no toxic side effects to the liver and kidneys; nor is there any danger of the occasional sudden death syndromes associated with the legal pharmaceutical glaucoma drugs and drops.

Hepatitis C

Hepatitis C is a viral disease of the liver that afflicts an estimated four million Americans. Chronic hepatitis C is typically associated with fatigue, depression, joint pain, and liver impairment, including cirrhosis and liver cancer. Patients diagnosed with hepatitis C frequently report that cannabis treats both the symptoms of the disease as well as the nausea associated with antiviral therapy.

Huntington's Disease

Huntington's disease (HD) is an inherited degenerative brain disorder characterized by motor abnormalities and dementia produced by selective lesions in the cerebral cortex and the striatum. There are presently no known conventional therapies available to alleviate HD symptoms or delay HD-associated striatal degeneration. Cannabinoids may possess potential to moderate the advancement of the disease, but more research is necessary to determine whether or not marijuana is capable of delaying the progression of this disease.

Lung Cleaner and Expectorant

Cannabis is the best natural expectorant to clear the human lungs of smog, dust, and the phlegm associated with tobacco use. Marijuana smoke effectively dilates the airways of the lungs, the bronchi, opening them to allow more oxygen into the lungs. It is also the best natural dilator of the tiny airways of the lungs, the bronchial tubes, making cannabis the best overall bronchial dilator for many people. Many joggers and marathon runners feel cannabis use cleans their lungs, allowing better endurance.

Migraine Headache Relief

While tobacco constricts arteries, cannabis opens them. Because migraine headaches are the result of artery spasms, combined with over-relaxation of veins, the vascular changes cannabis causes in the covering of the brain (the meninges) usually make migraines disappear.

Multiple Sclerosis

Multiple sclerosis (MS) is a chronic degenerative disease of the central nervous system that causes inflammation, muscular weakness, and a loss of motor coordination. Over time, MS patients typically become permanently disabled and, in some cases, the disease can be fatal. According to the U.S. National Multiple Sclerosis Society, about 200 people are diagnosed every week with the disease—often striking those only 20 to 40 years of age.

Clinical and anecdotal reports of cannabinoids' ability to reduce MS-related symptoms such as pain, spasticity, depression, fatigue, and incontinence are plentiful. Studies suggest that cannabinoids may also inhibit MS progression, in addition to providing symptom management. Sativex® is an oromucosal spray of a formulated extract of the cannabis sativa plant that contains the principal cannabinoids THC and CBD, as well as specific minor cannabinoids and other non-cannabinoid components. GW Pharmaceuticals developed Sativex to be administered as an oral spray, whereby the active ingredients are absorbed in the lining of the mouth, either under the tongue or inside the cheek. GW's licensing partners are commercializing Sativex for MS spasticity in 16 countries outside the United States.

Nausea Relief

"Marijuana is the best agent for control of nausea in cancer chemotherapy," according to Dr. Thomas Ungerleider, who headed California's Marijuana for Cancer research program from 1979 to 1984. It can also provide effective nausea relief caused by motion sickness. Pharmaceutical nausea-control drugs come in pills that are often swallowed by the patient, only to be thrown back up. Because cannabis can be ingested as smoke, it stays in the system and keeps working even if vomiting continues.

Parkinson's Disease

Parkinson's disease (PD) is a disorder of the brain that causes muscular tremors resulting in difficulty walking, controlling movement, and coordination. PD is caused by a change in the homeostasis of the endocannabinoid system in the body. The nerve cells that produce dopamine are slowly destroyed without which the brain cannot properly process messages. The result is loss of muscle function that worsens over time.

There is no cure for Parkinson's disease. A few pharmaceutical drugs have been developed to control the symptoms, but, as with many pharmaceutical drugs, the side effects are usually severe. Our bodies naturally produce the cannabinoids that are also present in marijuana. Cannabinoids influence various body processes such as pain and inflammation. Therefore, if someone consumes marijuana, it can assist those natural chemicals to function more efficiently. Cannabinoids can relieve symptoms, such as dystonia (painful, prolonged muscle contractions that cause involuntary repetitive twisting and sustained muscle contractions) and dyskinesia (a disease that causes repetitive, unintentional movements that may be described as twitching), which are prevalent in patients suffering from the Parkinson's disease.

Rheumatoid Arthritis

Rheumatoid arthritis (RA) is an inflammatory disease of the joints characterized by pain, stiffness, and swelling, as well as an eventual loss of limb function. Rheumatoid arthritis is estimated to affect about one percent of the population, primarily women. It is possible that cannabinoid therapy could provide symptomatic relief of joint pain and swelling, as well as suppressing joint destruction and disease progression. Throughout South America until the 1960s, rheumatism was treated with hemp leaves and/or flower tops heated in water or alcohol and placed on painful joints. In fact, this form of herbal medicine is still widely used in rural areas of Mexico, Central and South America, and by California Latinos for relief of rheumatism and arthritis pain.

Relaxation and Sleep

Cannabis lowers blood pressure, dilates the arteries, and reduces body temperature an average of one-half degree, thereby relieving stress. Evening cannabis smokers often report more relaxation and restful sleep. Prescription sleeping pills (the so-called "legal, safe and effective" drugs) are often just synthesized analogs of truly dangerous plants like mandrake, henbane, and belladonna.

References

[1] Quit Smoking Now Participant Workbook, The Florida AHEC Network, Co. 2010, Florida AHEC Network. www.flahec.org

[2] Malony, Jennifer and Chaushuri, Sabira (April 24, 2017) Tobacco's Surprise Reabound. Wall Street Journal.

[3] Malony, Jennifer and Chaushuri, Sabira (April 24, 2017) Tobacco's Surprise Reabound. Wall Street Journal.

[4] McDonald, Jim, (May 9, 2016). FDA Ban on Vaping: The Ugly Truth. Retreived from http://vaping360.com/fda-ban-on-vaping-the-ugly-truth/)

[5] McDonald, Jim, (May 9, 2016). FDA Ban on Vaping: The Ugly Truth. Retreived from http://vaping360.com/fda-ban-on-vaping-the-ugly-truth/)

[6] McDonald, Jim, (May 9, 2016). FDA Ban on Vaping: The Ugly Truth. Retreived from http://vaping360.com/fda-ban-on-vaping-the-ugly-truth/)

[7] Biles, Mary. (January 7, 2017) 7 Ways Cannabis Can Protect The Brain. Wake Up World. (Retrieved from https://wakeup-world.com/2017/01/07/7-ways-cannabis-can-protect-the-brain/)

[8]Biles, Mary. (January 7, 2017) 7 Ways Cannabis Can Protect The Brain. Wake Up World. (Retrieved from https://wakeup-world.com/2017/01/07/7-ways-cannabis-can-protect-the-brain/)

[9]Biles, Mary. (January 7, 2017) 7 Ways Cannabis Can Protect The Brain. Wake Up World. (Retrieved from https://wakeup-world.com/2017/01/07/7-ways-cannabis-can-protect-the-brain/)

[10]Biles, Mary. (January 7, 2017) 7 Ways Cannabis Can Protect The Brain. Wake Up World. (Retrieved from https://wakeup-world.com/2017/01/07/7-ways-cannabis-can-protect-the-brain/)

[11]Walia, Arjun. (August 23, 2013). 20 Medical Studies That Show Cannabis Can Cure Cancer. (Retrieved from http://www.collective-evolution.com/2013/08/23/20-medical-studies-that-prove-cannabis-can-cure-cancer/)

[12]Smith, Dana (October 5, 2016) Harvard Goes All In and Says Cannabis Reduces Tumor Growth. Retrieved from (https://cannabis.net/blog/medical/cannabis-can-reduce-tumor-growth-says-harvard-university)

[13]Smith, Dana (October 5, 2016) Harvard Goes All In and Says Cannabis Reduces

Tumor Growth. Retrieved from (https://cannabis.net/blog/medical/cannabis-can-reduce-tumor-growth-says-harvard-university)

[14]Smith, Dana (October 5, 2016) Harvard Goes All In and Says Cannabis Reduces Tumor Growth. Retrieved from (https://cannabis.net/blog/medical/cannabis-can-reduce-tumor-growth-says-harvard-university)

[15]National Institute on Drug Abuse. (Retrieved from https://www.drugabuse.gov/publications/marijuana/marijuana-safe-effective-medicine)

[16]National Institute on Drug Abuse. (Retrieved from https://www.drugabuse.gov/publications/marijuana/marijuana-safe-effective-medicine

[17]Results from the 2015 National Survey on Drug Use and Health: Detailed Tables, SAMHSA, CBHSQ. Retrieved from (http://www.samhsa.gov/data/sites/default/files/NSDUH-DetTabs-2015/NSDUH-DetTabs-2015/NSDUH-DetTabs-2015.htm. Accessed October 11, 2016.)

[18]Results from the 2015 National Survey on Drug Use and Health: Detailed Tables, SAMHSA, CBHSQ. Retrieved from

(http://www.samhsa.gov/data/sites/default/files/NSDUH-DetTabs-2015/NSDUH-DetTabs-2015/NSDUH-DetTabs-2015.htm. Accessed October 11, 2016.)

[19] Zapotosky, Matt, and Barrett, Devlin. (Aug. 15, 2017) DEA says Justice Department has "effectively shut down" marijuana research. Washington Post. Retrieved from (http://www.thecannabist.co/2017/08/15/marijuana-research-justice-department-dea/86116/)

[20] Zapotosky, Matt, and Barrett, Devlin. (Aug. 15, 2017) DEA says Justice Department has "effectively shut down" marijuana research. Washington Post. Retrieved from (http://www.thecannabist.co/2017/08/15/marijuana-research-justice-department-dea/86116/)

[21] Peake, Gage. (Aug. 15, 2017) Is Jeff Sessions' Justice Department Actively Blocking Cannabis Research? Leafly. (Retreived from https://www.leafly.com/news/politics/jeff-sessions-justice-department-actively-blocking-cannabis-research)

[22] Peake, Gage. (Aug. 15, 2017) Is Jeff Sessions' Justice Department Actively Blocking Cannabis Research? Leafly. (Retreived from https://www.leafly.com/news/politics/jeff-

sessions-justice-department-actively-blocking-cannabis-research)

[23]Peake, Gage. (Aug. 15, 2017) <u>Is Jeff Sessions' Justice Department Actively Blocking Cannabis Research?</u> Leafly. (Retreived from https://www.leafly.com/news/politics/jeff-sessions-justice-department-actively-blocking-cannabis-research)

Chapter 3 Big Pharma

"Hell is empty and all the devils are here."
Shakespeare, The Tempest

Prior to 1973, it was illegal in the U.S. to profit from healthcare. The Health Maintenance Organization Act (HMO) of 1973 passed by President Nixon changed that. The HMO Act authorized for profit independent practice associations and HMOs in which HMOs may contract with associations that, in turn, contract with individual physicians for services and compensation. State laws vary on such issues as whether HMOs may deny patient access to medical specialists without first going through the primary care provider.

The pharmaceutical companies have been corrupting how the healthcare industry delivers services for many years. They prey on the weakest members of society, those who will die if they cannot pay for their medicine. Patent monopolies create a problem for people paying for drugs that would most likely be affordable in a free market. Medicine should not be a luxury that only rich people can afford, but it is because the pharmaceutical companies control the government, unlike in any other first world country. They produce a drug, create a patent, monopolize the market, and then demand prices that can only be paid by very wealthy people (or people who live in countries with socialized medicine). How many taxpayers want a law that does not allow the government to negotiate drug prices for Medicare? Probably none, unless they work in the pharmaceutical industry and personally get rich from letting poor elderly sick people suffer and die.

When these corporations break the law and get caught, they are assessed a fine which comes nowhere near the profits they made by breaking the law. That is why they keep breaking the law. It works for them. Pharmaceutical companies buy the drafting of laws from politicians. Their unethical and damaging behavior makes it clear that they put profit before people. Conservatives usually say they fear a corrupt government more than they fear a corrupt corporation. However, if that corrupt corporation provides medicine, clean water, safe food, electricity, Internet service, or anything people need to live a decent life, it is just as bad as having a corrupt government. The Food and Drug Administration (FDA) does not test any of the drugs it approves. Instead, the agency relies entirely on the testing done by the advocates presenting their products for approval. The prices charged make it obvious that the concern is far more about maximizing profit, not curing diseases and saving lives.

According to Greg Ip, a writer for the Wall Street Journal, one federal study found that over one year, roughly 10 percent of generics (weighted by share of Medicaid purchases) more than doubled in price due to lack of competition.[1] Big Pharma is an enormous monopoly. It is very difficult for generic manufacturers to prove to the FDA that their drug has the same quality, strength, purity, and stability as the branded drug. Ip believes that imports of generics from countries with governmental negotiated prices should not be as controversial as patent-protected drugs because they involve far less expensive and risky research. Big Pharma makes the rules and the government goes along with it, most likely in exchange for some type of quid pro quo they won't tell us about.

The oligarchs own and control national governments who do their bidding. What makes Big Pharma unique in the U.S. is that the industry outspends all others on lobbying/bribing the government, including both Congress and the FDA. Professor

Donald W. Light, Joel Lexchin, and Jonathan J. Darrow have evidence that about 90 percent of all new drugs approved by the FDA over the last 30 years have little or no advantages compared to the existing drugs. We cannot trust the FDA to carry out its historic mission to protect the public from harmful and ineffective drugs. The bar for "safe" is too low and, over the past 30 years, approved drugs have caused an epidemic of harmful side effects, even when properly prescribed.

Donald W. Light, Ph.D. received his doctorate degree in sociology from Brandeis University and is a professor of comparative health policy at Rowan University, School of Osteopathic Medicine. He has written extensively about health care policy, the sociology of the medical profession, the U.S. health care systems, as well as pharmaceutical policy. He is a founding fellow of the Center for Bioethics at the University of Pennsylvania, and was a Fellow for a year at the Edmond J. Safra Center for Ethics at Harvard University in 2012. According to Light, Lexchin, and Darrow: "institutional corruption has occurred at three levels. First, through large-scale lobbying and political contributions, the pharmaceutical industry has influenced Congress to pass legislation that has compromised the mission of the FDA. Second, largely as a result of industry pressure, Congress has underfunded FDA enforcement capacities since 1906. Finally, industry has commercialized the role of physicians and undermined their position as independent, trusted advisers to patients."[2]

Light believes that ever since the pharmaceutical industry started making large contributions to the FDA for reviewing its drugs, the FDA has sped up the review process. This has resulted in drugs being approved that are significantly more likely to cause serious harm, hospitalizations, and deaths. Most new FDA policies are likely to increase the epidemic of harms. Regulations prohibit the FDA from comparing the effectiveness of new drugs or from assessing their cost-effectiveness, and this keeps the pharmaceutical companies happy.

In the U.S., many people die annually due to unnecessary surgeries, medical errors, infections acquired at the hospitals, and adverse side effects from medications. In addition, "testing and FDA criteria approval provide little or no information to clinicians on how to prescribe new drugs, a vacuum filled by company-shaped evidence that misleads physicians to prescribe drugs that are less safe and effective than indicated by evidence that the FDA possesses."[3] The proportion of new products with clinical advantages seems to have moved from about 1 in 8 down to 1 in 12, while the proportion with serious harms has gone up from 1 in 5 towards 1 in 3 as the number of drugs given priority status increases.[4]

According to an article in the Wall Street Journal entitled "Doctors Attack Drug Prices," Jeannie Whalen states that the average price of new cancer drugs in the U.S. increased five to tenfold over 15 years, to more than $100,000 a year in 2012. Ayalew Tefferi, hematologist at the Mayo Clinic, believes that pharmaceutical companies charge high prices to increase their profits long after they recoup the money they spent on research and development.[5] Tefferi is right. That is why Medicare Part D must be changed.

Any elderly person without supplemental insurance to Medicare will never be able to afford brand name medicine because of the cost. Big Pharma claims they spend all their money on research and development of new drugs to improve our health. In truth, they spend more on advertising than on research. Why do I have to keep watching commercials for diseases that I do not have? This is where their money is going, into advertising and TV commercials so people will ask their doctors for whatever they saw on TV. Fewer dollars are spent for researching and developing better drugs. Why would they want to cure anything when they make all their money on treatment?

Science journalist Matthew Herper had an interesting idea how to solve the drug patent problem. He suggested giving a new drug's inventor the exclusive right to sell the drug for 15 years after the day the drug is approved by regulators, and don't start the clock until the FDA approves the drug. In the current system, patents protect drugs from copycat versions for 20 years after the drug is developed. This makes pharmaceutical companies angry because it can take eight years or more after development to accumulate enough data to get a drug past the FDA. Once the patent expires, 80 percent of the brand name sales can vanish within a year as generic competitors enter the market.[6]

Drug companies file patent upon patent to try to extend the life of a single drug and then turn to litigation to stifle generics. Big Pharma's biggest loophole is clear: when a generic drug is challenged in court, the FDA is forced by law to freeze its approval for 30 months unless the case is settled before that. As a result, generic companies are constantly suing to invalidate extra patents; and, brand name drugmakers sue to keep generic versions off the market. The patients who can't afford the medicine always lose and these patent shenanigans slow medical innovation.

The U.S. Federal Trade Commission (FTC) should begin to crack down on the patent games drug giants play. Current law encourages pharmaceutical companies to conduct their clinical trials as quickly as they can and still satisfy the FDA. Herper believes this should be changed so generic drugmakers and branded pharmaceutical companies mark the day—15 years after a drug is approved, exclusivity will expire.[7]

The FTC has challenged the practice of pay-for-delay through at least 10 enforcement actions in the past decade, including two in 2017. On Aug. 3, 2017, the U.S. Senate passed an FDA-funding bill that would prevent baseless price increases on decades-old prescription drugs that are without competition. The bill instructs the FDA to speed up the review of generic drug applications when drugs on the market have little or no competitors. Another piece of legislation, the Creating and Restoring Equal Access to Equivalent Samples (CREATES) Act, would allow generic drug manufacturers to bring action in federal court for injunctive relief and authorizes judges to award damages to deter future delays. If the CREATES Act becomes law, generic drug companies would be able to sue branded companies that try to prevent generic drugmakers from obtaining samples of the branded drug to perform necessary tests.

The FDA has a special category of drugs called Drug Efficacy Study Implementation (DESI) that were introduced before 1962. FDA approval of these DESI drugs required proving safety but not efficacy. This led to developers of new drugs getting a new period of market exclusivity that lasts three years. According to Mark L. Baum, CEO of Imprimis Pharmaceuticals, Inc. and author of a Wall Street Journal article entitled "How FDA Rules Made a $15 Drug Cost $400," for many older medicines, government forces the original, name-brand version off the market. The FDA monopoly protection is given for what is essentially a generic version of a DESI drug, and this merely enriches sharp-dealing companies while making the drugs unaffordable to patients. The FDA is enriching monopolists for off-patent inexpensive medicine it did not develop in the first place.[8] How can anything be more corrupt than that?

New FDA policies are likely to make everything worse. Strong public demand that government "do something" about periodic drug disasters has played a central role in developing the FDA. Once mass marketing takes over, the FDA devotes only a small percentage of its budget to protect physicians or patients from receiving biased information. Evidence indicates why we can no longer trust the FDA to carry out its historic mission to protect the public from harmful and ineffective drugs.

Although it now embraces the industry rhetoric about "breakthrough" and "life-saving" innovation, the FDA in effect serves as the regenerator of patent-protected high prices for minor drugs in each disease group, as their therapeutic equivalents lose patent protection. The billions spent on promoting them results in the inverse benefit law: the more widely most drugs are marketed, the more diluted become their benefits but more widespread become their risks of harm.

The FDA also legitimates industry efforts to lower and widen criteria prescribing drugs, known by critics as "the selling of sickness." Regulations conveniently prohibit the FDA from comparing the effectiveness of new drugs or from assessing their cost-effectiveness. FDA officers propose to approve the drugs without ever knowing if they are therapeutic or not. Are the agencies in other countries as corrupt as the FDA or does this only happen in America?

Corrupt patent law is the main cause of health insurance being unaffordable in the U.S. It is legal in the U.S. (but not in most other nations) for the makers of branded drugs to pay the makers of generic drugs to delay introducing cheaper unbranded equivalents, after patents on the brands have expired. This is the root of the problem.[9] Patent-protected drugs are often essential for people's health or even their lives. Allowing a drug company to have a monopoly where it can charge whatever it can force you to pay makes little sense. This is like negotiating the pay of firefighters when they show up at your burning house with your family inside. This would give us much worse fire service and many very wealthy firefighters. The pharmaceutical companies make small improvements warranting new patents, effectively making their intellectual property semipermanent.

A Harvard study done on the opioid epidemic in September 2016 exposed the fraudulent marketing practices of Big Pharma, the patent schemes enabled by federal government, how generic drugs are routinely stifled, and possible ways to address the injustice.[10] The non-rigorous patenting standards and ineffectual policing of both fraudulent marketing and anticompetitive actions launched and prolonged the opioid epidemic. These regulatory issues are not unique to prescription opioids, but rather, they are reflective of the wider pharmaceutical market. The regulatory system is thoroughly corrupt and in need of reform.

OxyContin®

Using aggressive marketing tactics for OxyContin, Purdue Pharma successfully turned extended-release oxycodone into a blockbuster. Between 1996 and 2000, the company more than doubled its U.S. marketing team and created lucrative incentives and powerful tools to bolster sales. As part of its marketing campaign, Purdue funded professional societies advocating for more aggressive pain management. Purdue succeeded because of low patenting standards that enabled the company to secure and extend market exclusivity for extended-release oxycodone, providing motivation for its aggressive marketing. A history of tepid enforcement against pharmaceutical companies engaging in illegal marketing further incentivized Purdue to make false claims about the safety and effectiveness of the drug. Both practices helped drive opioid overuse and misuse, with tragic public health consequences.[11]

Purdue was able to patent extended-release oxycodone in the U.S. despite the fact that its constituent elements—the active ingredient oxycodone and the controlled-release system Contin—had been developed decades earlier. German scientists Martin Freund and Dr. Edmund Speyer first synthesized oxyCodone in 1916 in an effort to create a less addictive analgesic than morphine, which Bayer had been forced to pull from worldwide markets three years earlier. As expiration of market exclusivity for extended-release morphine approached, Purdue had to find a way to sustain its revenues. An internal debate ensued, with the company's vice president for research advocating for the development of other controlled-release opioids. Purdue ultimately adopted the recommendation, combining Contin and oxycodone to form extended-release oxycodone. The U.S. Patent and Trademark Office (USPTO) granted Purdue a patent for OxyContin on Nov. 30, 1993.[12]

Pharmaceutial companies routinely use citizen petitions to delay the entry of generic drugs into the marketplace–a very profitable game.

A citizen petition is a process provided by the FDA for individuals and community organizations to make requests or changes to health policy. Companies use this to counter the parts of the Drug Price Competition and Patent Term Restoration Act that make generic drugs more available. Citizen petitions are part of the basic law governing everything the FDA does. At any time, any "interested person" can request that the FDA issue, amend, or revoke a regulation or order, or take any other form of administrative action.

Non-rigorous patenting standards also enabled Purdue to extend its market exclusivity for extended-release oxycodone. As expiration of the primary patent for this drug approached, Purdue secured secondary patents on an abuse-deterrent formulation of the drug. This action forced patients who had been taking the original formulation to switch to the newer one. The company additionally filed a citizen petition asking the FDA to refuse to accept generic versions of the original extended-release oxycodone formulation because it was unsafe, which was a lie. The FDA acquiesced, effectively preventing the marketing of low-cost, therapeutically equivalent products. Then, generic drug manufacturers challenged the secondary patents.[13]

Purdue insisted that, unlike short-acting pain medications that must be taken every 4 to 6 hours, OxyContin tablets are taken every 12 hours, providing smooth and sustained pain control all day and all night. Purdue was fully aware of the inadequacy of the 12-hour dosing regimen for many patients and thus caused many to suffer more chronic pain. Clinical trial data and follow-up reports from patients who received the drug indicated that the drug often wore off after six to eight hours. Senior management at Purdue nevertheless instructed sales representatives to press prescribers not to prescribe extended-release oxycodone at shorter intervals. The fear was that the drug would lose its competitive advantage over alternative opioid medications, and Purdue executives did not care how much pain the patients would suffer as a result of the lies.[14]

Purdue eventually agreed to pay the federal government $600 million. The three executives agreed to $34.5 million in fines but avoided jail time, of course. Purdue has earned an estimated $31 billion in total revenues from OxyContin since its launch. Rather than deterring fraudulent marketing, the penalties simply became a cost of doing business.[15]

In response to growing opioid misuse and abuse, states focused on decreasing the supply of opioids on the market, without addressing the underlying demand for opioids within the U.S. In 2010, Florida enacted legislation mandating that pain management clinics register with the state, adopt minimum safety standards (e.g., use of tamper-proof and counterfeit-proof prescription pads), and submit to annual inspections.[16] Reckitt Benckiser succeeded in forestalling generic entry by introducing a modified version of buprenorphine/naloxone tablets.

In 2010, the company received FDA approval for a film formulation of the drug, having submitted a patent for both the film and its underlying delivery system in 2008. Reckitt Benckiser subsequently announced its intention to stop producing the tablet formulation of buprenorphine/naloxone, and in September 2012 filed a citizen petition requesting that the FDA not approve any generic versions of it. Non-rigorous patenting standards have enabled pharmaceutical companies to obtain a steadily increasing number of patents on drugs, extending the market exclusivity of these products.[17] Who gets hurt? Always the patients.

Secondary patenting is most harmful in the context of hard switches. In such instances, patients have no recourse but to use the costly new product, which will not be eligible for substitution when generic versions of the original product emerge. Even without hard switches, secondary patenting can help maintain high drug prices. When drug manufacturers introduce a modified, patent-protected product onto the market, they generally promote it heavily and cease advertising of the original. Like Purdue and Reckitt, many pharmaceutical companies have used citizen petitions to delay generic entry.[18]

Pharmaceutical companies have often engaged in false or misleading marketing. Over the past 25 years, the industry has paid billions to settle claims of illegal marketing, including making false or misleading claims or failing to disclose known risks. In 2012, GlaxoSmithKline paid $3 billion to settle civil claims and criminal charges that it downplayed the risk of the antidepressant paroxetine (Paxil®) in adolescents, promoted the antidepressant bupropion (Wellbutrin®) for unapproved uses, and hid data showing the increased risk of heart attacks from the diabetes drug rosiglitazone (Avandia®). Almost every major pharmaceutical company has been caught in similar marketing scandals. However, the industry remains highly profitable, supporting criticism that monetary penalties generally represent "a quite small percentage of . . . global revenue and often a manageable percentage of the revenue received from the product under scrutiny."[19]

The Problem with Citizen Petitions

The FDA has already taken action to address the misuse of citizen petitions by brand-name drug manufacturers. The FDA could in theory better exercise its existing authority to summarily deny citizen petitions filed "with the primary purpose of delaying the approval of an application" and that "does not on its face raise valid scientific or regulatory issues." In practice, however, it is unlikely the rule will bring about meaningful change. Most citizen petitions submitted with the primary aim of delay raise valid scientific or regulatory issues, which the FDA must investigate. In the case of buprenorphine/naloxone, for example, the agency would have been hard pressed to label the issue of accidental opioid exposure facially invalid. A more practical solution to combat "sham" citizen petitions would be for the FDA to impose time restrictions on filing.[20]

Niney-two percent of citizen petitions filed against generics come from brand-name drug companies. In theory, citizen petitions about drug safety are supposed to be exactly what they sound like: a way for anyone to bring concerns straight to the FDA. In practice, however, many citizen petitions are filed by pharmaceutical companies to fight off a competitor's cheaper generic drug.[21]

Patents grant exclusive rights to companies as an incentive to develop new drugs. However, once a drug patent has expired, the only incentive is to be creative about reducing generic competitors. Gaming the FDA's citizen petition is common. The FDA can deny petitions that it finds frivolous, but it never does. The agency tends to err on the side of caution because the consequences of approving an unsafe drug are so high and because they care more about profit than people.

The scope of the problem is bigger than the FDA. Michael Carrier, a law professor at Rutgers, who has studied the citizen petition process, noted that the issue sits at the junction of several areas of law: antitrust law, patent law, state drug laws, and the Hatch-Waxman Act that established the generic approvals system in 1984. Carrier cites EpiPen® as an example of where pharmaceutical company Mylan used multiple delay tactics against a competitor. An EpiPen® is used to treat life-threatening allergic reactions, including anaphylaxis, in people who have a history of serious allergic reactions. Mylan and Teva, the company seeking to manufacture a generic EpiPen, settled a lawsuit in 2012, in which Teva agreed not to enter the market until June 2015. Months before the settlement period was supposed to end, Mylan filed a citizen petition about Teva's product. Then, weeks before the FDA was supposed to respond to that petition, it filed a supplement petition containing the Mylan-commissioned study questioning Teva's version. Carrier notes that Mylan waited years to file its citizen petition. The last-minute timing raised Carrier's suspicions.[22]

Two devious tactics by manufacturers of brand-name drugs to delay competition from cheaper generic drugs were appropriately slapped down recently by federal and state officials. One tactic involves buying off the competition. According to the FTC, the pharmaceutical company Cephalon, which makes Provigil®, a drug used to treat sleep disorders, sued four generic drug makers in 2005-06. The suit claimed patent infringement and Cephalon later paid more than $300 million collectively to drop their challenges to Provigil's patents. The companies also had to stop selling their generics for six years, until April 2012. One of the four companies paid off by Cephalon was Teva Pharmaceutical Industries, based in Israel, which later bought Cephalon and now has to answer for Cephalon's improper scheme. On May 28, the FTC announced that Teva had agreed to settle a lawsuit filed by the government for $1.2 billion, the largest amount ever secured by the agency.

Buprenorphine/Suboxone®

Another tactic in the pharmaceutical world is known as "forced switching" or "product hopping."[23] Reckitt Benckiser had a patent for its opiate-treatment drug Suboxone that was about to expire in 2009. Suboxone is a blend of the painkiller buprenorphine and the opiate blocker naloxone. By combining the drug with naloxone—which causes the immediate onset of withdrawal symptoms if the product is inappropriately melted and injected—Reckitt Benckiser made it harder to abuse, greatly broadening its appeal as a drug for treating opioid dependency. At stake was the loss of the company's 85 percent hold on the market for medication-assisted treatment, which was booming thanks to the growing opiate epidemic. Hundreds of millions of dollars stood to be lost from the patent's expiration.[24]

The company spin-off company Indivior and a third company called MonoSol Rx gamed the pharmaceutical regulatory process using deceptive practices to maintain a chokehold on the emerging market for medicine-based addiction treatment. The case against Reckitt Benckiser accuses the company of "product hopping," meaning a company tweaks its product slightly, often without any actual improvements, and then applies for a new patent to keep profits high. In Reckitt Benckiser's case, the product switch was from the orange Suboxone tablets it had been successfully marketing to a new dissolvable film strip that was developed by co-defendant MonoSol Rx.[25]

The plaintiffs accused the company of undermining the market for generics through a "multi-step scheme" that began in 2010 with an aggressive effort to get prescribers to stop dispensing its own Suboxone tablets and replace them with the new film version. Over the next two years, Reckitt Benckiser compensated doctors for being advocates of the drug, lobbied legislators on the benefits of Suboxone film, and penalized employees for not meeting sales targets for the new drug. It also raised the price of its tablets, making them more expensive than the newer film version, even though the pills are cheaper to make.²

In September 2012, with generics getting closer to approval, Reckitt Benckiser announced its intention to take tablet versions of its drug off the market on the grounds that the pills posed a safety threat to children who might inadvertently eat them. On the same day, it filed a citizen petition with the FDA calling on the agency to postpone approval of generics in the interest of public safety. The company based its child-safety claims on a single study it had paid for itself. According to the plaintiffs, it used the findings to sow fear among medical professionals and encourage them to dispense only Suboxone film. The FDA rejected Reckitt Benckiser's petition to essentially ban the product it had been happily selling for seven years—and that it continues to sell throughout Europe, where Suboxone tablets are still under patent.[27]

In June 2013, the FTC opened an investigation into whether Reckitt Benckiser abused public regulatory processes and fought for nearly two years to obtain more than 20,000 documents the company was fighting to withhold. Legal experts disagree whether product hopping is a crime, but it is clearly wrong. In my opinion, it is wrong because Reckitt Benckiser tried to exploit the hysteria over the increasing use of opioids to increase profit by blocking their competition.

The FTC has argued that it is a crime if it has the effect of coercively undermining consumer choice. In December 2013, federal agents raided Reckitt Benckiser's West Virginia offices after the Department of Justice launched a criminal probe into the company's Suboxone business. According to one estimate, between 2009 and 2013 when the FDA finally approved generic buprenorphine/naloxone, more than $1 billion in annual sales were generated. 20 percent of the company's profit base, and approximately 3 million Americans had been treated with the drug.[28]

FDA Corruption Explained

When the FDA finds scientific fraud or misconduct, the agency doesn't notify the public, the medical establishment, or even the scientific community that the results of a medical experiment are inaccurate. For more than a decade, the FDA has shown a pattern of hiding misconduct. As a result, nobody ever finds out which data is bogus, which experiments are tainted, and which drugs might be on the market under false pretenses. The FDA has repeatedly hidden evidence of scientific fraud, not just from the public but also from its most trusted scientific advisers, even as they were deciding whether or not a new drug should be allowed to be sold.[28]

Scientists and medical professionals should know the truth so they can advise patients of the risks associated with medications. The FDA protects the pharmaceutical companies, not the citizens, and it has been doing this for a long time. Perhaps if the FDA were abolished, we would have access to medicine and would need less synthetic poison to treat our illnesses. Abolishing the corrupt Controlled Substances Act and the FDA would enable more people to have access to medicine that works and is not patentable.

The FDA generates a lot of paperwork, including Establishment Inspection Reports (Form 483), and, in the worst cases, Warning Letters. If you manage to locate these documents, you'll see that, most of the time, key portions are redacted. This includes blacked out information that describes what drug the researcher was studying, the name of the study, and precisely how the misconduct affected the quality of the data.[29] These redactions make it impossible to figure out which study is tainted, which is exactly what both the FDA and the pharmaceutical companies want. Telling the truth is not good for Big Pharma's profit margin.

On occasion, the FDA has approved and promoted statements about drugs that, according to its own inspectors, are based on lies. Approximately 100 drugs, including chemotherapy compounds and prescription painkillers, had been approved for sale in the U.S. at least in part on the strength of Cetero's tainted tests. The vast majority of tests were on generic versions of brand-name drugs that Cetero scientists had often run critical tests to determine whether the generics did, in fact, act the same in the body as the originals. For example, one of these generic drugs was ibuprofen, sold as gelatin capsules by one of the nation's largest grocery-store chains for months before the FDA received assurance they were safe. Cetero had been caught faking data from thousands of drug trials. That suddenly worthless data had been used to establish the safety or effectiveness of approximately 100 drugs, mostly generics, that were being sold in the U.S. The FDA refuses to release the names of the drugs whose approval data were undermined by fraud.[30]

The only reason the FDA has a right to refuse is because it controls the federal government. The FDA covers up drug-related misconduct by publishing a listing of generic drugs in the U.S., known as the Orange Book. Prescription drugs in this book are often given what's called a therapeutic equivalence code. This code is a two-letter designation that signals the quality of the scientific evidence that a generic is "bioequivalent" to the name-brand drug. AB-rated drugs are drugs that meet the necessary bioequivalence standards established by the FDA. At the pharmacy, generic substitution is the process by which a generic equivalent is dispensed rather than the brand-name drug. Even though the FDA updates the Orange Book monthly, no drugs lost their AB rating in the months after the Cetero scandal broke.

In the year and a half after the Cetero fraud was first announced, only four generic drugs (in various dosages) were downgraded to a lower rating, none of which appeared to be linked to the Cetero problem. A written statement issued by the agency's press office noted that the FDA requested additional data from the companies whose drugs were implicated in the Cetero affair and, "If the data were not provided within 6 months or the data provided did not support a finding of bioequivalence, the FDA said it would consider changing the generic product's therapeutic equivalence rating in the Orange Book from AB to BX."[31] The whole point of science-based medicine is to keep us from having to guess whether or not pills are safe to take, and if we can't trust the FDA, who can we trust?

Vivitrol®

The National Institute on Drug Abuse, Substance Abuse Mental and Health Services Administration, and professional medical organizations all recommend medication-assisted treatment for opioid addiction. Both methadone and Suboxone, called opioid-maintenance therapy, reduce cravings and prevent withdrawal, helping people to avoid the harmful behaviors associated with addiction. Many lawmakers, law enforcement and corrections officials, see lurking risks in any substance with street value — any substance that activates the opioid receptors in the brain. As a result, methadone and buprenorphine are two of the most heavily regulated drugs in America, even more than the highly addictive painkillers that have touched off the addiction crisis. The third medication, Vivitrol, sidesteps much of the debate. Approved to treat opioid addiction in 2010, Vivitrol is a monthly injection of extended-release naltrexone. It is not an opioid. Instead, it blocks opioid receptors in the brain. If the patient has chronic pain as well as an addiction problem, Vivitrol won't help.[32]

Alkermes is a niche player in the pharmaceutical industry, and Vivitrol is central to the company's growth plans. Although the drug was first approved to treat alcohol addiction in 2006, it wasn't until the company began marketing Vivitrol to law enforcement and policymakers that sales took off. Vivitrol is more expensive than opioid maintenance — around $1,000 a shot. It also requires patients to stop using opioids and go through a painful detox before they can begin taking it, which makes it a worse alternative to buprenorphine or methadone. It is meant only for criminals and not patients who want to avoid a very painful detox process. Why pays for this expensive drug? Taxpayers of course, as criminals rarely have money to pay medical bills. It is marketed very heavily to inmates and parolees. If you can't make profit from pain pill addicts, why not exploit prisoners for profit? Alkermes has no problem doing that.

Indiana lawmakers voted to explicitly allow Medicaid insurers to use prior authorizations for buprenorphine, and specifically exempted Vivitrol from those conditions. The final version of the bill removed the Vivitrol exemption, but most insurers under Indiana Medicaid will pay for Vivitrol without a prior authorization. Alkermes has pushed for increased regulations on buprenorphine for the sole purpose of selling more Vivitrol. For example, under an Ohio law, doctors treating more than 30 patients with buprenorphine must now apply for a special license from the pharmacy board. That adds new rules and a significant administrative burden to how doctors run their practice. Lobbyists for Alkermes applauded the bill. Alkermes tried a similar approach at the federal level, too. Leading up to the passage of the Comprehensive Addiction and Recovery Act in 2016, the company sought increased federal regulation of buprenorphine. The company circulated a document that presented slanted material about buprenorphine. The focus was on the drug's potential for diversion and abuse while largely ignoring its benefits for individuals and for public health.[33]

Matthew Henson, Director of Public Relations at Alkermes circulated the white paper, which he described as a "working document" meant to educate federal lawmakers about medication-assisted treatment options. The document doesn't mention Vivitrol. As lawmakers sought to expand access to treatment, the white paper called for stricter regulation of buprenorphine through a bill dubbed the Opioid Addiction Treatment Modernization Act, introduced in the House in

June 2015. Alkermes' lobbyists disparaged opioid maintenance therapy using the same language. Pushing for opioid abstinence, however, could help Alkermes sell more Vivitrol because it is the only drug that is a non-opioid treatment for opioid addiction.[34] It amazes me how many companies want to exploit addicts for profit, the weakest most downtrodden among us and the folks who desperately need our help to become healthy again.

Subsys®

The U.S. opiate drug problem isn't limited to illegal narcotics. The sale of dangerously addictive painkillers prescribed by our doctors has quadrupled in the past decade. One company in particular is pushing pain to the legal edge of aggressive medical marketing. Specialty pharmaceutical company Insys Therapeutics, with the help of several physicians across the country now under investigation, is putting profits before patients as it makes millions from your pain. Insys is subject to investigations regarding the sales and marketing practices of its main product, Subsys (Fentanyl), a painkiller delivered as an oral spray.[35]

According to FDA guidelines, Subsys is only meant to be used to treat late-stage cancer pain. Fentanyl products are "the most potent and dangerous opioids on the market," said Dr. Andrew Kolodny, executive director of Physicians for Responsible Opioid Prescribing and chief medical officer of the Phoenix House Foundation. According to some physicians, fentanyl is approximately 100 times more powerful than morphine and gets into the bloodstream faster because it is sprayed under the tongue. The potency of Subsys also comes with a high price tag. One package of 30 sprays can cost between $900 and $3,000, depending on the dosage, and those prices keep increasing. The fentanyl class of drugs had an average prescription price of $160 in 2016, according to Express Scripts, the largest pharmacy benefits manager in the U.S.[36] Who better to profit from than people in tremendous pain dying of cancer? They will spend every last dime to kill the pain and Insys Therapeutics knows it.

While it is legal for physicians to prescribe medications for indications outside of FDA guidelines if they see fit, it is illegal for pharmaceutical companies to market a drug for off-label use. Insys not only marketed Subsys off-label but also paid medical professionals to write more prescriptions. Connecticut-based nurse practitioner Heather Alfonso pleaded guilty to accepting approximately $83,000 from Insys in return for prescribing the highly addictive Subsys. The Connecticut U.S. Attorney called it kickbacks. According to court transcripts of Alfonso's plea agreement, the money was allegedly paid to Alfonso as part of Insys Therapeutics' speaker program. In Alfonso's words, this was "basically dinner at a nice restaurant" with people who had no license to prescribe controlled substances like Subsys. Insys often assisted with the prior authorization process for off-label prescriptions, according to legal documents.[37] Only doctors are allowed to do this, not pharmaceutical companies, but pharmaceutical companies do not care about laws, especially laws that interfere with profit.

A lawsuit alleges that "the Company's management was aware that only about 10 percent of prescriptions approved through the Prior Authorization Department were for cancer patients; the majority were written for peripheral neuropathy, lower back pain and sciatica." The lawsuit goes even further and alleges there was "encouragement to doctors to disregard FDA mandated dosing, violation of patient privacy rights, fraudulent Medicare and private insurance claims, and kickbacks to doctors."[38]

Dr. John N. Kapoor, the owner of Insys Therapeutics, was arrested and charged with leading a nationwide conspiracy to use bribes and fraud to distribute a fentanyl spray intended for cancer patients. The founder and former CEO of Insys and still a member of its board, faces federal charges of racketeering, conspiracy to commit fraud, and conspiracy to violate the Anti-Kickback statute. In addition to fines, the racketeering and fraud charges carry possible prison sentences of up to 20 years. The kickback charge can bring up to five years. Prosecutors say the company paid doctors to prescribe Subsys. FDA reports of adverse events and possible related complications include hundreds of deaths.

Prescribing a possibly fatal synthetic version of fentanyl to people with back pain is evil. Those people might be better off with Embeda® (a combination of morphine for pain and naltrexone to prevent feelings of euphoria) to control their pain. The best doctors only resort to opioid therapy if the patient is unable to have surgery followed by physical therapy, as that is the very best cure. An elderly person with terminal cancer who cannot undergo surgery followed by physical therapy deserves pain control. New legislation passed in 2018 is making it much more difficult for surgery patients to purchase the narcotic pain medication they need after their operations. Because of the addicts, the pain patients suffer more now.

Neurontin (Gabapentin) and Lyrica

In 1994, Neurontin (the brand name of generic Gabapentin) was approved by the FDA to treat seizures. Gabapentin was approved for use as an anticonvulsant or anti-epileptic drug. Gabapentin is often combined with other anticonvulsant medications to prevent seizures and associated symptoms. The severity of this drug's side effects became a matter of increasing public concern in 1996.

The first prominent Gabapentin lawsuit was filed by Dr. David Franklin, a Pfizer employee. This lawsuit alleged that the company was defrauding the government, that some doctors received illegal payments in return for prescribing Gabapentin. Since the cost of this medication was often paid for by Medicaid, Dr. Franklin claimed that federal funds had been fraudulently used. He also claimed that Pfizer was illegally marketing Gabapentin for ADHD, bipolar disorder, migraines, and nerve pain.

It is legal for a doctor to prescribe Gabapentin for a purpose other than controlling epilepsy or neuralgia; however, it is illegal for pharmaceutical companies to advertise using the drug for non-FDA approved purposes. Doctors decide what is best for their patients while pharmaceutical companies usually decide what is best for their profit margin, thus these companies cannot be trusted to market drugs for non-FDA approved uses. Dr. Franklin's lawsuit resulted in Pfizer agreeing to pay $430 million to the Department of Justice to resolve both civil and criminal allegations of illegally marketing Gabapentin for bipolar disorder, migraines, and nerve pain.

Many Gabapentin lawsuits concerning side effects were soon launched. Often, the foundation of these lawsuits was the claim that prescription information failed to sufficiently warn doctors or patients of the risk of suicidal thoughts. More than 1,200 cases concerning Gabapentin side effects were filed in the wake of the 2004 Gabapentin lawsuit. However, no lawsuit concerning a suicide resulted in a settlement until 2010. Pfizer's Lyrica for fibromyalgia also caused the same problem—suicidal thoughts in people with no history of depression.

The lawsuit in 2010 focused on racketeering law. Insurance company Kaiser sued Pfizer over its illegal aggressive promotion of

Gabapentin as a multi-use off-label drug, resulting in a $141 million settlement. Individual Gabapentin lawsuits concerning the drug's side effects are still being filed by the loved ones of suicide victims. These lawsuits seek compensation from Pfizer, claiming that the drug-maker failed to warn that suicidal thoughts were a possible side effect of taking the drug.

Pfizer agreed to pay $325 million to wrap up claims that its Parke-Davis unit touted the epilepsy drug Gabapentin for uses not approved by the FDA, costing healthcare payers millions in unnecessary spending. Pfizer's Warner-Lambert unit pleaded guilty to two violations of the Food, Drug & Cosmetic Act and paid civil and criminal penalties for promoting Gabapentin as a treatment for bipolar disorder, ADHD, migraine headaches and other types of pain.[39]

Pfizer said it would pay $190 million to settle a federal antitrust lawsuit claiming that the company was responsible for illegal maneuvering to keep cheaper generics off the market. Parke-Davis was a unit of Warner-Lambert, which Pfizer acquired in 2000. The claims about off-label marketing go back to 1994. Pfizer deliberately expanded the promotion of off-label uses after the Warner-Lambert buyout.[40]

The off-label allegations are among many leveled against not only Pfizer, but almost every Big Pharma company. In addition to Pfizer's DOJ settlement involving Gabapentin, the company agreed to pay $2.3 billion to resolve Justice Department allegations that it sold a variety of drugs for off-label uses, including the now-withdrawn blockbuster painkiller, Bextra. That settlement included a record-setting $1.3 billion criminal penalty. In the business world criminals pay fines — you can't put an entire company in jail. Pfizer recently said it would pay $491 million to resolve claims that its Wyeth unit, acquired in a 2009 megamerger, touted the transplant-rejection drug Rapamune for a variety of off-label uses.[41]

Pfizer also marketed Lyrica for off-label uses, which was initially approved for treatment of diabetic peripheral neuropathy and post-herpetic peripheral neuropathy, and subsequently approved for the treatment of fibromyalgia. Contrary to the approved intended uses, Pfizer marketed Lyrica for the treatment of chronic pain, neuropathic pain (other than diabetic peripheral neuropathy and post-herpetic peripheral neuropathy), perioperative pain, and migraines. Pfizer encouraged its sales force to promote Lyrica as superior to its own Gabapentin because no generic was yet available.

Citalopram

There is a disconnection between the FDA's drug approval process and the reports in medical journals. When the FDA analyzes and publishes its clinical trials in medical journals, pharmaceutical corporations have free rein to shape the analyses. The FDA conducts independent analyses of the data submitted by the corporations, and it may deny or delay approval. A detailed example of deliberate corporate bias has finally been documented through materials released in litigation. This exposé was reported by Drs. Jon Jureidini, Jay Amsterdam, and Leemon McHenry. This example concerned a clinical trial of an antidepressant drug in children and adolescents.[42]

The drug, citalopram, was already approved for use by adults, and its off-label use for children would spread if there was published supportive evidence. An Investigational New Drug protocol and plan of analysis were filed by Forest Laboratories with the FDA in 1999. The trial was completed in 2002, and the results were published in the American

Journal of Psychiatry in 2004–but the FDA did not accept the results as sufficient to approve this drug for children or adolescent patients. By that time, the patent on citalopram had expired and Forest Laboratories introduced a virtual twin drug, Escitalopram (single active enantiomer). Single-enantiomer drugs not only are critical in new drug development, but they also can be used as a defense strategy by innovator drug companies from generic drug competition. By developing single enantiomers (each molecule of a pair of molecules that are mirror images of each other) of previously approved racemates, a pharmaceutical company can extend the product's life cycle. That more expensive version of citalopram was heavily promoted, and it was approved in 2009 for children's use. Even then the FDA specifically noted that safety and efficacy were not established in children under age 12. Since then, new analyses suggest that most antidepressant drugs have little evidence of efficacy in children older than 12.[43]

Perhaps Congress should mandate that the FDA strictly analyze all data from clinical trials according to the registered protocols and analysis plans. That requirement should apply to new drugs or to approved drugs being tested for new indications. It should apply also to publications reporting new trials of approved drugs. Corporations and investigators should be prohibited from publishing their own in-house statistical analyses unless verified by FDA oversight. The pharmaceutical corporations always claim their publications undergo peer review. However, that is not a barrier to pervasive corporate bias because the peer reviewers for medical journals don't see all the real data. They see only the data the corporation wants them to see. Only the FDA sees all the data. That gives them too much power.[44]

Risperdal®

Risperdal is a billion-dollar antipsychotic medicine with many benefits and a few problematic side effects. It can cause strokes among the elderly and it can cause boys to grow large breasts. Johnson & Johnson (J&J) marketed Risperdal aggressively to the elderly and to boys, while allegedly manipulating and hiding the data about breast development. J&J got caught, pleaded guilty to the crime, and has paid more than $2 billion in penalties and settlements. That is very little compared to the $30 billion in sales of Risperdal around the world.[45]

J&J's antipsychotic medicine prior to Risperidal® ended its patent life and sales plunged as generics gained market share. In 1994, J&J released Risperdal as a successor, but the FDA said it wasn't necessarily better than the previous version and was effective primarily for schizophrenia in adults. That's a small market, and J&J wanted annual revenues of at least $1 billion. To achieve that, J&J reinvented Risperdal as a drug for a broad range of problems, targeting everyone from seniors with dementia to children with autism. The company also turned to corporate welfare and paid doctors consulting fees and successfully lobbied for Texas to adopt Risperdal in place of generics. This meant that the state paid $3,000 a year for each Medicaid patient taking Risperdal®, rather than $250 a year for a generic.[46]

Even though Risperdal wasn't approved for the elderly, J&J formed a sales force called ElderCare, with 136 people to market it to seniors. The FDA protested and noted there were "an excess number of deaths" among the elderly who took the drug. At the same time, J&J was also expanding into another forbidden market: children. The company began peddling the drug to pediatricians and by 2000, more than 20 percent of Risperdal was going to children and adolescents.

By 2004, Risperdal was a $3-billion-a-year drug. One challenge was that a J&J study had found Risperdal caused 5.5 percent of boys to develop large breasts, a condition known as gynecomastia. J&J covered this up.[47] Risperdal is a good drug that helps some people, but it was marketed too broadly and the system failed to protect consumers. J&J will likely have to pay a total of $6 billion in settlements for its misconduct, but the company made $18 billion in profits on Risperdal just within the United States.[48] Once again, the profit exceeds the fine by so much that breaking the law makes sense if profit is your only goal and you don't care about those who suffer.

Pradaxa®
After only several years on the market, the blood thinner Pradaxa became the subject of more than 4,000 state and federal lawsuits. These lawsuits claimed the drug caused sudden uncontrollable gastrointestinal, rectal and brain bleeding, and heart attacks that resulted in hundreds of deaths. In May 2014, the drug's manufacturer, Boehringer Ingelheim Pharmaceutical Company, announced it would pay $650 million to settle the lawsuits in order to avoid lengthy litigation. Boehringer Ingelheim heavily marketed Pradaxa as safe and effective. Doctors wrote millions of prescriptions for the new blood thinner after the FDA approved it in October

2010. In 2011, Boehringer spent $464 million to promote Pradaxa through direct-to-consumer advertising and other means of marketing.

One of the drug's key selling points was its convenience. Boehringer Ingelheim touted Pradaxa as a "one-size-fits-all" drug that did not require doctor checkups to adjust dosage. Pradaxa was touted as not requiring blood tests or dietary restrictions, unlike warfarin, an older medication Pradaxa was intended to replace. In 2011, more than 540 patients died after using Pradaxa, and thousands of other people reported suffering from serious side effects.[49]

The number of Pradaxa adverse event reports surpassed those of all other monitored drugs in 2011. Emergency room doctors and trauma surgeons began to voice concerns because patients were rushed to the hospital with life-threatening bleeding that could not be easily stopped. The medical community recognized the bleeding risk associated with blood thinners, and experts have criticized that Pradaxa was sold for five years without a remedy to stop its blood-thinning effects. The FDA did not approve Praxbind, a fast-acting Pradaxa antidote, until October 2015.[50]

More than 4,000 people who suffered damaging side effects from Pradaxa filed lawsuits against Boehringer Ingelheim. Some people filed Pradaxa lawsuits because they didn't want other families to endure the same suffering they had experienced. The plaintiffs alleged Boehringer Ingelheim willfully endangered the public through its use of deceptive marketing practices, failure to disclose risks, and failure to provide adequate treatment methods for patients who experience severe bleeding. In addition, lawsuits claimed Pradaxa's manufacturer did not adequately label the drug. According to these lawsuits, original labeling and prescribing information printed between October 2010 and March 2011 did not include adequate dosing information with respect to patient's weight. Nor was there a warning that there were any established methods for treating patients who suffered from excessive bleeding. Moreover, labeling failed to provide adequate warnings about gastrointestinal bleeding, specifically in patients with gastrointestinal issues. Labeling also ignored stating the risk of bleeding in older patients and other at-risk populations.[51]

Several people filed lawsuits against Pradaxa's manufacturer. Their lawsuit claims the company's aggressive marketing did not take into account patient safety. Walter Daumler said he watched his sister, Doris, bleed to death because of Pradaxa. Daumler had been told by doctors that there was nothing they could do because at the time there was no antidote for the hemorrhaging caused by the blood thinner. Roy Heady was hospitalized for a brain hemorrhage after switching from warfarin (Coumadin®) to Pradaxa. Charles Jackson suffered intestinal bleeding after taking Pradaxa for only three weeks. Harold Asher lost his wife, Barbara Jean, after she switched to Pradaxa. She was rushed to the hospital where she died because doctors couldn't stop the Pradaxa bleed, according to court documents. According to legal reports, all the plaintiffs were hospitalized for a brain hemorrhage after switching from warfarin to Pradaxa. In May 2014, Boehringer Ingelheim announced it would pay $650 million to settle all 4,000 state and federal Pradaxa lawsuits. Pradaxa sales at the time exceeded $2 billion in the U.S.[52] The crooks never lose any money with this game they play with the legal system and they never spend a single day in jail. They won't stop unless unjust patent laws are changed.

Dr. Burzynski's Antineoplaston Therapy for Cancer

If you think the FDA is corrupt based on the pills I have discussed so far, you will be shocked to find out how the FDA treated Stanislaw R. Burzynski, M.D., Ph.D., who found a cure for some types of cancerous tumors. The more people he saved because of his treatment, the harder the FDA tried to shut down his research. Big Pharma wants to treat cancer, not cure it, as there is far less profit in a cure than in ongoing treatment.

According to Burzynski, when the body does not have enough antineoplastons, cells that begin to develop abnormally are not corrected and tumors form and grow. Burzynski's antineoplaston therapy (a special combination of proteins and amino acids) was curing some lethal cancerous tumors, even the ones that attach themselves to the spinal cord and brain. In similar situations, other U.S. doctors and oncologists send you home to die. Traditional oncologists offer no hope to people with a glioma attached to the spinal cord and brain.

Burzynski believes that antineoplaston therapy supplies the body with the substances needed to correct the abnormal development of the cell and allow it to develop or die a natural cell death, while healthy cells remain unaffected. In 1977, he established the Burzynski Clinic in Houston, TX.[53] Burzynski was curing patients who had already endured the maximum chemotherapy and radiation treatments doled out by standard American oncologists. Many of his patients testified that his natural medicine saved them and their children's lives.

Burzynski discovered an advanced, cutting edge and non-toxic gene-targeting cure for even the most lethal forms of cancer, including terminal brain cancers of small children (childhood brainstem gliomas). He pioneered the use of biologically active peptides for the treatment of cancer. Burzynski wasn't just curing one kind of cancer or something rare. Rather, he was curing 40 different kinds of cancer–including breast, lung, and brain cancer. These naturally occurring human peptides are deficient in cancer patients and these peptides play a major role in preventing the growth of cancer cells.

The FDA did not deny in court that Burzynski's treatments worked. However, they still tried to shut him down for shipping medications over state and international lines. FDA officials did not want his name and treatment method to be nationally or internationally recognized for fear his treatment would become mainstream and undermine the whole westernized and allopathic chemical-cancer-industrial-complex we know today. The FDA has had success shutting down natural cures that have had a high cure rate on newly diagnosed cancer patients. The FDA had repeatedly attempted to shut down the Burzynski Clinic by crippling Burzynski's finances by dragging him through the courts, wasting nearly $100 million in taxpayer money. This is all on court record.[54]

The FDA seized 12,000 patient records from Burzynski's office. Eventually, the FDA stole Burzynki's ideas, intentionally diluted the most important ingredients, reran his tests, and lied to Americans and the world, saying his treatments never worked. In its attempt to bury the great cancer cure, the FDA patented the diluted version and destroyed the records of the real version. If that isn't corruption, I don't know what is.

In 2010, drug companies spent more than $500 million buying drug approvals from the FDA. To date, the FDA has approved 25 weakened versions of Burzynski's treatment and they target only a gene or two, instead of the 100 genes or more that Burzynski did. Burzynski's treatment does not include the side effect of creating new cancers in the body, which chemotherapy causes. There's no nerve damage, kidney damage, or infertility. In fact, many other gene-targeted cancer medications have been given accelerated FDA-approval without even demonstrating a single cure or any survival benefit. The FDA "approves" chemical cancer treatments with less than a 3 percent cure rate, and "ignores" natural cancer treatments with a 90 percent or higher cure rate. Also ignored is a 25-50 percent cure rate for the deadliest of brain cancers and conventional treatments have never even cured one.[55] It is pretty obvious that the FDA works for Big Pharma and is not a government agency that protects U.S. citizens from harmful drugs as it claims it does.

Because each person's genetic makeup is different, Burzynski and his team perform genetic tests and customize the treatment for each patient. Personalized cancer therapy requires a thorough understanding of each patient's genetic makeup to unravel the biology of the cancer. One of the strongest aspects of recovery is that patients and their caretakers receive training for administering all therapies at home, as well as nutritional counseling.

Through clinical research and trials, the doctors at the Burzynski Clinic are able to determine if investigational drugs are effective and safe. Using different phases, the physicians and scientists test small groups for safe-dose ranges and side effects. Then larger groups are tested and the effectiveness is compared to commonly used therapies. Quality control of clinical trials maintain strict, written study protocols that are FDA reviewed and approved prior to patient enrollment. All of this helps Burzynski Clinic doctors tailor treatment for each person, who has different responses to type and frequency, financial considerations, monitoring requirements, etc. Since 1993, patients with a variety of advanced cancers have enrolled in Phase II clinical trials of antineoplastons. Currently, new FDA-reviewed Phase II and III clinical trials are undergoing IRB review and approval.[56]

Burzynski's treatment plan is superior to chemotherapy because personalized gene-targeting cancer therapy protects the healthy cells from harm. On the other hand, chemotherapy harms the cancer patient's immune system and should be used only as a last resort. In courts of law across the U.S., patients and their relatives tell judges that Burzynki's treatment saved their lives, ones that had been called "terminal" by the mainstream institution and cancer industrial complex of America. Hospitals and oncologists had "sent them home to die." These doctors had exhausted all their means of prescribing chemicals and dangerous radiation, so they told the patients outright there was nothing they could do to save their lives. Using the body's natural biochemical defense system, Burzynski, with his antineoplastons, targeted molecular switches that regulate cell function; moreover, by using amino acid derivatives he protected the healthy cells from harm. This is the ultimate difference from chemotherapy, which damages healthy cells and cripples immunity.[57]

Forty years ago, a doctor presented a theory about cancer treatment that was the polar opposite of the conventional "paradigm." Cancer cells are like terrorist infiltrators, and you wouldn't bomb your own city because some stray "radical cells" are wandering loose in the downtown area, or in the suburbs. This is what health professionals suggest as the first order of business. They want to bomb those cancer cells by pouring toxins into the entire area, or the whole body for that matter, as long as you kill those cancer cells. Many good cells and good bacteria get killed by chemotherapy and radiation.

Cancer is often a disease of the blood and the gene malfunctions can't be turned off with a chemotherapy "switch." Humans need their good gut bacteria (flora) for immunity from everything else, besides just the cancer. To kill the immune system is like disarming your own forces, and then stepping into battle. That's one health battle you're likely to lose.

Antineoplastons balance levels of oncogenes and tumor suppressor genes, the two kinds involved in cancer growth. If cancer can't grow, it dies. A body that still has a working immune system can fight, but chemotherapy weakens the body's immune system. With chemotherapy and radiation, patients are vomiting throughout the day and night, suffering loss of appetite, loss of energy, loss of hair, loss of immunity, and essentially loss of hope. Medical marijuana can treat their symptoms but cannot cure their cancer yet. Since Sessions opposes research on high quality medical marijuana, if it does cure cancer, the government does not want us to know about it.

Burzynski has never been given funding for research from the FDA, even after receiving approval for clinical trials. He has no valid indictments, despite decades of harassment. The natural cure clinic goes about its legal ways and cures people of cancer, without the help of the FDA or any U.S. regulatory agency. This should encourage millions of people who are wondering whether or not they should try chemotherapy and/or radiation for their cancer. If I were diagnosed with cancer, I would want to try antineoplastons and gene targeting natural therapies. I would know this treatment is tailored for my personal gene case study, body needs, and particular point in time with cancer development. Chemotherapy would be my last resort.

The U.S. National Cancer Institute (NCI) has distributed hundreds of millions of dollars to conventional cancer research, which as we all know has been a failure. In fact, the federal government has prohibited taxpayer money from funding Burzynski's highly successful research. Cancer patients are only allowed per the government to participate in Burzynski's trials if they have already gone through conventional cancer treatments that have been deemed unsuccessful. With the exception of a few cases where exemptions were granted, most of Burzynski's patients have come to him in extremely poor health as a result of the brain-frying, immune system-destroying chemotherapy and radiation treatments to which they were previously summoned. Yet the success rate of Burzynski's treatment is far superior to conventional treatments.

Burzynski's "Cancer is Serious Business" film was released in 2011. The movie tells the true story of a man who won the largest legal battle against the FDA in American history.

His gene-targeted medicines already got FDA approval up to the final phase of clinical trials. By delaying final approval as long as possible, the FDA holds out on releasing a cure for cancer to the public, for fear people may all start lining up for it, instead of chemotherapy and radiation.

The FDA's four federal grand juries that spanned 10 years couldn't indict Burzynski. Perhaps that was because he wasn't doing anything wrong, except saving people from a failed medical system. He was never found guilty of any wrongdoing. Meanwhile, mainstream oncology is leaving millions dead.

Since Burzynski's compounds are not licensed drugs, the FDA restricts the Burzynski Clinic to clinical trials. That way, the compounds can still be sold and administered as therapy, but the cure will never be on TV telling Americans how and where to find this treatment. Antinooplastons can cure some of the most incurable forms of terminal cancer. Various cancer survivors are presented in "Cancer is Serious Business" who chose these medications instead of surgery, chemotherapy, or radiation—with full disclosure of medical records to support their diagnosis and recovery.

Burzynski's ability to successfully treat incurable cancer with such consistency has baffled the medical industry. His success prompted numerous investigations by the Texas Medical Board that relentlessly took Burzynski as high as the state supreme court in its failed attempt to halt his practices. What was the true motivation of the U.S. government's relentless persecution of Burzynski? If antineoplastons are approved for public use, this will allow a single scientist to hold an exclusive license to manufacture and sell these medicines on the open market, before they become generic. Pharmaceutial companies will not profit from the most effective gene-targeted cancer treatment the world has ever seen. As usual, it is all about who gets the profit.

By the mid-1990s, Burzynski had already registered over 60 clinical trials. He had put together over 70 protocols to treat every type of cancer his clinic was addressing. Imagine if the FDA demanded this much work from pharma companies making the insane drugs thrown together in a lab, never tested for safety or efficacy, marketed on TV, and sold to pharma-dispensing doctors? The FDA couldn't even put together a task force big enough to review all of the protocols Burzynski submitted.

The American Cancer Society has denounced Burzynski and his treatment entirely, as has Cancer Research UK. Their poor state of research is based entirely on funding handouts from pharma lobbyists pushing chemical drugs. Nobody is paying them to research natural cures. Burzynski's treatment has a 50 percent cure rate for "incurable" brainstem gliomas, when conventional treatments have zero. This has been proven clinical trial after clinical trial.

Sloan Kettering Cancer Center jumped on the homeopathic alternative medicine bandwagon and accused Burzynski of having no evidence to support the anticancer effects in humans. It did not know that numerous people testified about their survival in court because of antineoplaston therapy; Sloan Kettering researchers haven't taken one look at all the clinical trials and research.

The Hamburg FDA Scandal

Former FDA Commissioner Dr. Margaret Hamburg allegedly used her position with the FDA to run a huge fraud and racketeering conspiring to generate millions of dollars in illegal drug company profits for her husband's hedge fund company, Renaissance Technologies. This is according to a federal lawsuit filed in Washington, D.C. in April 2016.

The lawsuit alleges that as FDA commissioner, Hamburg acted in a conspiracy to get a dangerous drug approved, even though the drug had serious and sometimes deadly side effects.[59]

The criminal complaint states that the defendants, including Hamburg, operated a criminal conspiracy from 2009-15 to suppress warnings about the drug, Levaquin®. The complaint also states that the defendants, including Hamburg, engaged in a conspiracy to reap large profits by not disclosing to plaintiffs and the public the full extent of the deadly side effects of Levaquin. Hamburg allegedly acted illegally and outside her commissioner authority to suppress information to the plaintiffs and the public that Levaquin was a dangerous drug and could be deadly. The complaint also alleges that more than 5,000 people died because of actions relating to the conspiracy.[60]

Hamburg allegedly appointed Johnson and Johnson (J&J) officials to major FDA advisory committees and colluded with J&J to suppress information about Levaquin. The lawsuit states that from 2009 until 2015, the plaintiffs in the lawsuit suffered from mitochondrial toxicity, nervous system adverse events, and various multi-system disabilities related to taking the drug. The plaintiffs—Terry Aston,

John Fratti, Linda Martin, David Melvin, and Jennifer Wilcox—claim that after taking Levaquin they suffered muscle twitching, abdominal pain, kidney and liver damage, hair loss, depression, psychosis, and hearing and vision problems, among many other issues.[61]

The lawsuit was filed by Larry Klayman, a former federal prosecutor. It charged Hamburg and her husband, Peter Brown (an executive with the hedge fund firm Renaissance Technologies), with collusion, conspiracy, and racketeering, along with J&J to conceal those deadly risks. Hamburg also came under fire when she approved a highly addictive painkiller drug called Zohydro® ER. In December 2012, an FDA advisory panel of experts voted against approval of Zohydro ER. The panel cited concerns over that drug's potential for overdose. Indeed, 28 law enforcement agencies and addiction experts had expressed concern that approval of a pure hydrocodone drug would lead to an increase in overdoses and deaths. Fifteen anti-addiction groups wrote a letter of complaint to the Secretary of Health and Human Services. Despite the safety concerns by the medical and law enforcement community, and despite the expert panel's overwhelming rejection of the drug, Hamburg approved it. The lawsuit provides documentation showing that from 2011 to 2015, Hamburg's husband's hedge fund, Renaissance Technologies, held millions in stock in Alkermes, the manufacturer of Zohydro® ER.[62]

Alkermes is the same company that tried to sell expensive naloxone called Vivitrol to addicts despite the painful detox they'd have to go through. Besides, buprenorphine is better for addiction treatment as it does not require a painful detox but instead helps with withdrawal symptoms. Alkermes makes a fortune getting people hooked on Zohydro ER, who then get locked up for turning to the streets when doctors cut off the prescription. Alkermes is ready to sell them Vivitrol to treat the addiction. Both Alkermes and Renaissance Technologies were given the FDA green light to rake in profits from both the sale of a highly addictive drug and the sale of a treatment for that drug-induced addiction! What better way to make money? Get them hooked on poison and then sell them the treatment.

The plaintiffs are seeking the following:

- "For general (non-economic), special (economic), actual and compensatory damages in excess of $120,000,000;

- For damages trebled in the amount of J&J's gross sales pursuant to 15 U.S.C. § 1117 of the Lanham Act;
- With regard to the RICO counts, trebled damages with attorneys' fees and costs;
- For damage to person, business, and/or property, including but not limited to,
- past, present, and future financial loss such as lost earnings and loss of earning;
- capacity, medical, hospital, and incidental expenses, emotional distress and pain;
- and suffering damages according to proof;
- For consequential damages in a sum reasonable to a jury;
- For punitive damages in excess of $750,000,000 to impress upon Defendants the seriousness of their egregious conduct and to deter similar conduct in the future;
- For attorneys' fees, treble damages, expenses, and costs of this action; and
- For such further relief as this Court deems necessary, just, and proper."

The trial is not over, but I suspect Hamburg and her husband will pay a fine and serve no time in jail.

Talc Lawsuit Against Johnson & Johnson

In October 2017, a California judge threw out a $417 million verdict against Johnson & Johnson (J&J) in a lawsuit filed by a woman who claimed she developed ovarian cancer after using its talc-based products like Johnson's Baby Powder for feminine hygiene. The ruling by Los Angeles Superior Court Judge Maren Nelson marked the latest setback facing women and family members who accuse J&J of not adequately warning consumers about the cancer risks of its talc-based products. The decision followed a jury's decision in August to hit J&J with the largest verdict to date in the litigation, awarding California resident Eva Echeverria $70 million in compensatory damages and $347 million in punitive damages. Nelson reversed the jury verdict and granted J&J's request for a new trial. Nelson said the August trial was underpinned by errors and insufficient evidence on both sides, culminating in excessive damages.[63]

Mark Robinson, who represented Echeverria in her lawsuit, said he would file an appeal immediately. J&J officials say the company faces lawsuits by 4,800 plaintiffs nationally, asserting talc-related claims. Many of those cases are in California, where Echeverria's case was the first to go to trial, and in Missouri where J&J has faced five trials. The Missouri litigation led to four verdicts against J&J in which juries issued verdicts totaling $307 million. The company has only won one case. However, the Missouri cases, which have largely been brought by out-of-state plaintiffs, have faced jurisdictional questions. The Supreme Court issued a ruling in June that limited where personal injury lawsuits could be filed. A Missouri appellate court in February 2016 threw out a $72 million jury verdict awarded to the family of a deceased Alabama woman. It was ruled the case should not have been tried in St. Louis.[64] Why do the pharmaceutical companies always win when the issue hits the highest court? Is it possible that judges are in cahoots with these people and are being paid off? J&J is responsible for numerous deaths as well as all the other companies mentioned in this chapter. It is time to hold all of them accountable and do more than fine them a few million dollars.

Monsanto and Seed Patents
The majority of seeds are controlled by industrial giants — Monsanto, Du Pont, Syngenta and Bayer. Patents on Monsanto seeds prevent farmers from saving or

exchanging seed, therefore undermining the farmers' rights or seed sovereignty. Patents also create monopolies even though a seed is clearly not an invention, even if it is modified by a corporation. In a genetically engineered crop, the original seed comes from farmers. Monsanto, as the "inventor" and patent holder, sells the seeds subject to a limited licensing agreement. This means farmers are permitted to plant the purchased seed in only one growing season. Growers are allowed to sell or consume the resulting crop, but they may not replant it. This type of patent law has enabled Monsanto to maintain a stranglehold on the production of the food and fiber all human beings need to survive. A "natural" seed may only provide 25 bushels per acre, while a gene-seed could get up to 65+ bushels per acre. Therefore, a farmer has no other way to make enough money to compete with other farmers unless patented seeds are bought.

Patents on seed, which allow corporations to own seed, are wrong for many reasons. Seed is constantly creating and recreating itself. To treat seed as a corporate invention and grant corporations patents on seed is unethical. All seed has been evolved by nature and perfected by farmers over millennia. The corporation takes farmers' varieties, uses the trait found commercially useful, and applies for a patent. Patent rights violate farmers' right to save, use, reuse, breed, and exchange seed as their commons. No corporation should have the right to a self-replicating natural product.[65]

Monsanto's argument is when farmers save seed from a crop grown from patented seed and then use that seed for another crop, they are illegally replicating, or "making" Monsanto's proprietary seeds. Instead farmers should legally use the seeds by planting them only one time and purchasing more seeds for each subsequent planting. Seeds, unlike computer chips or iPhones, for example, are essential to life. If people are denied a computer chip or iPhone, they don't go hungry. If people are denied seeds, the potential consequences are far more serious, and Monsanto sues people who try to replant seeds if they cannot afford to buy new ones every year. In many cases, farmers are forced to buy pesticide resistant seeds, or else their crops may be killed from the mist of pesticide used by farmers from nearby.

Bowman vs. Monsanto Co., Case No. 11-796

The Bowman vs. Monsanto case arose after Vernon Hugh Bowman, an Indiana farmer, bought transgenic soybean crop seeds from a local grain elevator for his second crop of the season. Monsanto originally sold the seed from which these soybeans were grown to farmers under a limited-use license. It prohibited the farmer-buyer from using the seeds for more than a single season or from saving any seed produced from the crop for replanting. The farmers sold their soybean crops (also seeds) to the local grain elevator, from where Bowman then bought seeds. After Bowman replanted the seeds for his second harvest, Monsanto filed a lawsuit claiming that he infringed on their patents by replanting soybeans without a license. In response, Bowman argued that Monsanto's claims were barred under the doctrine of patent exhaustion, because all future generations of soybeans were embodied in the first generation that was originally sold.

The U.S. Supreme Court unanimously affirmed the decision of a federal court that the patent exhaustion doctrine does not permit a farmer to reproduce patented seeds by planting and harvesting saved crop seeds without the patent holder's permission. On May 13, 2013, the Supreme Court ruled that Bowman's conduct infringed Monsanto's patents. The decision held that when a farmer plants a harvested and saved seed, thereby growing another soybean crop, that action constitutes an unauthorized "making" of the patented product.[66]

Justice Elena Kagan, writing for the Court, emphasized that the decision was narrow, but the implications for agricultural biotechnology are significant. The decision clarifies the application of patent law in the context of biotechnology crops, where the patented technology is naturally self-replicating. The law that patent exhaustion applies only to the item sold and not to reproductions applies to patented seeds that naturally self-replicate. This court decision is consistent with the Court preferring an oligarchy to a constitutional republic.

Footnotes

[1]Ip, Greg. A Cure for Swelling Drug Prices: Competition. Wall Street Journal.

[2]Light, Donald W., Lexchin, Joel, and Darrow, Jonathan J., Institutional Corruption of Pharmaceuticals and the Myth of Safe and Effective Drugs. (Sept. 2013) Journal of Law and Medicine & Ethics, 590

[3]Light, Donald W., Lexchin, Joel, and Darrow, Jonathan J. Institutional Corruption of Pharmaceuticals and the Myth of Safe and Effective Drugs. (Sept. 2013) Journal of Law and Medicine & Ethics, 595.

[4]Light, Donald W., Lexchin, Joel, and Darrow, Jonathan J. Institutional Corruption of Pharmaceuticals and the Myth of Safe and Effective Drugs. (Sept. 2013) Journal of Law and Medicine & Ethics, 597.

[5]Whalen, Jeannie (July 23, 2015). Doctors Attack Drug Prices. Wall Street Journal.

[6]Herper, Matthew (May 2, 2002). Solving the Drug Patent Problem. Retrieved from http://www.forbes.com/2002/05/02/0502patents.html)

[7]Herper, Matthew (May 2, 2002). Solving the Drug Patent Problem. Retrieved from

http://www.forbes.com/2002/05/02/0502patents.html)

[8]Baum, Mark L., (April 6, 2017) How FDA Rules Made a $15 Drug cost $400. New York Times.

[9]Light, Donald W., Lexchin, Joel, and Darrow, Jonathan J. (July 17, 2013). Risky Drugs Why FDA Cannot Be Trusted. Edward J. Safra Center for Ethics. Retrieved from (http://ethics.harvard.edu/blog/risky-drugs-why-fda-cannot-be-trusted).

[10]Sarpatwari, Ameet, Sinha, Michael S., Kesselheim, Aaron S., The Opioid Epidemic: Fixing a Broken Pharmaceutical Market. (Retrieved from http://harvardlpr.com/wp-content/uploads/2017/07/SarpatwariSinhaKesselheim.pdf)

[11]Sarpatwari, Ameet, Sinha, Michael S., Kesselheim, Aaron S., The Opioid Epidemic: Fixing a Broken Pharmaceutical Market. (Retrieved from http://harvardlpr.com/wp-content/uploads/2017/07/SarpatwariSinhaKesselheim.pdf

[12]Sarpatwari, Ameet, Sinha, Michael S., Kesselheim, Aaron S., The Opioid Epidemic: Fixing a Broken Pharmaceutical Market. (Retrieved from http://harvardlpr.com/wp-

content/uploads/2017/07/SarpatwariSinhaKesselheim.pdf

[13]Sarpatwari, Ameet, Sinha, Michael S., Kesselheim, Aaron S., The Opioid Epidemic: Fixing a Broken Pharmaceutical Market. (Retrieved from http://harvardlpr.com/wp-content/uploads/2017/07/SarpatwariSinhaKesselheim.pdf

[14]Sarpatwari, Ameet, Sinha, Michael S., Kesselheim, Aaron S., The Opioid Epidemic: Fixing a Broken Pharmaceutical Market. (Retrieved from http://harvardlpr.com/wp-content/uploads/2017/07/SarpatwariSinhaKesselheim.pdf

[15]Sarpatwari, Ameet, Sinha, Michael S., Kesselheim, Aaron S., The Opioid Epidemic: Fixing a Broken Pharmaceutical Market. (Retrieved from http://harvardlpr.com/wp-content/uploads/2017/07/SarpatwariSinhaKesselheim.pdf

[16]Sarpatwari, Ameet, Sinha, Michael S., Kesselheim, Aaron S., The Opioid Epidemic: Fixing a Broken Pharmaceutical Market. (Retrieved from http://harvardlpr.com/wp-content/uploads/2017/07/SarpatwariSinhaKesselheim.pdf

[17]Sarpatwari, Ameet, Sinha, Michael S., Kesselheim, Aaron S., The Opioid Epidemic:

Fixing a Broken Pharmaceutical Market. (Retrieved from http://harvardlpr.com/wp-content/uploads/2017/07/SarpatwariSinhaKesselheim.pdf

[18]Sarpatwari, Ameet, Sinha, Michael S., Kesselheim, Aaron S., The Opioid Epidemic: Fixing a Broken Pharmaceutical Market. (Retrieved from http://harvardlpr.com/wp-content/uploads/2017/07/SarpatwariSinhaKesselheim.pdf

[19]Sarpatwari, Ameet, Sinha, Michael S., Kesselheim, Aaron S., The Opioid Epidemic: Fixing a Broken Pharmaceutical Market. (Retrieved from http://harvardlpr.com/wp-content/uploads/2017/07/SarpatwariSinhaKesselheim.pdf

[20]Sarpatwari, Ameet, Sinha, Michael S., Kesselheim, Aaron S., The Opioid Epidemic: Fixing a Broken Pharmaceutical Market. (Retrieved from http://harvardlpr.com/wp-content/uploads/2017/07/SarpatwariSinhaKesselheim.pdf

[21]Zhang, Sarah (March 8, 2017). How Pharma Companies Use 'Citizen Petitions' to Keep Drug Prices High. (Retrieved from https://www.theatlantic.com/health/archive/2017/03/pharma-citizen-petitions-drug-prices/518544/)

[22] Zhang, Sarah (March 8, 2017). <u>How Pharma Companies Use 'Citizen Petitions' to Keep Drug Prices High</u>. (Retrieved from https://www.theatlantic.com/health/archive/2017/03/pharma-citizen-petitions-drug-prices/518544/)

[23] <u>Sneaky Ways to Raise Drug Profits</u>. (June 8, 2015) New York Times Editorial Board. (Retrieved from http://www.nytimes.com/2015/06/08/opinion/sneaky-ways-to-raise-drug-profits.html?ref=opinion)

[24] Moraff, Christopher (10/5/16) <u>Suboxone Creator's Shocking Scheme to Profit Off Heroin Addicts</u>. (Retrived from http://www.thedailybeast.com/articles/2016/10/05/suboxone-creator-said-its-pills-killed-kids-to-make-1-billion.html)

[25] Moraff, Christopher (10/5/16) <u>Suboxone Creator's Shocking Scheme to Profit Off Heroin Addicts</u>. (Retrived from http://www.thedailybeast.com/articles/2016/10/05/suboxone-creator-said-its-pills-killed-kids-to-make-1-billion.html)

[26] Moraff, Christopher (10/5/16) <u>Suboxone Creator's Shocking Scheme to Profit Off Heroin Addicts</u>. (Retrived from http://www.thedailybeast.com/articles/2016/10

/05/suboxone-creator-said-its-pills-killed-kids-to-make-1-billion.html)

[27]Hagopian, Joachim. (March 7, 2016) The Evils of Big Pharma Exposed. Global Research. (Retrieved from http://www.globalresearch.ca/the-evils-of-big-pharma-exposed/5425382).

[28] Seife, Charles. Are Your Medications Safe? Slate. (Retrived from http://www.slate.com/articles/health_and_science/science/2015/02/fda_inspections_fraud_fabrication_and_scientific_misconduct_are_hidden_from.html)

[29] Seife, Charles. Are Your Medications Safe? Slate. (Retrived from http://www.slate.com/articles/health_and_science/science/2015/02/fda_inspections_fraud_fabrication_and_scientific_misconduct_are_hidden_from.html)

[30] Seife, Charles. Are Your Medications Safe? Slate. (Retrived from http://www.slate.com/articles/health_and_science/science/2015/02/fda_inspections_fraud_fabrication_and_scientific_misconduct_are_hidden_from.html)

[31] Seife, Charles. Are Your Medications Safe? Slate. (Retrived from http://www.slate.com/articles/health_and_scie

nce/science/2015/02/fda_inspections_fraud_fabrication_and_scientific_misconduct_are_hidden_from.html)

[32]Harper, Jake. (June 12, 2017). <u>Drugmaker Tries To Cash In On The Opioid Epidemic, One State Law At A Time</u>. Side Effects Public Media. Retreived from (http://www.npr.org/sections/health-shots/2017/06/12/523774660/a-drugmaker-tries-to-cash-in-on-the-opioid-epidemic-one-state-law-at-a-time)

[33]Harper, Jake. (June 12, 2017). <u>Drugmaker Tries To Cash In On The Opioid Epidemic, One State Law At A Time</u>. Side Effects Public Media. Retreived from (http://www.npr.org/sections/health-shots/2017/06/12/523774660/a-drugmaker-tries-to-cash-in-on-the-opioid-epidemic-one-state-law-at-a-time)

[34]Harper, Jake. (June 12, 2017). <u>Drugmaker Tries To Cash In On The Opioid Epidemic, One State Law At A Time</u>. Side Effects Public Media. Retreived from (http://www.npr.org/sections/health-shots/2017/06/12/523774660/a-drugmaker-tries-to-cash-in-on-the-opioid-epidemic-one-state-law-at-a-time)

[35]Gusovsky, Dina. (Wed., Nov. 4, 2015) <u>The pain killer: A drug company putting profits</u>

above patients. CNBC. Retrieved from (https://www.cnbc.com/2015/11/04/the-deadly-drug-appeal-of-insys-pharmaceuticals.html)

[36]Gusovsky, Dina. (Wed., Nov. 4, 2015) The pain killer: A drug company putting profits above patients. CNBC. Retrieved from (https://www.cnbc.com/2015/11/04/the-deadly-drug-appeal-of-insys-pharmaceuticals.html

[37]Gusovsky, Dina. (Wed., Nov. 4, 2015) The pain killer: A drug company putting profits above patients. CNBC. Retrieved from (https://www.cnbc.com/2015/11/04/the-deadly-drug-appeal-of-insys-pharmaceuticals.html

[38]Gusovsky, Dina. (Wed., Nov. 4, 2015) The pain killer: A drug company putting profits above patients. CNBC. Retrieved from (https://www.cnbc.com/2015/11/04/the-deadly-drug-appeal-of-insys-pharmaceuticals.html

[39]Staton, Tracy (June 2, 2014). Pfizer adds another $325M to Neurontin settlement tally. Total? $945M. Fierce Pharma. (Retrieved from https://www.fiercepharma.com/sales-and-marketing/pfizer-adds-another-325m-to-neurontin-settlement-tally-total-945m)

[40]Staton, Tracy (June 2, 2014). Pfizer adds another $325M to Neurontin settlement tally. Total? $945M. Fierce Pharma. (Retrieved from https://www.fiercepharma.com/sales-and-marketing/pfizer-adds-another-325m-to-neurontin-settlement-tally-total-945m)

[41]Staton, Tracy (June 2, 2014). Pfizer adds another $325M to Neurontin settlement tally. Total? $945M. Fierce Pharma. (Retrieved from https://www.fiercepharma.com/sales-and-marketing/pfizer-adds-another-325m-to-neurontin-settlement-tally-total-945m)

[42]Carroll, Bernard J., (June 22, 2016) Corruption of FDA Clinical Trials Reports: The Problem and a Proposed Remedy. Naked Capitalism. Retreived from (https://www.nakedcapitalism.com/2016/06/corruption-of-fda-clinical-trials-reports-the-problem-and-a-proposed-remedy.html)

[43]Carroll, Bernard J., (June 22, 2016) Corruption of FDA Clinical Trials Reports: The Problem and a Proposed Remedy. Naked Capitalism. Retreived from (https://www.nakedcapitalism.com/2016/06/corruption-of-fda-clinical-trials-reports-the-problem-and-a-proposed-remedy.html)

[44]Carroll, Bernard J., (June 22, 2016) Corruption of FDA Clinical Trials Reports: The Problem and a Proposed Remedy. Naked

Capitalism. Retreived from (https://www.nakedcapitalism.com/2016/06/corruption-of-fda-clinical-trials-reports-the-problem-and-a-proposed-remedy.html)

[45] Kristof, Nicolas. (September 17, 2015). When Crime Pays: J&J's Drug Risperdal. New York Times. Retrieved from https://www.nytimes.com/2015/09/17/opinion/nicholas-kristof-when-crime-pays-jjs-drug-risperdal.html?ref=opinion&_r=0)

[46] Kristof, Nicolas. (September 17, 2015). When Crime Pays: J&J's Drug Risperdal. New York Times. Retrieved from https://www.nytimes.com/2015/09/17/opinion/nicholas-kristof-when-crime-pays-jjs-drug-risperdal.html?ref=opinion&_r=0

[47] Kristof, Nicolas. (September 17, 2015). When Crime Pays: J&J's Drug Risperdal. New York Times. Retrieved from https://www.nytimes.com/2015/09/17/opinion/nicholas-kristof-when-crime-pays-jjs-drug-risperdal.html?ref=opinion&_r=0

[48] Kristof, Nicolas. (September 17, 2015). When Crime Pays: J&J's Drug Risperdal. New York Times. Retrieved from https://www.nytimes.com/2015/09/17/opinion/nicholas-kristof-when-crime-pays-jjs-drug-risperdal.html?ref=opinion&_r=0

[49] Miller, Emily. *Pradaxa Settlements & Lawsuit History.* Drugwatch. (Retreived from https://www.drugwatch.com/pradaxa/lawsuit/)
[50] Miller, Emily. *Pradaxa Settlements & Lawsuit History.* Drugwatch. (Retreived from https://www.drugwatch.com/pradaxa/lawsuit/)
[51] Miller, Emily. *Pradaxa Settlements & Lawsuit History.* Drugwatch. (Retreived from https://www.drugwatch.com/pradaxa/lawsuit/)
[52] Miller, Emily. *Pradaxa Settlements & Lawsuit History.* Drugwatch. (Retreived from https://www.drugwatch.com/pradaxa/lawsuit/)

[53] Burzynski, Stanilaw R., MD. TruthWiki. (Retrieved from (http://www.truthwiki.org/dr-stanislaw-r-burzynski-the-burzynski-clinic/)

[54] Burzynski, Stanilaw R., MD. TruthWiki. (Retrieved from (http://www.truthwiki.org/dr-stanislaw-r-burzynski-the-burzynski-clinic/)

[55] Burzynski, Stanilaw R., MD. TruthWiki. (Retrieved from (http://www.truthwiki.org/dr-stanislaw-r-burzynski-the-burzynski-clinic/)

[56] Burzynski, Stanilaw R., MD. TruthWiki. (Retrieved from (http://www.truthwiki.org/dr-stanislaw-r-burzynski-the-burzynski-clinic/)

[57] Nathan, Geoffrey. (April 25, 2016) *Former FDA Commissioner in Massive Conspiracy and Rackeetering Lawsuit.* (Retrieved from https://www.federalcharges.com/news/2016-

04-25-former-fda-commissioner-named-in-massive-conspiracy-and-rackeetering-lawsuit/)

[58]Nathan, Geoffrey. (April 25, 2016) Former FDA Commissioner in Massive Conspiracy and Rackeetering Lawsuit. (Retrieved from https://www.federalcharges.com/news/2016-04-25-former-fda-commissioner-named-in-massive-conspiracy-and-rackeetering-lawsuit/)

[59]Nathan, Geoffrey. (April 25, 2016) Former FDA Commissioner in Massive Conspiracy and Rackeetering Lawsuit. (Retrieved from https://www.federalcharges.com/news/2016-04-25-former-fda-commissioner-named-in-massive-conspiracy-and-rackeetering-lawsuit/)

[60]Nathan, Geoffrey. (April 25, 2016) Former FDA Commissioner in Massive Conspiracy and Rackeetering Lawsuit. (Retrieved from https://www.federalcharges.com/news/2016-04-25-former-fda-commissioner-named-in-massive-conspiracy-and-rackeetering-lawsuit/)

[61]Bellon, Tina and Raymond, Nate (October 20, 2017) California Judge Tosses $417 Million Talc Cancer Verdict Against Johnson & Johnson. Reuters. (Retrieved from https://www.reuters.com/article/us-johnson-

johnson-cancer-lawsuit/california-judge-tosses-417-million-talc-cancer-verdict-against-johnson-johnson-idUSKBN1CQ003?il=0)

[60]Bellon, Tina and Raymond, Nate (October 20, 2017) <u>California Judge Tosses $417 Million Talc Cancer Verdict Against Johnson & Johnson.</u> Reuters. (Retrieved from https://www.reuters.com/article/us-johnson-johnson-cancer-lawsuit/california-judge-tosses-417-million-talc-cancer-verdict-against-johnson-johnson-idUSKBN1CQ003?il=0)
[63]Miller, Emily. <u>Pradaxa Settlements & Lawsuit History.</u> Drugwatch. (Retreived from https://www.drugwatch.com/pradaxa/lawsuit/)
[64]Miller, Emily. <u>Pradaxa Settlements & Lawsuit History.</u> Drugwatch. (Retreived from https://www.drugwatch.com/pradaxa/lawsuit/)
[65]<u>Who Owns the Seed.</u> (June 5, 2012). Seed Freedom. (Retrieved from http://seedfreedom.info/who-owns-the-seed/)
[66]<u>Who Owns the Seed.</u> (June 5, 2012). Seed Freedom. (Retrieved from http://seedfreedom.info/who-owns-the-seed/)

Chapter 4: Unsafe Water and Toxic Processed Food

"Let me ask you one question
Is your money that good?
Will it buy you forgiveness?
Do you think that it could?
I think you will find
That when death takes its toll
All the money you made cannot buy back your soul."
Bob Dylan, Masters of War

The plutocrats are polluting the water we drink, poisoning the food we eat, and polluting the air we breathe. The International Bottled Water Association (IBWA) Bottled Water Code of Practice, sometimes referred to as the "Model Code," was first published in 1982. At that time, the FDA regulations for bottled water were limited in scope. IBWA developed a set of standards that could be used as minimum standards to which association members would subscribe. State agencies would be encouraged to adopt the standards as a model for their own bottled water regulations.

A key provision of the Code of Practice, and a principal benefit of membership, is IBWA's requirement for an annual unannounced inspection of each member bottlers' facility by an independent third-party food safety organization, currently NSF International for domestic companies. The program confirms the member's conformance with the technical and regulatory requirements of the Code of Practice and rewards members for achieving superior performance at the plant.

The IBWA Code of Practice has adopted many of the state requirements for bottled water. However, there are some instances where an individual state requirement may not be included in the Code of Practice. Examples are source and finished product monitoring requirements for certain substances and bulk water hauling regulations. If a bottler sells in a particular state, compliance with the state bottled water regulations must be ensured. This is to prevent disasters, such as what happened to the citizens of Flint, Michigan, where the state's environmental agency did not require pipes be treated with anti-corrosive agents. This would have kept lead from leaching off the pipes into the water system.

Gov. Rick Snyder's administrators knew in 2016 that the Flint River was not a safe drinking water source. All state governors have a fiduciary duty to put people before cost. Snyder intentionally allowed poisoned drinking water into Flint so he could save a few bucks after he gave businesses billions in tax cuts. The system is rigged against us; the only way to fight back is to install water filters in our homes to remove all toxins before we drink the water. In Flint, the regional Environmental Protection Agency (EPA) administrator has resigned, two state environmental officials have been suspended, and there is proof that Gov. Snyder knew the citizens were being poisoned and did nothing about it.[1]

The Flint water crisis began with an April 2014 decision by a state-appointed emergency manager to switch the city's water source from Lake Huron water to a local corrosive river. The state's environmental agency oversaw the switch and failed to require the use of corrosion control agents, which allowed lead to leach off water pipes and flow into households across the city.[2]

Another important issue is that only 90 out of 100,000 potential contaminants are regulated by the EPA. No amount of lead in drinking water is considered safe. The health based goal is zero.[3] Early exposure to lead impairs brain development and is often associated with later violent or criminal behavior. The lead industry hates regulation and millions of children continue to suffer brain impairment because of its greed. The EPA's action level for lead is 15 parts per billion. Seven locations in Flint, Michigan, tested above 1,000 parts per billion. According to Nicholas Kristof, a journalist for the New York Times stated that "lead poisoning in many places in America is even worse than in Flint. Kids are more likely to suffer lead poisoning in Pennsylvania, Illinois or New York State than in Flint. A starting point of this public health revolution should be to protect infants and fetuses from toxic substances, which means taking on the companies that buy lawmakers to prevent regulation."[4]

According to Michael Moore, who lives in Flint and was hospitalized with pneumonia, Gov. Snyder nullified the free elections in Flint, deposed the mayor and city council, and then appointed his own man to run the city a few years ago. To save money, government officials decided to unhook the people of Flint from their fresh water drinking source, Lake Huron, and instead, make the public drink from the toxic Flint River. When the governor and his staff members discovered just how toxic the water was, they kept quiet and covered up the extent of the damage being inflicted on Flint's residents. Most notable was the lead affecting the children, causing irreversible and permanent brain damage.

A few months after Gov. Snyder removed Flint from the clean fresh water the people had been drinking for decades, someone from General Motors complained to Gov. Snyder that the Flint River water was causing their car parts to corrode when being washed on the assembly line. The Governor was appalled to hear that GM property was being damaged. He jumped through a number of hoops and quietly spent $440,000 to hook GM back up to the Lake Huron water. The rest of Flint businesses and homes were kept on the Flint River water. While the children in Flint were drinking lead-filled water, there was one address in Flint that got clean water: the GM factory.

In addition to daily exposing every child in Flint to lead poisoning, there are many other diseases afflicting Flint's citizens. The number of cases in Flint of Legionnaires disease has increased tenfold since the switch to the river water. Doctors are now discovering another half-dozen toxins found in the blood of Flint's citizens, causing concern about other health catastrophes that may soon come to light. In addition, thanks to corrupt Gov. Snyder, all homeowners in Flint are now stuck with a house that's worth nothing. That's a total home value of $2.4 billion down the economic drain. People in Flint, one of the poorest cities in the U.S., don't have much to their name; and, for many their only asset is their home. In addition to being poisoned, they now have a net worth of zero.[5]

Many U.S. cities have been found to have unsafe levels of lead in the water, including Durham and Greenville, North Carolina, Columbia, South Carolina, and Jackson, Michigan. Officials in those states waited six months to disclose the contamination, and there have been scores of additional places in recent years. The EPA tells us that streams tapped by water utilities serving a third of the population are not yet covered by clean-water laws that limit levels of toxic pollutants. Even purified water often travels to homes through pipes that are in stunning disrepair, potentially open to disease and pollutants. Although Congress banned lead water pipes in 1986, between 3.3 million and 10 million older ones remain, primed to leach lead into tap water by forces as simple as jostling during repairs or a change in water chemistry.[6]

A hospital in Flint stopped using the water because it was damaging its medical instruments. Finally, after out-of-state toxicity experts confirmed that Flint's water constituted a major public health emergency, Gov. Snyder and crew were forced to switch from denial to damage control. He has since apologized to Flint residents and is trying to save face (and his job) by promising to "fix" the mess he made. Unfortunately, the poison is not only in the water. The situation in Flint reveals there is a much deeper contamination poisoning our country's political morals. There is an insidious right-wing belief that poor people are moochers whose misfortunes can be ignored—even when their misfortunes stem directly from the discriminatory practices of evil elites like Gov. Snyder. What happened in Flint proves that our government cannot be run like corporations because corporations exist to reward only a few winners, whereas the purpose of government is to serve all its citizens. Everyone has a right to safe drinking water and the problem in Flint could have been avoided by continuing to use the water used in Detroit and the other wealthy cities.[7]

Nick Lyon, director of the Michigan Department of Health and Human Services and four other officials involved with Flint's lead-contaminated water issue were charged with involuntary manslaughter. Lyon was accused of misconduct in office and involuntary manslaughter, becoming the highest-ranking member of Gov. Snyder's administration to be targeted in the criminal probe. The manslaughter charge carries a penalty of up to 15 years in prison and a $7,500 fine, while the misconduct charge carries a prison sentence of up to five years and a $10,000 fine.[8] Lyon; former Flint Emergency Manager Darnell, Earley; former Michigan Department of Environmental Quality Drinking Water Chief, Liane Shekter-Smith; State Water Supervisor, Stephen Busch; and former Flint Water Department Manager Howard Croft have been accused of failing to alert the public about an outbreak of Legionnaires' disease in the Flint area. Earley, Shekter-Smith, Busch, and Croft already have been charged with less-serious crimes.[9]

Michigan Attorney General Bill Schuette wants to file charges against Gov. Snyder. When asked why Snyder has not been charged, Schuette said no "crime has been established." The state's chief medical officer, Dr. Eden Wells, was charged with obstruction of justice and lying to a police officer.[10]

Schuette filed charges against six more state employees on July 29, 2016, for their alleged involvement in lead contamination of the water supply in Flint. Three other employees were previously charged, bringing the total to nine. Environmental employees face allegations of tampering with or altering lead in water tests, while those in the health department faced allegations of concealing tests that showed elevated lead levels in blood. The multiple felony and misdemeanor charges carry sentences of one to five years in prison and fines of up to $10,000.[11]

The charges stem from a criminal investigation by Schuette's office, which created a team of investigators who have said the scope of potential criminal charges that could be considered include misconduct in office and involuntary manslaughter. Those charged include Health and Human Services employees Nancy Peeler, head of the childhood lead poisoning prevention program; Corrine Miller, a state epidemiologist; and Robert Scott, acting coordinator of the state's childhood lead poisoning prevention program. They were charged with misconduct in office for "willfully and knowingly misleading [colleagues] regarding the reports of the increase in blood lead levels of children . . . in and around Flint." The three state environmental employees charged are Water Regulators Patrick Cook and Adam Rosenthal and former state Water Chief Liane Shekter Smith. Rosenthal was charged with tampering with evidence for "knowingly and intentionally" altering or destroying lead and copper test results on three occasions between February and August 2015.[12] Surely these employees must have known that lead causes brain damage in children! Do you think they were concerned that everyone who owned a home in Flint now owned property with no market value because of the toxic water? These citizens were literally trapped in their poisoned homes, because for many of these poor people, their home was their only asset. They now can't sell it and leave.

Attorney General Schuette filed criminal charges against two state environmental employees and one city employee who allegedly tampered with evidence, distorted lead results, and failed to require the use of corrosion control chemicals that would have prevented lead from leaching off water pipes and flowing into Flint households. The city employee, Mike Glasgow, struck a plea deal with Schuette's office, and a judge took the agreement under advisement. The allegations that Michigan Department of Health and Human Services employees hid evidence of elevated lead levels in blood were raised by researchers from Virginia Tech, who helped uncover the contamination issue. Researchers reviewed years of blood lead level data and found, in the months after the city switched water sources, a noticeable spike.[13]

The Environmental Protection Agency (EPA) tried to roll back standards for a huge source of toxic water pollution: coal-fired power plants. This is the latest installment in EPA Administrator Scott Pruitt's agenda, and it might be coming to the tap water near you. The Trump administration wants to pause Obama-era regulation aimed at limiting the dumping of toxic metals by the nation's power plants into public waterways.[14] To make America great again, wouldn't it help to poison some of our citizens with mercury, arsenic, and lead? Trump's attempt to halt these clean water protections for mercury, arsenic, and lead from coal power plants is very foolish and dangerous, because power plants represent the largest industrial source of toxic wastewater pollution in the country.

Coal-fired power plants are the biggest source of toxic water pollution, as they discharge very nasty and dangerous chemicals like lead, arsenic, and cadmium that are linked to a host of serious health problems. Unfortunately, the federal standards for that pollution were almost nonexistent and 30 years out of date, thanks to the political clout of the coal industry. The EPA was ordered to act and the agency finalized updated standards in 2015, which went into effect in January 2016. Power plants have been busy complying with the standard since then, which could turn off the spigot of this toxic brew into our streams, rivers, and lakes.[15]

Almost 40 percent of all coal plants discharge toxic pollution within 5 miles of a downstream community's drinking water intake. Coal-plant wastewater has contaminated more than 23,000 miles of waterways, including nearly 400 water bodies used as drinking water sources. However, a polluter lobby group had petitioned the EPA to review the rule, and Pruitt has been happy to oblige. In 2017, he informed a court that he would act on the decision and revisit the standard, even though it had been the law of the land for well over a year.[16] Pruitt resigned in July 2018 because of numerous ethics violations.

The Environmental Working Group (EWG) published results of a study that reveals Tampa Bay's drinking water exceeds the maximum chromium levels the California

Office of Environmental Health Hazard Assessment deems safe. As news of this cancer-causing toxin in Tampa's water spreads, citizens wonder how serious is the risk. In 1993, a single mother named Erin Brockovich almost single-handedly put an end to local water contamination by the Pacific Gas and Electric Company of California. Her work shed light on the toxins infiltrating local drinking water supplies, which led to California's current public health goals concerning water. The contaminant in question was chromium-6, a cancer-causing toxin linked with liver damage, reproductive problems, lung cancer, and developmental harm–the same contaminant in Tampa Bay's water.[17]

Chromium, a metallic element, is odorless and tasteless. Two forms of chromium occur naturally in water: chromium-3 and chromium-6. Chromium-3 is important for human dietary health and is in many fruits, vegetables, meats, and grains. Chromium-6 stems from natural chromium deposit erosion or industrial processes and is a carcinogen. Factories with poor storage, leaking containers, or inefficient industrial waste removal practices can leak chromium-6 into the environment–and eventually into our groundwater. Experts have linked chromium-6 with liver and kidney damage, pulmonary congestion, asthma, respiratory irritation, and respiratory cancer. Even minor exposures to chromium-6 can cause adverse health problems.[18]

According to the EWG, 20 different areas in Florida showed levels that exceed 0.02 parts per billion (ppb) for the contaminate chromium. These regions include the City of Sarasota, the University of South Florida, the City of Tampa Water Department, and the City of St. Petersburg. Pasco County showed the highest level of chromium-6 at 0.491 ppb. Content was also high in Hillsborough County, Pinellas County, Manatee County, and Sarasota County. The study suggests that negligent manufacturing waste practices caused the chromium-6 contamination. Coal-burning power plants often dump ash containing chromium-6 into unlined pits, threatening hundreds of thousands of water supplies. Studies show that common methods to treat drinking water supplies may actually increase levels of chromium-6, a known carcinogen. Experts say those at greatest risk of harm from this toxin are infants, children, those who take antacids, and those with poorly functioning livers.[19]

The 1972 Clean Water Act is the country's main tool for controlling source water pollution, but the law is limited by enforcement issues and legal ambiguity over which bodies of water it governs. Protecting tap water quality means fighting two battles: one against pollution as it enters waterways, and another against polluted water when it arrives at a treatment plant. Most U.S. water systems are fed by groundwater, which is usually cleaner than surface water since it is filtered by soil and rocks. However, big cities tend to rely on rivers and lakes, so more Americans tend to use surface-water systems.

A typical water-treatment plant uses the following five steps to clean up so-called "raw water" before delivering it to customers:

- **Coagulation:** As untreated water flows into the treatment plant, it is first mixed with alum and other chemicals that form small, sticky particles called "floc," which attract bits of dirt and other debris.
- **Sedimentation:** The combined weight of the dirt and floc becomes heavy enough to sink to the bottom of the tank, where it settles as sediment. The clearer water then flows on to the next step in the process.
- **Filtration:** After larger dirt particles are removed, the water passes through a series of filters designed to clean out

smaller stowaways, including some microbes. These filters are often made of sand, gravel ,and charcoal, mimicking the natural soil-filtration process that usually keeps groundwater pure in nature.

- **Disinfection:** Water treatment used to end with filtration, but disinfectants have been added to kill any microbes that might have made it past the filters. Typically, a small amount of chlorine is added to the filtered water, although other disinfectant chemicals may also be used.
- **Storage:** Once disinfectants are added, the water is placed in a closed tank or reservoir to let the chemicals work their magic. Eventually, the water flows from its storage area through pipes into homes and businesses.[20]

Before the days of synthetic chemicals and oil spills, bacteria and viruses were the main dangers lurking in water. Lakes, rivers, and streams contain a wide variety of microbes, some of which can wreak gastrointestinal havoc if they get into our bodies. While treatment plants now remove most of these microbes, some have been known to get through. Small private wells face the highest risks since the EPA doesn't regulate them. This is especially the case in rural areas where livestock manure mixes with runoff, sometimes contaminating a well's groundwater supply.[21]

Chlorine is the main disinfectant used to treat U.S. drinking water, but treated water may also contain disinfectant byproducts such as bromate, chlorite, and haloacetic acids. Chlorine is toxic to humans as well as microbes, and while small amounts make tap water safer, too much can have the opposite effect. Health problems may include: eye and nose irritation, stomach discomfort, anemia, and even neurological problems in infants and young children. Bromate and haloacetic acids have also been linked to liver and kidney problems, as well as increased cancer risk. In addition, inorganic chemicals are one of the world's oldest water pollutants, but humans have also helped spread them around. Arsenic has a long history of poisoning wells as it erodes from natural deposits, but today it is also in runoff from orchards and in waste from manufacturers of electronics. Metals like copper, lead, and mercury can leach from natural deposits, too. Today, however, they're better known for seeping out of corroded pipes or being emitted by mines, factories, and refineries. Many have severe neurological effects.[22]

Radiation is another potent carcinogen that can get into the water supply. Radioactive atoms, known as radionuclides, are mainly a naturally occurring water pollutant, emanating from natural deposits of radium, uranium, and other radioactive metals. Drinking radiation-tinged water over time is a big risk factor for cancer, which is similar to breathing radon gas, that is often trapped in basements after drifting up from the soil below.[23]

Hydraulic Fracking

Hydraulic fracking is one of the most controversial types of underground injection systems. Drillers pump pressurized water, sand, and chemicals down a newly drilled well, forcing them through perforations in its casing so they blast out to the surrounding shale, opening new cracks and widening old ones. Water may constitute up to 99 percent of this mixture, while the sand serves as a "propping agent" to keep the cracks open after the water is pumped out. This technology has existed for decades, but recent breakthroughs now let drillers use more water — 2 to 5 million gallons per well — while new "slickwater" fracking chemicals help slash friction. That increases the water pressure and, thus, the amount of fracturing. After a well has been drilled into rock, a fluid (usually water mixed with viscous chemicals) is injected at high pressure, expanding deep fractures in the rock. These fractures are then filled with a "propping agent" (usually sand suspended in chemicals) to keep the cracks from closing once the pressure is released. The new, wider cracks then allow the oil or gas to flow more freely to the surface, improving the well's productivity.[24] Fracking is controversial because many people believe it can cause earthquakes, but most of the controversy has focused on how it affects water supplies. Very little comprehensive data exists to show how much fracking chemicals wind up in groundwater, and drilling companies aren't required to disclose what chemicals they inject into their wells.

A Harvard study published in 2016 found the drinking water of millions of Americans contains polyfluoroalkyl and perfluroalkyl substances (PFAS) that cause cancer and immunodeficiency. Levels of a widely used class of industrial chemicals linked with cancer and other health problems exceed federally recommended safety levels in public water supplies for millions in the U.S. This is according to a study led by researchers from the Harvard T.H. Chan School of Public Health and the Harvard John A. Paulson School of Engineering and Applied Sciences.[25] PFAS used to be known as PFCs, which stands for perfluorinated chemicals, for which the compounds were historically known. PFCs are the stain, water, and grease repellant chemicals found in many products people use every day.

According to Xindi Hu, a doctoral student in the Department of Environmental Health at T.H. Chan School of Public Health, "Chemicals with unknown toxicities, such as PFAS, were allowed to be used and released to the environment, and we now have to face the severe consequences. The actual number of people exposed may be even higher than our study found, because government data for levels of these compounds in drinking water is lacking for almost a third of the U.S. population—about 100 million people."[26] That is very scary. There is no way to know how many toxins we have been exposed to.

PFAS have been linked with cancer, high cholesterol, and obesity.[27] Although several major manufacturers have discontinued the use of some PFAS, the chemicals continue to persist. Concentrations of six types of PFAS in drinking-water supplies were studied, using data from more than 36,000 water samples collected nationwide by the EPA from 2013 to 2015. They also looked at industrial sites that manufacture or use PFAS: at military fire-training sites and civilian airports where firefighting foam containing PFAS is used and at wastewater-treatment plants. Discharges from these plants, which are unable to remove PFAS from wastewater by standard treatment methods, could contaminate groundwater. The study found that PFAS were detectable at the minimum reporting levels required by the EPA in 194 out of 4,864 water supplies in 33 states across the United States. Drinking water from 13 states accounted for 75 percent of the detections: California, New Jersey, North Carolina, Alabama, Florida, Pennsylvania, Ohio, New York, Georgia, Minnesota, Arizona, Massachusetts, and Illinois, in order of frequency of detection.[28]

Texas officials were aware of a citywide lead problem since 2015—one the city still hasn't corrected and one Destiny and John Walton first learned about in a September letter to residents. City and state officials even knew, from recent tests, that water in the Walton family's cramped, one-bedroom rental house near railroad tracks was carrying sky-high levels of lead. The Waltons got their first inkling of a problem when blood tests detected high levels of lead in their son's growing body. Then they learned that their tap water contained lead—about 28 times the federal limit.[29]

Millions of Americans face similar risks because the nation's drinking-water enforcement system doesn't make small utility companies play by the same safety rules as everyone else. These companies that serve only a few thousand people or less don't have to treat water to prevent lead contamination until after lead is found. Even when safety tests are skipped or water isn't treated after lead is found, federal and state regulators do not always force these small utility companies to comply with the law.

In 2016, USA TODAY network journalists reviewed records from the EPA and all 50 states. The journalists visited small communities across the country and interviewed more than 120 people stuck using untested or lead-tainted tap water. The investigation found:

- About 100,000 people get their drinking water from utilities that discovered high lead but failed to treat the water to remove it. Dozens of utilities took more than a year to formulate a treatment plan and even longer to begin treatment.

- 4 million Americans get water from small operators who skipped required tests or did not conduct the tests properly, violating a cornerstone of federal safe drinking water laws. The testing is required because, without it, utilities, regulators and people drinking the water can't know if it is safe. In more than 2,000 communities, lead tests were skipped more than once. Hundreds repeatedly failed to properly test for five or more years.

- About 850 small water utilities with a documented history of lead contamination—places where state and federal regulators are supposed to pay extra attention—have failed to properly test for lead at least once since 2010.[30]

This two-tiered system exists in both law and practice. Regulators are more lenient with smaller water systems because they lack resources, deeming some lost causes when they don't have the money, expertise, or motivation to fix problems. The nation's Safe Drinking Water Act allows amateurs to operate smaller water systems even though the risks for people drinking the water are the same. Officials in West Virginia, for example, labeled more than a dozen of the smaller water systems "orphans" because they didn't have owners or operators. Enforcement efforts for those utilities amounted to little more than a continuous stream of warning letters when operators failed to test year after year. All the while, residents continued drinking untested and potentially contaminated water.[31]

Virginia Tech's Marc Edwards, is one of the nation's top experts on lead in drinking water who helped identify the crisis in Flint, Michigan. Edwards believes people in America's forgotten places—rural outposts, post-industrial communities, and towns where the poor tend to live—are most at risk from the dangers of lead exposure. These dangers include: irreversible brain damage, lowered IQ, behavioral problems, and language delays. Edwards said the effects of lead poisoning could make it even more difficult for families in these communities to climb out of poverty. "I'm worried about their kids," he said. "The risk of permanent harm here is horrifying." Destiny and John Walton fear lead has already harmed their son Adam. At an age when other children use dozens of words, Adam said just three: "mama," "dada," and "no." They Waltons wish they had known about lead in the water earlier so they could have protected Adam.[32]

South Florida Water Problems

South Florida is located above two huge underground stores of water: the Biscayne and Floridan Aquifers. Miami gets most of its drinking water from the upper Biscayne Aquifer, while the government has used the lower portion of the Floridian to dump waste and untreated sewage. This continues despite the multiple studies that have warned waste could one day seep into the drinking water.

Environmentalists are concerned that Florida Power & Light (FPL) wants to dump radioactive waste into the water. A small group of activists called Citizens Allied for Safe Energy (CASE) tried to stop the FPL plan, but their legal petition was shot down. CASE had filed a petition with the U.S. Nuclear Regulatory Commission (NRC), but the NRC threw out CASE's complaint, saying the environmental group had filed too late in the FPL's approval process.[33]

FPL is going to build two nuclear reactors at the controversial Turkey Point Nuclear Generating Station south of Miami. FPL officials told the U.S. Nuclear Regulatory

Commission about the plan to store contaminated water used to clean the reactors, as well as radioactive waste ("radwaste") in the Boulder Zone. In October 2017, the NRC issued a report, stating the FPL plan would pose "no environmental impacts" to the South Florida environment, which is a lie. Approximately one month later, CASE filed a legal petition demanding that the NRC hold a hearing on the FPL radioactive waste plan.

Everyone who lives in South Florida knows nothing below us is hermetically sealed. A hermetically sealed container is so tightly closed that no air can leave or enter it. Environmentalists say the plan would likely leak carcinogens such as cesium, strontium 90, and tritium right into the drinking-water aquifers. CASE's November complaint cited both governmental data and FPL engineers. In separate hearings it was admitted that waste could leak upward from the Boulder Zone into the Biscayne Aquifer. The Ground Water Atlas of the United States, a government document, warns the Boulder Zone "is thought to be connected to the Atlantic Ocean, possibly about 25 miles east of Miami, where the sea floor is almost 2,800 feet deep along the Straits of Florida."

Also, "an upward hydraulic gradient from the Floridan [Aquifer] to the Biscayne [Aquifer]," an FPL engineer testified in January 2016 means that "The Floridan is under pressure. Therefore, you have flow from the Floridan into the Biscayne and not vice versa." Since filing that complaint, CASE also uncovered yet another governmental study, which confirms the Boulder Zone can leak into "underground sources of drinking water" in South Florida.[34]

A 2015 study from the United States Geological Survey states that many tectonic faults and other fissures exist under Biscayne Bay and the "Miami Terrace," the seafloor immediately east of the Miami shoreline. The report states that recent studies by the U.S. Geological Survey of seismic-reflection profiles acquired in onshore canals and offshore in Biscayne Bay and the Atlantic continental shelf have indicated the presence of toctonic faults. These studies substantiate the utility of this approach for locating feasible vertical-fluid flow pathways. The strike-slip fault spans confining units of the Floridan aquifer system and could provide high permeability passageways for groundwater movement. If present near wastewater injection utilities, these features represent a plausible physical system for the upward migration of liquid waste or sewage discharged into a river or the sea injected into the Boulder Zone.[35]

FPL officials insist that any radioactive-waste discharges will be carefully monitored to ensure they won't leak, but most Floridians know they are not telling the truth. Miami-Dade County officials said cooling canals from Turkey Point were already leaking waste into Biscayne Bay. This ordeal, along with FPL officials' alleged refusal to take proper responsibility for the damage, led to a lawsuit filed in the U.S. Southern District of Florida and the Tropical Audubon Society. The lawsuit claims FPL officials have violated numerous sections of the U.S. Clean Water Act, as well as a pollution-abatement contract. The legal action comes after regulators found more than 200 times the daily level of tritium, a radioactive isotope, in the Biscayne Bay water. Tritium is linked to nuclear power production, which led regulators to point their fingers at the only giant smoking gun in the area: Turkey Point, which sits on the Bay's shores near Homestead, about 25 miles south of downtown Miami. While tritium at that amount isn't believed to be dangerous to people, its presence indicates that the plant's cooling canals are leaking.[36] This is a huge problem nobody knows how to rectify!

Until the 1970s, employees at FPL had been dumping hot cooling water straight into the Bay, until a court order put a stop to all that. Then a 5,800-acre, two-miles-wide-by-five-miles-long cooling canal was built that is adjacent to the Bay. The leak from those canals carries a host of potential environmental problems for sensitive ecosystems.

"The cooling canal system is unlined and underlain by porous limestone geology, including the Biscayne Aquifer," the suit says. "The contaminated water in the cooling canal system has for many years discharged, and continues to discharge from the cooling canal system into Biscayne Bay" right from the pipes.[37]

During 2016, plumes of toxic algae turned South Florida's emerald waters dark brown and smothered its inlets under a fetid blanket of guacamole green goop that killed fish, suffocated oyster beds, and triggered a ferocious outcry from coastal residents. This has led to the closing of beaches, the declaration of a state of emergency, and the desperate, heart-breaking efforts of people using garden hoses to save manatees, affectionately known as sea cows, caked in toxic slime and struggling to breathe.[38]

Lake Okeechobee's fertilizer-infused water turns the ocean dark brown, causing ecological and economic calamity for South Florida's Treasure Coast. None of the reports explained how this calamity is man-made. Many people were determined to turn Everglades sawgrass into cash crops. Environmental degradation is only part of the price the public pays so private companies can turn sugar into money. These tropical wetlands have been drained and maintained for decades at great expense for the benefit of Florida's sugar cane industry. Billions of dollars have been spent on a regional flood control system that keeps the cane fields from flooding during periods of heavy rain and irrigated during droughts. Adding to the public cost, a national sugar program requires American consumers to pay twice the world price for sugar through a blend of import quotas, tariffs, and loan guarantees. Congress has kept the program in place specifically for the sugar industry since 1934. Critics of the U.S. sugar policy say sugar can be imported at half the price and without environmental damage here.[39]

In future decades, rising temperatures and shifting rain patterns likely will worsen the plague of toxic algae. Because only a fraction of the sugar cane fields is being tried to solve the algae problem, some see it as a test of whether special interests can win. For 6,000 years, excess groundwater has spilled over the southern rim of Lake Okachobee, nourishing the Everglades before draining into the Florida Bay. To prepare for the sugar cane fields, engineers raised and fortified the lake's southern shore, funneling all that excess groundwater through an array of canals, levees, and pumping stations into two rivers that then dump it into the sea along Florida's eastern and western coasts.[40]

This cleared the way for the cane fields, but choked off water to the rest of the Everglades. It also infected rivers and South Florida's coastlines with toxic algae. It also created a seeping dike that, if a bad storm comes along, could lay waste to everything and everybody in its path. The 143-mile-long dike, named in the 1930s after former-president Herbert Hoover, had been built piecemeal over 135 years, beginning in the 19th century. It leaks and is in constant need of inspection and repair. The higher the level of the lake, the higher the risk of a failure. The sea is its only safety valve when the lake becomes too full.[41]

Water is not the only problem. The FDA is not keeping unsafe food out of the country. The media has reported serious mistakes made by the FDA in the recent past. A glimpse into the last few decades of FDA oversight shows how little the FDA has done to improve the food system in this country, how it has allowed us to eat harmful food additives, and how it has failed to act after an ingredient has been found to be unsafe. There are several products that have been deemed "FDA Approved" which were yanked from market years after they were shown to be extremely dangerous. Unless many people die, the FDA does nothing.

Sulfites

Sulfites were being used as preservatives in wine, raisins, and other foods and were thought to be safe. In 1982, the FDA proposed that sulfites formally be declared "generally recognized as safe," or GRAS, a legal category of substances added to food. This action was recommended even though several years before California researchers found that sulfites could trigger asthma attacks. The problem arose because restaurants had begun soaking iceberg lettuce and peeled, raw potatoes in a sulfite solution.

The sulfites prevented browning but resulted in high levels in the foods.[42]

The Center for Science in the Public Interest (CSPI) publicized the sulfite problem and then, even in those pre-Internet days, heard from many people who suffered asthma attacks after eating a restaurant salad or drinking a glass of wine. Then there was publicity from more than a dozen people whose family members died after eating sulfite-laced foods. With people dying, CSPI petitioned the FDA to ban sulfites, but the agency did nothing. 60 Minutes ran, and then re-ran, a story on this topic, but still the FDA did nothing.[43]

The FDA approved sulfite preservatives on fresh produce in 1982, despite evidence that sulfites could trigger asthma attacks. Soon after, many people got sick and some died after eating salads laced with sulfites in restaurants. The Center for Science in the Public Interest (CSPI) claimed to have documented over a dozen deaths, and petitioned the FDA to ban its use—yet the FDA failed to act for four years. The FDA finally banned sulfites on fresh produce in 1986 and subsequently limited it in other foods.[44]

Partially Hydrogenated Oils/Trans Fat

Until 1990, artificial trans fat, which forms when partially hydrogenated vegetable oil is manufactured, was generally thought to be innocuous. However, researchers conducted a study showing that trans fat promoted heart disease by raising "bad" LDL cholesterol. In 1993, CSPI called on the FDA to require trans fat to be listed on the new Nutrition Facts labels. It took the FDA 13 years to comply. Meanwhile, new research showed that trans fat was the single most harmful fat in our diet. Walter Willett, chairman of the nutrition department at the Harvard School of Public Health, estimated that trans fat was causing tens of thousands of fatal heart attacks annually. In 2004, CSPI petitioned the FDA to ban partially hydrogenated oil. Eight years later, in 2002, the FDA still had not done so, and some foods still contain copious amounts of the deadly fat. (Denmark, Austria, Switzerland, and Iceland have all essentially banned the use of partially hydrogenated oil.)[45]

Partially hydrogenated oils are used in pies, crackers, cakes, cookies, and in fried foods at restaurants. When partially hydrogenated oils are manufactured they create artificial trans fats. Trans fat raises the "bad" LDL cholesterol and lowers the good "HDL" cholesterol, increasing the risk of heart disease. The FDA has still not made a final determination to ban it, despite pleas from the American Heart Association and the American College of Cardiology.[46]

Caramel Coloring

The FDA defended the presence of a cancer-causing contaminant (4-methylimidazole) in the caramel coloring used in Coke, Pepsi, and other soft drinks. In stark contrast, the state of California adopted a regulation requiring colas to have a cancer-warning notice unless their levels of 4-MI were under 30 micrograms (most brands had about five times as much). After failing to fend off the requirement, companies quickly began marketing colas made with less-contaminated caramel colorings, but only in California.[47]

Antibiotics in Animal Feed for Growth Promotion

The meat industry uses significantly more antibiotics than the healthcare industry and it has been reported that animals receive 80 percent of the antibiotics produced in this country (estimated at 29 million pounds per year). The reason that industrial farms are systematically feeding their animals antibiotics is to produce bigger animals that grow faster on less food—thereby increasing their profits. Antibiotics also help the animals survive the poor conditions in which they may be raised. The Center for Disease Control (CDC) warns that this use is contributing to antibiotic-resistant infections in humans and harming public health. Recent reports done in 2014 indicate that antibiotic resistance can be blamed for at least 2 million illnesses and 23,000 deaths in the U.S.[48]

In 2013, the FDA issued guidelines for the industry (that went into effect in December 2016) that recommends halting the use of antibiotics to fatten up animals, along with veterinary oversight of antibiotic use. The FDA's guidance is voluntary and not legally enforceable, which means that if it reduces profits, companies can ignore the FDA's warning. According to Pew Charitable Trusts, there's a huge loophole that will still permit antibiotics for "disease prevention" in "the absence of any threat from a specific bacterial disease." This may allow veterinarians to rationalize a prescription for routine antibiotics. The European
Union banned antibiotics in animal feed for growth promotion in 2006.[21] Unlike some Americans, they do not want to poison their citizens.

The International Agency for Research on Cancer (IARC) has classified processed meat as a carcinogen. It has also classified red meat as a probable carcinogen. IARC is the cancer agency of the World Health Organization. Processed meat includes hot dogs, ham, bacon, sausage, and some deli meats. It refers to meat that has been treated in some way to preserve or flavor it. Processes include salting, curing, fermenting, and smoking. Red meat includes beef, pork, lamb, and goat.[49]

Twenty-two experts from 10 countries reviewed more than 800 studies to reach their conclusions. They found that eating 50 grams of processed meat every day increased the risk of colorectal cancer by 18 percent. That's the equivalent of about four strips of bacon or one hot dog. For red meat, there was evidence of increased risk of colorectal, pancreatic, and prostrate cancer.[50]

High Fructose Corn Syrup

Many Americans are consuming huge doses of sugar, especially high fructose corn syrup. It is sweeter and cheaper than regular sugar and is in every processed food and sugar-sweetened drink. In recent history, we've gone from 20 teaspoons of sugar per person per year to about 150 pounds of sugar per person per year. That's a half pound a day for every man, woman, and child in America. The average 20-ounce soda contains 15 teaspoons of sugar, all of it high fructose corn syrup. When you consume sugar in those doses, it becomes a toxin.[51]

As part of the chemical process used to make high fructose corn syrup, the glucose and fructose—which are naturally bound together—become separated. This allows the fructose to mainline directly into your liver, which turns on a factory of fat production in your liver called lipogenesis. This can lead to fatty liver—the most common disease in America today, affecting 90 million Americans. High fructose corn syrup is the driver of the current epidemic of heart attacks, strokes, cancer, dementia, and Type 2 diabetes. It contains dangerous chemicals and contaminants.[52]

Chloralkali is used in making high fructose corn syrup, and it contains mercury. Also, there are trace amounts of mercury found in beverages containing high fructose corn syrup. It may not be a problem if consumed occasionally, but the average person in the country consumes more than 20 teaspoons a day of high fructose corn syrup and the average teenager has 34 teaspoons a day. Over time, this can accumulate in the body, causing health problems. If you see this ingredient on a label, I guarantee you the food is processed junk.[53]

Artificial Sweeteners are Poison

The chemical additive aspartame is a carcinogenic substance that nobody should consume. According to the Huffington Post, Donald Rumsfeld made a fat bonus when aspartame became legal. Rumsfeld is a political figure known for being the secretary of defense under both President Gerald Ford and President George W. Bush. Dr. John Olney, who founded the field of neuroscience called excitotoxicity, attempted to stop the approval of aspartame with Attorney James Turner back in 1996. The FDA's own toxicologist, Dr. Adrian Gross, told Congress that without a shadow of a doubt, aspartame can cause brain tumors and brain cancer. It also violated the Delaney Amendment, which forbids putting anything in food that is known to cause cancer. (For more information, see http://www.mpwhi.com/parliament_is_right_on_independent_aspartame_studies.htm.) According to the top doctors and researchers on this issue, aspartame causes headaches, memory loss, seizures, vision loss, comas and cancer. It worsens or mimics the symptoms of such diseases and conditions as fibromyalgia, multiple sclerosis, lupus, attention deficit disorder, diabetes, Alzheimer's, chronic fatigue and depression. Further dangers highlighted is that aspartame liberates free methyl alcohol. The resulting chronic methanol poisoning affects the dopamine system of the brain, causing addiction. Methanol, or wood alcohol, constitutes one third of the aspartame molecule and is classified as a severe metabolic poison and narcotic.[54]

The effects of aspartame are documented by the FDA's data. Dr. Betty Martini works with doctors around the world in an effort to remove aspartame from food, drinks, and medicine. According to Martini, aspartame has brought more complaints to the FDA than any other additive and is responsible for 75 percent of such complaints to that agency. The EPA found aspartame to be a potentially dangerous chemical. Martini also says it is a "deadly neurotoxic drug masquerading as an additive. It interacts with all antidepressants, L-DOPA, Coumadin, hormones, insulin, all cardiac medication, and many others. It also is a chemical hyper-sensitization drug so that it interacts with vaccines, other toxins, other unsafe sweeteners like Splenda, which has a chlorinated base like dichlorodiphenyltrichloroethane (DDT) which can cause autoimmune disease. DDT is a colorless, tasteless, and almost odorless crystalline chemical compound originally developed as an insecticide.

The FDA has known this for a quarter of a century and done nothing.[55]

In 1985, Monsanto purchased G.D. Searle, the chemical company that held the patent to aspartame. Monsanto was untroubled by aspartame's clouded past, including the report of a 1980 FDA Board of Inquiry. Three independent scientists confirmed that aspartame "might induce brain tumors." The FDA had previously banned aspartame based on this finding, only to have then-Searle Chairman Donald Rumsfeld vow to "call in his markers," to get it approved. Ronald Reagan was sworn in as president on Jan. 21, 1981. Rumsfeld, while still CEO at Searle, was part of Reagan's transition team. This team hand-picked Dr. Arthur Hull Hayes, Jr., to be the new FDA commissioner. Hayes, a pharmacologist, had no previous experience with food additives before being appointed director of the FDA. On Jan. 21, 1981, the day after his inauguration, Reagan issued an executive order eliminating the FDA commissioner's authority to take action. Searle then re-applied to the FDA for approval to use aspartame in food sweetener. Hayes, Reagan's new FDA commissioner, appointed a five-person Scientific Commission to review the board of inquiry's decision. It soon became clear that the panel would uphold the ban by a 3-2 decision. Hayes installed a sixth member on the commission, and the vote became deadlocked. He then personally broke the tie in aspartame's favor.[56] Chemical food additives are poison, but the FDA is going to continue to lie about how safe they are to consume.

Aspartame has a patent in Europe that shows it is made from the waste products of genetically modified E. coli bacteria. Though this fact was reported as early as 1999, not much attention was paid at the time to aspartame and its maker Monsanto. The patent refers to "cloned microorganisms" later revealed to be genetically modified E. coli bacteria. They are modified to produce an especially large peptide used to create aspartame. The cultivated and well-fed bacteria then produce proteins, which contain the aspartic acid/phenylalanine amino acid segment required to produce the sweetener. The bacteria waste is then treated to turn the large peptide and a free carboxyl group into a dipeptide. The dipeptides are then treated with alcohol and methanol to produce aspartame.[57]

Splenda is just as bad as aspartame. To make Splenda, regular sugar is chemically altered, replacing hydrogen-oxygen groups with chlorine. While there are only small amounts of chlorine in Splenda, studies have suggested that if consumed regularly for a long period of time, these levels could accumulate in the body, leading to adverse health outcomes. Sucralose passes through your GI tract undigested, but new studies show that sucralose is actually metabolized, according to study coauthor Susan S. Schiffman, PhD, an adjunct professor at North Carolina State University. Splenda reduces good gut bacteria by altering the amount and quality of the beneficial microbes that are in your belly by 50 percent or more and this alteration in bacterial counts is associated with weight gain and obesity.[58]

Splenda also makes other medicine you take less effective by limiting the absorption of therapeutic drugs, such as those for cancer and heart disease. It releases toxins if you bake with it because it decomposes during baking, which releases potentially toxic compounds called chloropropanols. Splenda can alter insulin responses and blood sugar levels and has been associated with Irritable Bowel Syndrome. Sugar substitutes with sucralose are linked to type 2 diabetes, heart disease, metabolic syndrome, and obesity.[59]

rBGH Milk

rBGH is a genetically engineered artificial hormone injected into dairy cows to make them produce more milk. Despite opposition from scientists, farmers and consumers, the U.S. currently allows dairy cows to be injected with recombinant bovine growth hormone (rBGH). Monsanto was required to submit a scientific report on rBGH to the FDA so the agency could determine the growth hormone's safety. Margaret Miller put the report together, and in 1989 shortly before she submitted the report, Miller left Monsanto to work for the FDA. Her primary job was to determine whether or not to approve the report she wrote for Monsanto—Monsanto literally approved its own report! Miller was assisted by another former Monsanto researcher, Susan Sechen. The results of the study were not made available to the public until 1998, when a group of Canadian scientists obtained the full documentation and completed an independent analysis of the results. The documents showed that the FDA had never even reviewed Monsanto's original studies (on which the approval for Posilac {rBGH} had been based). In the end, the point was moot whether or not the report had contained all of the original data.[60]

Although rBGH has been banned in every industrialized nation in the world except for the United States, Monsanto continues to claim that rBGH-derived milk is no different from the natural stuff. This is despite documentation that rBGH milk contains substantially higher levels of a potent cancer tumor promoter called IGF-1. This poses a serious risk to the entire U.S. population, which is now exposed to high levels of IGF-1 in dairy products. Elevated blood levels of IGF-1 are among the leading known risk factors for breast cancer, and are also associated with other major cancers, particularly colon and prostate.[61]

For many nutritionists, the obesity epidemic is inextricably linked to the sales of packaged foods, which grew 25 percent worldwide from 2011 to 2016. This compares to 10 percent in the U.S., according to Euromonitor, a market research firm. An even starker shift took place with carbonated soft drinks; sales in Latin America have doubled since 2000, overtaking sales in North America in 2013, the World Health Organization reported. The same trends are mirrored with fast food, which grew 30 percent worldwide from 2011 to 2016. This compares to 21 percent in the United States, according to Euromonitor. Take, for example, Domino's Pizza, which in 2016 added 1,281 stores—one "every seven hours," noted its annual report—all but 171 of them overseas.[62] Big Food isn't just destroying the health of Americans, but those living overseas as well.

Brazil faces a new nutritional challenge: over the last decade, the country's obesity rate has nearly doubled to 20 percent, and the number of people who are overweight has nearly tripled to 58 percent. Each year, 300,000 people are diagnosed with Type 2 diabetes, a condition with strong links to obesity. Specific examples in Brazil also highlight the food industry's political prowess. In 2010, a coalition of Brazilian food and beverage companies refused measures that sought to limit junk food ads aimed at children.[63]

It is hard to overstate the economic power and political access enjoyed by food and beverage conglomerates in Brazil, which are responsible for 10 percent of the nation's economic output and employ 1.6 million people. In 2014, food companies donated $158 million to members of Brazil's National Congress, a threefold increase over 2010, according to Transparency International Brazil. A study the organization released last year found that more than half of Brazil's current federal legislators had been elected with donations from the food industry–before the Brazilian Supreme Court banned corporate contributions in 2015. The single largest donor to congressional candidates was the Brazilian meat giant JBS, which gave candidates $112 million in 2014. Coca-Cola gave $6.5 million in campaign contributions that year and McDonald's donated $561,000.[64]

The Food Guide Pyramid of the 1990's was bad advice that often led to obesity. Carbohydrates, particularly refined carbohydrates (breads, pasta, rice, and cereals) break down to sugar. We were told to eat six to 11 daily servings, which stores in your body as fat. In addition to the 152 pounds of sugar we eat yearly, we're getting 146 pounds of flour that also break down to sugar. Altogether, that's nearly a pound of sugar daily for every American! All those refined carbs create inflammation that triggers most chronic diseases, including diabetes, obesity, and heart disease. Equally flawed was the very top (smallest part) of the Food Guide Pyramid, which advised consuming fats and oils sparingly. According to Dr. Mark Hyman, instead of following the outdated, clearly poor advice from the old Food Guide Pyramid, you should eat a whole foods diet. This includes mostly vegetables, some fruits, and plenty of healthy fats like eggs, coconut oil, and olive oil. Avoid highly processed, factory-manufactured foods. Choose fresh vegetables, fruits, whole grains, beans, nuts, seeds, and lean animal proteins such as fish, chicken, and eggs.[65] Hyman is the Director of Cleveland Clinic's Center for Functional Medicine and the Founder of The UltraWellness Center in Massachusetts. He is convinced that the problem with the U.S. government's original Food Guide Pyramid, released in 1992, was that it conveyed the wrong dietary advice. Its 2005 replacement was vague and very confusing. The Food Guide Pyramid failed to show that whole wheat, brown rice, and other whole grains are healthier than refined grains. The pyramid pointed Americans to the type of low-fat diet that can worsen blood cholesterol profiles and make it harder to keep weight in check. It grouped healthy proteins (fish, poultry, beans, and nuts) into the same category as unhealthy proteins (red meat and processed meat), and overemphasized the importance of dairy products.[66] If you want to be healthy, eat less sugary carbs and eat more protein, nuts, and salmon.

Hydroquinone

Not only does the FDA not ensure that our drinking water and our foods are safe, it also ignores problems with products meant for women's skin. Hydroquinone is a compound used in a variety of skin products, usually targeted at customers who are looking to reduce the appearance of dark spots, freckles, acne scars, and other problem spots on the body. Hydroquinone has been the subject of much controversy over the years, and there have been many groups calling for the FDA to put a ban on the compound. In some countries, hydroquinone is already illegal. While hydroquinone is still FDA-approved and legal in the U.S., it poses some serious health risks that medical sources acknowledge. If you're thinking about using hydroquinone, there are a variety of reason you should stay away from it.

Skin Irritation

Regular use of hydroquinone can cause serious irritation of the skin, especially for people who already have sensitive skin or allergies. In some cases, hydroquinone can cause extreme redness, itching, or even a burning sensation when it is applied to the skin. Hydroquinone works to reduce the amount of melanin your skin produces, which in turn makes your skin lighter in appearance. Then your skin becomes more susceptible to dangerous carcinogenic rays that can lead to dangerous sunburns. Over a prolonged period of time, this can lead to an increased risk of certain types of skin cancer. Most manufacturers tell users to limit their sun exposure when using hydroquinone treatments—and this is impossible if you live in Florida. Some people are surprised by how severe a sunburn can be or how irritated their skin becomes after of prolonged sun exposure and using topical products that contain hydroquinone.

Ochronosis

Ochronosis is a long-term skin condition that is caused by exposure to certain chemicals. When ochronosis occurs, the skin becomes considerably darker and thicker than normal. The skin on the top of your foot is very different from the skin on your heel. That's the difference between healthy skin and skin affected by ochronosis. Some scientists and researchers have made a connection between long-term use of skin lightening products that contain hydroquinone and this skin condition.

On Aug. 29, 2006, the FDA proposed a ban on over-the-counter sales of cosmetic products containing hydroquinone, a skin-bleaching (lightening) ingredient. According to the FDA, approximately 65 companies sell in the U.S. over 200 different types of skin-lightening products containing hydroquinone. Currently, products that contain up to 2 percent hydroquinone may be sold in the U.S. without a prescription, and prescription skin-lightening products may contain up to 4 percent hydroquinone. Examples of prescription products containing hydroquinone are Lustra, Tri-Luma, and EpiQuin Micro.

The reason cited for the proposed ban is that studies in rodents show "some evidence" that hydroquinone may act as a carcinogen, although its cancer-causing properties have yet to be proved in humans. Dome-shaped yellowish spots and grayish-brown spots also have been observed in ochronosis among black women and men in South Africa, Britain, and the U.S. Ochronosis has been observed in conjunction with hydroquinone use even in individuals who have used hydroquinone-containing cosmetics for a short time. Some studies also report abnormal function of the adrenal glands and high levels of mercury in people who have used hydroquinone-containing cosmetics. For these reasons, hydroquinone has already been banned in Japan, the European Union, and Australia. America? The FDA allows it to be sold for profit in the U.S. despite the risks.

Hydroquinone-topical solutions can make skin more sensitive to sunlight (photosensitivity). People using these preparations should wear protective clothing and sunscreen when in sunlight. Exposure to ultraviolet light can cause severe sunburn when using hydroquinone. Applying hydroquinone to skin that is sunburned, windburned, chapped, or irritated can worsen these conditions.

Given how the FDA does not protect Americans, I strongly suggest you buy bottled spring water, make sure your chicken has no antibiotics added, limit fish intake because of the mercury content, avoid all processed meat, avoid meat that is high in fat and cholesterol (beef and pork), limit processed foods made with high fructose corn syrup or toxic artificial sweeteners, eat fewer products that contain refined sugar, and do not use any makeup that is not hypoallergenic. If the FDA and the EPA won't protect you from dangerous carcinogens, you have to protect yourself.

Footnotes

[1] LeFever, Jenna (February 26, 2016). Bombshell: Emails Show Michigan Governor Knew About Flint's Contaminated Water A Year Earlier. Reverbpress. (Retrieved from http://reverbpress.com/news/us/bombshell-emails-show-michigan-governor-knew-about-flints-contaminated-water-a-year-earlier/)

[2] Felton, Ryan (July 29, 2016) Flint water crisis: attorney general files charges against six more employees. The Guardian. (Retrieved from https://www.theguardian.com/us-news/2016/jul/29/flint-water-crisis-attorney-general-files-charges-six-more-state-employees)

[3] Mcginty, Jo Craven. (March 12, 2016). With Drinking Water, Safe Enough is the Goal. Wall Street Journal.

[4] Kristof, Nicholas. (February 2, 2016) Are You a Toxic Waste Disposal Site? New York Times. (Retrieved from http://www.nytimes.com/2016/02/14/opinion/sunday/are-you-a-toxic-waste-disposal-site.html?emc=edit_nk_20160213&nl=nickkristof&nlid=71338060&te=1&_r=0

[5]Moore, Michael, Ten Things They Won't Tell You About the Flint Water Tragedy, but I Will. (Retrieved from http://michaelmoore.com/10FactsOnFlint/).

[6]Wines, Michael and Schwartz, John. (Feb. 8, 2016) Unsafe Lead Levels in Tap Water Not Limited to Flint. New York Times. (Retrieved from

http://www.nytimes.com/2016/02/09/us/regulatory-gaps-leave-unsafe-lead-levels-in-water-nationwide.html?emc=edit_th_20160209&nl=todaysheadlines&nlid=71338060)

[7]Strether, Lambert. (February 7, 2016) Jim Hightower: What Really Poisoned the Water in Flint, Michigan. Naked Capitalism. (Retrieved from http://www.nakedcapitalism.com/2016/02/jim-hightower-what-really-poisoned-the-water-in-flint-michigan.html).

[8]Fleming, Leonard N. and Oosting, Jonathan. (June 14, 2017) Health chief, 4 others get Flint manslaughter charges. The Detroit News. Retrieved from (http://www.detroitnews.com/story/news/michigan/flint-water-crisis/2017/06/14/flint-water/102838154/?fref=gc&dti=242494922822456)

[9]Fleming, Leonard N. and Oosting, Jonathan. (June 14, 2017) Health chief, 4 others get Flint

manslaughter charges. The Detroit News. Retrieved from (http://www.detroitnews.com/story/news/michigan/flint-water-crisis/2017/06/14/flint-water/102838154/?fref=gc&dti=242494922822456)

[10]Fleming, Leonard N. and Oosting, Jonathan. (June 14, 2017) Health chief, 4 others get Flint manslaughter charges. The Detroit News. Retrieved from (http://www.detroitnews.com/story/news/michigan/flint-water-crisis/2017/06/14/flint-water/102838154/?fref=gc&dti=242494922822456)

[11]Felton, Ryan (July 29, 2016) Flint water crisis: attorney general files charges against six more employees. The Guardian. (Retrieved from https://www.theguardian.com/us-news/2016/jul/29/flint-water-crisis-attorney-general-files-charges-six-more-state-employees)

[12]Felton, Ryan (July 29, 2016) Flint water crisis: attorney general files charges against six more employees. The Guardian. (Retrieved from https://www.theguardian.com/us-news/2016/jul/29/flint-water-crisis-attorney-general-files-charges-six-more-state-employees)

[13]Felton, Ryan (July 29, 2016) Flint water crisis: attorney general files charges against six more employees. The Guardian. (Retrieved from https://www.theguardian.com/us-news/2016/jul/29/flint-water-crisis-attorney-general-files-charges-six-more-state-employees)

[14]Hitt, Mary Anne, (April 17, 2017) <u>Trump and Pruitt Attack EPA Clean Water Standard</u>. Huffington Post. (Retrieved from https://www.huffingtonpost.com/entry/trump-pruitt-attack-epas-clean-water-standard_us_58f515b5e4b01566972251af)

[15]Hitt, Mary Anne, (April 17, 2017) <u>Trump and Pruitt Attack EPA Clean Water Standard</u>. Huffington Post. (Retrieved from https://www.huffingtonpost.com/entry/trump-pruitt-attack-epas-clean-water-standard_us_58f515b5e4b01566972251af)

[16]Hitt, Mary Anne, (April 17, 2017) <u>Trump and Pruitt Attack EPA Clean Water Standard</u>. Huffington Post. (Retrieved from https://www.huffingtonpost.com/entry/trump-pruitt-attack-epas-clean-water-standard_us_58f515b5e4b01566972251af)

[17]Lipcon and Lipcon, Attorneys at Law. (Oct. 11, 2016) <u>Twenty Florida Towns are Drinking Toxic Cancer-Causing Water</u>. (Retrieved from

http://www.lipconlawfirm.com/twenty-florida-towns-drinking-toxic-cancer-causing-water/)

[18]Lipcon and Lipcon, Attorneys at Law. (Oct. 11, 2016) Twenty Florida Towns are Drinking Toxic Cancer-Causing Water. (Retrieved from http://www.lipconlawfirm.com/twenty-florida-towns-drinking-toxic-cancer-causing-water/)

[19]Lipcon and Lipcon, Attorneys at Law. (Oct. 11, 2016) Twenty Florida Towns are Drinking Toxic Cancer-Causing Water. (Retrieved from http://www.lipconlawfirm.com/twenty-florida-towns-drinking-toxic-cancer-causing-water/)

[20]Mclendon, Russell. (Aug. 11, 2016) How polluted is U.S. drinking water? MNN. (Retrieved from https://www.mnn.com/earth-matters/translating-uncle-sam/stories/how-polluted-is-us-drinking-water)

[21]Mclendon, Russell. (Aug. 11, 2016) How polluted is U.S. drinking water? MNN. (Rotrieved from https://www.mnn.com/earth-matters/translating-uncle-sam/storics/how-polluted-is-us-drinking-water)

[22]Mclendon, Russell. (Aug. 11, 2016) How polluted is U.S. drinking water? MNN. (Retrieed from https://www.mnn.com/earth-matters/translating-uncle-sam/stories/how-polluted-is-us-drinking-water)

[23]Mclendon, Russell. (Aug. 11, 2016) How polluted is U.S. drinking water? MNN.

(Retrieed from https://www.mnn.com/earth-matters/translating-uncle-sam/stories/how-polluted-is-us-drinking-water)

[24]Mclendon, Russell. (Aug. 11, 2016) <u>How polluted is U.S. drinking water?</u> MNN. (Retrieed from https://www.mnn.com/earth-matters/translating-uncle-sam/stories/how-polluted-is-us-drinking-water)

[25]Feldscher, Karen, Harvard Chan School Communications. (Aug. 9, 2016) <u>Unsafe levels of toxic chemicals found in drinking water of 33 states</u>. Harvard Gazette. (Retreived from https://news.harvard.edu/gazette/story/2016/08/unsafe-levels-of-toxic-chemicals-found-in-drinking-water-of-33-states/)

[26]Feldscher, Karen, Harvard Chan School Communications. (Aug. 9, 2016) <u>Unsafe levels of toxic chemicals found in drinking water of 33 states</u>. Harvard Gazette. (Retreived from https://news.harvard.edu/gazette/story/2016/08/unsafe-levels-of-toxic-chemicals-found-in-drinking-water-of-33-states/)

[27]Feldscher, Karen, Harvard Chan School Communications. (Aug. 9, 2016) <u>Unsafe levels of toxic chemicals found in drinking water of 33 states</u>. Harvard Gazette. (Retreived from https://news.harvard.edu/gazette/story/2016/0

8/unsafe-levels-of-toxic-chemicals-found-in-drinking-water-of-33-states/)

[28]Feldscher, Karen, Harvard Chan School Communications. (Aug. 9, 2016) <u>Unsafe levels of toxic chemicals found in drinking water of 33 states</u>. Harvard Gazette. (Retreived from https://news.harvard.edu/gazette/story/2016/08/unsafe-levels-of-toxic-chemicals-found-in-drinking-water-of-33-states/)

[29]Ungar, Laura and Nichols, Mark. <u>4 million Americans could be drinking toxic water and would never know</u>. USA TODAY. (Retrieved from https://www.usatoday.com/story/news/2016/12/13/broken-system-means-millions-of-rural-americans-exposed-to-poisoned-or-untested-water/94071732/)

[30]Ungar, Laura and Nichols, Mark. <u>4 million Americans could be drinking toxic water and would never know</u>. USA TODAY. (Retrieved from https://www.usatoday.com/story/news/2016/12/13/broken-system-means-millions-of-rural-americans-exposed-to-poisoned-or-untested-water/94071732/

[31]Ungar, Laura and Nichols, Mark. <u>4 million Americans could be drinking toxic water and would never know</u>. USA TODAY. (Retrieved from

https://www.usatoday.com/story/news/2016/12/13/broken-system-means-millions-of-rural-americans-exposed-to-poisoned-or-untested-water/94071732/

[32]Ungar, Laura and Nichols, Mark. 4 million Americans could be drinking toxic water and would never know. USA TODAY. (Retrieved from https://www.usatoday.com/story/news/2016/12/13/broken-system-means-millions-of-rural-americans-exposed-to-poisoned-or-untested-water/94071732/

[33]Iannelli, Jerry. (Jan. 16, 2017) FPL Wins Battle to Store Radioactive Waste Under Miami's Drinking Water Aquifer (Retrieved from http://www.miaminewtimes.com/news/fpl-wins-battle-to-store-radioactive-waste-under-miamis-drinking-water-aquifer-9059210)

[34]Iannelli, Jerry. (Jan. 16, 2017) FPL Wins Battle to Store Radioactive Waste Under Miami's Drinking Water Aquifer (Retrieved from http://www.miaminewtimes.com/news/fpl-wins-battle-to-store-radioactive-waste-under-miamis-drinking-water-aquifer-9059210

[35]Iannelli, Jerry. (Jan. 16, 2017) FPL Wins Battle to Store Radioactive Waste Under Miami's Drinking Water Aquifer (Retrieved from http://www.miaminewtimes.com/news/fpl-wins-battle-to-store-radioactive-waste-under-miamis-drinking-water-aquifer-9059210

[36]Iannelli, Jerry. (Jan. 16, 2017) FPL Wins Battle to Store Radioactive Waste Under Miami's Drinking Water Aquifer (Retrieved from http://www.miaminewtimes.com/news/fpl-wins-battle-to-store-radioactive-waste-under-miamis-drinking-water-aquifer-9059210

[37]Iannelli, Jerry. (Jan. 16, 2017) FPL Wins Battle to Store Radioactive Waste Under Miami's Drinking Water Aquifer (Retrieved from http://www.miaminewtimes.com/news/fpl-wins-battle-to-store-radioactive-waste-under-miamis-drinking-water-aquifer-9059210

[38]Stern, Marcus, Parker, Kait, Wilking, Spencer. (Dec. 8, 2016) Toxic Lake: The Untold Story of Lake Okeechobee. The Weather Channel. https://weather.com/news/news/florida-toxic-lake-okeechobee

[39]Stern, Marcus, Parker, Kait, Wilking, Spencer. (Dec. 8, 2016) Toxic Lake: The Untolr Slury of Lako Okeechobee. The Weather Channel. https://weather.com/news/news/florida-toxic-lake-okeechobee

[40]Stern, Marcus, Parker, Kait, Wilking, Spencer. (Dec. 8, 2016) Toxic Lake: The Untolr Story of Lake Okeechobee. The Weather Channel. https://weather.com/news/news/florida-toxic-lake-okeechobee

[41] Stern, Marcus, Parker, Kait, Wilking, Spencer. (Dec. 8, 2016) <u>Toxic Lake: The Untolr Story of Lake Okeechobee</u>. The Weather Channel. https://weather.com/news/news/florida-toxic-lake-okeechobee

[42] Jacobson, Michael F. (July 11, 2012) <u>FDA Is Not Protecting Consumers From Unsafe Food Additives</u>. Huffington Post. Retreived from https://www.huffingtonpost.com/michael-f-jacobson/food-additives-_b_1654034.html)

[43] Jacobson, Michael F. (July 11, 2012) <u>FDA Is Not Protecting Consumers From Unsafe Food Additives</u>. Huffington Post. Retreived from https://www.huffingtonpost.com/michael-f-jacobson/food-additives-_b_1654034.html)

[44] Foodbabe. 5 Ingredients That Should Have Never Been Approved By The FDA—Are You Eating Them? (Retreived from https://foodbabe.com/2015/01/08/5-ingredients-that-should-have-never-been-approved-by-the-fda-are-you-eating-them/)

[45] Foodbabe. 5 Ingredients That Should Have Never Been Approved By The FDA—Are You Eating Them? (Retreived from https://foodbabe.com/2015/01/08/5-ingredients-that-should-have-never-been-approved-by-the-fda-are-you-eating-them/))

[46] Foodbabe. 5 Ingredients That Should Have Never Been Approved By The FDA–Are You Eating Them? (Retreived from https://foodbabe.com/2015/01/08/5-ingredients-that-should-have-never-been-approved-by-the-fda-are-you-eating-them/)

[47] Jacobson, Michael F. (July 11, 2012) FDA Is Not Protecting Consumers From Unsafe Food Additives. Huffington Post. Retreived from https://www.huffingtonpost.com/michael-f-jacobson/food-additives-_b_1654034.html)

[48] Foodbabe. 5 Ingredients That Should Have Never Been Approved By The FDA–Are You Eating Them? (Retreived from https://foodbabe.com/2015/01/08/5-ingredients-that-should-have-never-been-approved-by-the-fda-are-you-eating-them/)

[49] Foodbabe. 5 Ingredients That Should Have Never Been Approved By The FDA–Are You Eating Them? (Retreived from https://foodbabe.com/2015/01/08/5-ingredients-that-should-have-never-been-approved-by-the-fda-are-you-eating-them/)

[50] World Health Organization Says Processed Meat Causes Cancer (October 26, 2015) Retrieved from (https://www.cancer.org/latest-news/world-health-organization-says-processed-meat-causes-cancer.html)

[51] Hyman, Mark, MD (Nov. 12, 2013). Why You Should Never Eat High Fructose Corn Syrup. (Retreived from https://www.huffingtonpost.com/dr-mark-hyman/high-fructose-corn-syrup_b_4256220.html)

[52] Hyman, Mark, MD (Nov. 12, 2013). Why You Should Never Eat High Fructose Corn Syrup. (Retreived from https://www.huffingtonpost.com/dr-mark-hyman/high-fructose-corn-syrup_b_4256220.html)

[53] Hyman, Mark, MD (Nov. 12, 2013). Why You Should Never Eat High Fructose Corn Syrup. (Retreived from https://www.huffingtonpost.com/dr-mark-hyman/high-fructose-corn-syrup_b_4256220.html)

[54] Hyman, Mark, MD (Nov. 12, 2013). Why You Should Never Eat High Fructose Corn Syrup. (Retreived from https://www.huffingtonpost.com/dr-mark-hyman/high-fructose-corn-syrup_b_4256220.html)

[55] Hyman, Mark, MD (Nov. 12, 2013). Why You Should Never Eat High Fructose Corn Syrup. (Retreived from https://www.huffingtonpost.com/dr-mark-

hyman/high-fructose-corn-syrup_b_4256220.html)

[56]Gennet, Robbie, (May 25, 2011) Aspartame vs. Splenda: Which Is Worse for You? The Huffington Post. (Retreived from https://www.huffingtonpost.com/robbie-gennet/donald-rumsfeld-and-the-s_b_805581.html)

[57]Gennet, Robbie, (May 25, 2011) Aspartame vs. Splenda: Which Is Worse for You? The Huffington Post. (Retreived from https://www.huffingtonpost.com/robbie-gennet/donald-rumsfeld-and-the-s_b_805581.html)

[58]Gennet, Robbie, (May 25, 2011) Aspartame vs. Splenda: Which Is Worse for You? The Huffington Post. (Retreived from https://www.huffingtonpost.com/robbie-gennet/donald-rumsfeld-and-the-s_b_805581.html)

[59]Butler, Kristen, (Aug. 27, 2013) Aspartame patent reveals E. coli feces used. Science News. (https://www.upi.com/Science_News/Blog/2013/08/26/Aspartame-patent-reveals-E-coli-feces-used/8131377527919/

[60]Girdwain, Jessica (Dec. 17, 2013) Is Sucralose—The Sweetener Most Commonly Known As Splenda—Really Safe? Prevention. (Retreived from

https://www.prevention.com/food/healthy-eating-tips/health-risks-sucralose)

[61]Girdwain, Jessica (Dec. 17, 2013) Is Sucralose—The Sweetener Most Commonly Known As Splenda—Really Safe? Prevention. (Retreived from https://www.prevention.com/food/healthy-eating-tips/health-risks-sucralose)

[62]Lies and Deception: How the FDA Does Not Protect Your Best Interest. Smart Publications. (Retreived from http://www.smart-publications.com/articles/lies-and-deception-how-the-fda-does-not-protect-your-best-interests)

[63]Jacobs, Andrew and Richtel, Matt. (September 16, 2017) How Big Business Got Brazil Hooked on Junk Food. New York Times. (Retrieved from (https://www.nytimes.com/interactive/2017/09/16/health/brazil-obesity-nestle.html?mcubz=0)

[64]Jacobs, Andrew and Richtel, Matt. (September 16, 2017) How Big Business Got Brazil Hooked on Junk Food. New York Times. (Retrieved from (https://www.nytimes.com/interactive/2017/09/16/health/brazil-obesity-nestle.html?mcubz=0

[65]Hyman, Mark, MD (February 25, 2016) Why the Food Pyramid Got It All Wrong

Rodale Wellness. (Retrieved from https://www.rodalewellness.com/health/why-the-food-pyramid-got-it-all-wrong)
[66]The Problems with the Food Guide Pyramid and MyPyramid. (Retrieved from https://www.hsph.harvard.edu/nutritionsource/mypyramid-problems/)

Chapter 5: Corruption on the High Seas

"I would never support an industry that is close to having a slave labor situation. The minimum wage law doesn't apply. They are third world workers and the ships are registered in foreign ports. They are not protected by any U.S. wage laws."
    Gershon Cohen

Maritime law deals with the application of law to events that occur on navigable waters, which generally include all the oceans of the world as well as large lakes or rivers that can be used for commercial shipping. No federal statute provides general rules for determining admiralty jurisdiction, and no statute comprehensively enumerates the various categories of cases that fall within admiralty jurisdiction. There are huge differences between maritime law and state law, especially where punitive damages are concerned.

Florida is one of the nation's premier maritime states, with more than 1,000 miles of coastline and many miles of navigable territorial waters. Florida is also the cruise capital of the world. Carnival Corporation and Royal Caribbean Cruises, Ltd. together control nearly three-fourths of the entire North American cruise industry. Norwegian Cruise Line is another major carrier. All three are incorporated outside the U.S. but maintain their principal places of business in Miami, Florida. All of their ships, which primarily sail from U.S. ports, are registered in foreign nations and fly foreign flags, so they and their operators are generally not subject to most U.S. corporate income tax, health, safety, and wage laws. A foreign-flagged vessel may transport passengers between two U.S. ports, with a distant foreign port in-between, and it can transport passengers between many U.S. ports, as long as a nearby foreign port is included in the itinerary. This is a critical reason why Canadian ports are included in cruises of Alaska's Inside Passage—they provide the foreign port. The only thing a foreign-flagged vessel cannot do is to transport passengers between two U.S. ports directly.

According to a Sun Sentinel article by Arlene Satchell dated July 17, 2013, cruise lines and their passengers and crew spent $7 billion in Florida in 2012. This is according to a study of the North American cruise industry released on July 16, 2013, by Cruise Lines International Association–(CLIA). Florida, home to the world's three busiest cruise ports–Port Miami, Port Everglades and Port Canavera–recorded the highest economic impact among all states, with 36 percent of the total amount Americans spend on cruising. More than 6 million of the 10.1 million cruise passengers who started cruises from U.S. ports last year left from Florida, according to the study. That's a 2.6 percent increase from 2011. For the 2012 budget year ended Sept. 30, Port Miami held the No. 1 spot as the world's busiest cruise port with 3.77 million cruise passengers. Port Canaveral and Port Everglades followed with 3.76 million and 3.69 million cruise passengers, respectively.

Maritime law is very unique, and its rules would seem absurd if applied to automobile personal injury law or premises liability matters. A collision between a trucking company's tractor-trailer and a car that results in the death of the car's driver may result in a multimillion dollar verdict from a jury. It would be unheard of for the court to cap the trucking company's liability at the value of the smashed tractor-trailer, any fees received for delivering the cargo, and an additional amount based on the size of the truck. However, in a maritime action, this is essentially what can be done! There are very strict limits about who you can sue, where you have to bring the suit and when you must bring the suit. There are also pre-suit notice requirements. If you fail to comply with these steps, no matter whose fault it is, you will be precluded from recovering.

Today, all cruise tickets contain the carriers' private restrictions on the time and locale of passenger lawsuits. Under federal forum provisions on cruise tickets, nondiversity passengers or suitors must initiate their suits in nonjury federal admiralty court. Diversity jurisdiction is a form of subject-matter jurisdiction in civil procedures in which a United States' district court has the power to hear a civil case. The persons who are parties are "diverse" in citizenship, which generally indicates they are citizens of different states or non-U.S. citizens. Most carriers' proprietary tickets require written claims to be presented within six months after an incident and lawsuits to be filed within one year. The geographical venue selected for passenger lawsuits by Carnival, Royal Caribbean, and Norwegian Cruise Line is Miami, Florida.

Designation Where At Law Causes of Action are Combined with Admiralty Claims

In order for the case to be heard under the court's admiralty jurisdiction, Rule 9(h) of the Federal Rules of Civil Procedure provides that when a case which is subject to jurisdiction of federal district courts under 28 U.S.C. § 1333, and is also subject to federal district court jurisdiction on some other basis, such as diversity of citizenship, the plaintiff may elect that all the causes of action be heard in admiralty by a statement identifying the claims as admiralty and maritime claims. Claims within the admiralty or maritime jurisdiction of the federal courts do not give rise to a right to a trial by jury. *United States v. La Vengeance,* 3 U.S. 297 (1796).

By invoking diversity of citizenship as the basis for jurisdiction instead of admiralty jurisdiction, or by not opting to designate his or her claim as an admiralty claim, the plaintiff gains the advantage of a jury trial. However, the plaintiff may lose the advantage of certain procedures available only in admiralty cases. This includes the remedies of arrest and maritime attachment provided for in the Supplemental Rules to the Federal Rules of Civil Procedure. It is very important to have a maritime attorney review your case before deciding whether or not to invoke diversity of citizenship as the basis of jurisdiction to get a jury trial. It is usually the best option, but not always.

Although cruise companies are prohibited from making contributions to U.S. political campaigns, many politicians are friends of the cruise lines. These politicians often help to pass legislation to increase the profits of cruise-line owners and disregard passenger safety issues. Every ship is governed by the laws of the country where it is registered. Bermuda, the Bahamas, Panama, or Liberia protect the cruise lines from high income taxes and U.S. labor laws. The flag state is technically responsible for enforcement of international regulations and conventions. However, flag-of-convenience registries often leave inspection and certification of safety equipment to the U.S. Coast Guard. A ship may never be fully inspected unless it stops in a port where inspections are done. Flags of convenience severely limit recourse to U.S. courts, regarding disputes over wages. The employment contract of a crew worker on a Bahamian-registered ship states that any dispute or claims "shall be governed and adjudicated pursuant to laws of the Bahamas, regardless of any other legal remedies that may be available."

Cruise lines, by being able to force passengers from all over the world to sue a carrier in a single U.S. locality within a very short time, have long enjoyed a home-court litigation advantage. Article III, §2, of the U. S. Constitution vests federal courts with original jurisdiction over all cases of admiralty and maritime jurisdiction. Pursuant to 28 USCS § 1333, "the district courts shall have original jurisdiction, exclusive of the courts of the States, of: (1) any civil case of admiralty or maritime jurisdiction, saving to suitors in all cases all other remedies to which they are otherwise entitled." The Savings-to-Suitors clause establishes the common-law right to bring a claim in the state or federal forum. State courts have jurisdiction in personam (made against a specific person only) concurrent with the admiralty courts.

In Romero v. International Terminal Operating Co., 358 U.S. 354 (1959), the U.S. Supreme Court recognized a state-federal "sharing of competence" in maritime common law matters. In Romero, the Supreme Court confirmed "the historic option of a maritime suitor pursuing a common law remedy to select his forum, state or federal." It was also ruled that "except in diversity cases, maritime litigation brought in state courts cannot be removed to the federal courts." In Lewis v. Lewis & Clark Marine, Inc., 531 U.S. 438, 454-55 (2001), the court reaffirmed that both a state forum choice and a trial by jury are remedies "saved" absolutely to maritime common law suitors in the U.S. by the Saving-to-Suitors Clause of 28 U.S.C. §1333(1).

All maritime common-law suitors otherwise required to sue in the U.S. have been entitled to initiate in state court and to remain there unless and until removed by a defendant to federal court on diversity grounds. Maritime common-law state court actions, which fail any requirement for federal diversity jurisdiction, *cannot* be removed to federal court. The traditional "removal" process places the burden on the removing defendant to prove to a federal judge that federal jurisdiction exists. If the defendant guesses wrong about the existence of federal jurisdiction, the federal court can then remand the case back to state court rather than dismissing it outright.

Carnival's current tickets expressly acknowledge there may be unspecified passenger lawsuits to which the federal courts lack subject-matter jurisdiction. State courts, rather than federal courts, have been the default jurisdiction for maritime suits in the U.S. arising from the common law. The expressly limited federal judicial system created by Congress in 1789 included a nonjury admiralty court. The intent was primarily for specialized causes of action unique to admiralty, e.g., actions in rem (made against or affecting a thing, and therefore affecting people as well) against vessels. Historically, the majority of maritime passenger lawsuits in the U.S. have been handled as state court jury actions.

A passenger's cruise ticket is a non-negotiable contract of adhesion (meaning the passenger can take it or leave it as is). In Carnival Cruise Lines, Inc. v. Shute, 499 U.S. 585 (1991), the court held that such a cruise ticket may "reasonably" dictate the geographical locality for passenger lawsuits. Shute began as an action voluntarily initiated by a passenger/suitor on the admiralty (nonjury) side of federal court, and it involved a former, purely geographical forum clause. Thus, Shute did not implicate the Saving-to-Suitors Clause at all. Throughout the last century, and for most of the current one, nearly all major cruise carriers have complied with the Saving-to-Suitors Clause. They do this by employing ticket provisions offering all passengers their "historic option" to sue the carrier in state court (subject to a defendant's right to remove an appropriate diversity case from state to federal court pursuant to 28 U.S.C. §1441).

In 2002, Carnival abruptly deviated from this norm and installed federal-forum provisions in passenger tickets for its Carnival Cruise Lines brand. The relevant clause reads:

> It is agreed by and between the guest and Carnival that all disputes and matters arising under, or in connection with or incident to this Contract or the Guest's cruise, including travel to and from the vessel, shall be litigated, if at all, before the United States District Court for the Southern District of Florida in Miami, or as to those lawsuits to which the Federal Courts of the United States lack subject matter jurisdiction, before a court located

in Miami-Dade County, Florida, to the exclusion of the courts of any other county, state or country.

Norwegian Cruise Line (NCL) adopted an identical clause in 2005. These provisions require suit in nonjury federal admiralty court for all claims failing any requirement for federal diversity jurisdiction. Federal forum provisions in cruise tickets are not authorized by any government regulation, statute, or treaty, but rather, they are the carriers' creation for proprietary use with their own passengers.

Why do cruise lines attempt to federalize all their passenger claims? One possible explanation is forum-shopping. A carrier cannot deny a nondiversity passenger/suitor a jury trial in state court. However, in federal court a jury trial can be denied and bench trials usually produce significantly lower damage awards than juries in comparable cases. In addition, economies of scale make state court the only common-sense "fit" for many relatively minor cruise-related disputes, which would be deterred altogether if they had to be pursued as federal cases. Enforcing federal-forum provisions in cruise tickets would decrease from approximately 60 to 15 the total number of state and federal judges now available to process a carrier's passenger suits in Miami. This represents a 75 percent reduction of judicial manpower to handle the bulk of an entire industry's customer litigation, arising from an ever-increasing number of cruise-ship injuries.

Title 46 U.S.C. §183c(a) is a specific maritime "nonwaiver" statute first enacted in 1936. This statute provides that it is illegal for the manager, agent, or owner of any vessel transporting passengers between ports of the U.S. or between any U.S. port and a foreign port to insert in any rule, regulation, contract, or agreement any provision or limitation:

- ☐ Purporting, in the event of loss of life or bodily injury arising from the negligence or fault of such owner or his servants, to relieve such owner, master, or agent from liability, or from liability beyond any stipulated amount, for such loss or injury, or

- ☐ Purporting in such event to lessen, weaken, or avoid the right of any claimant to a trial by court of competent jurisdiction on the question of liability for such loss, or injury, or the measure of damages. All such provisions of limitations contained in such rule, regulation, contract, or agreement are declared to be against public policy and shall be null and void and of no effect.

Whether or not any form of binding jury trial is available to cruise passengers in federal admiralty court is an open question. There are many reported cases that demonstrate that binding jury trials under Fed. R. Civ. P. 39(c) routinely take place in federal admiralty court. Cruise carriers do not agree in their passenger tickets to give such consent, and the world's largest cruise carrier, Carnival, has a long history of successfully opposing jury trials in federal admiralty court. A federal admiralty bench trial, or even a jury trial requiring the consent of a defendant, is not a constitutionally sufficient substitute for a jury trial of right.

In Sullivan v. Ajax Navigation Corp., and Celebrity Cruises, Inc., 881 F. Supp. 906 (S. D. N. Y. 1995), the court refused to enforce a federal-forum clause of Celebrity Cruises. The relevant clause was properly placed in the ticket, had the correct font size, and specifically required all passengers to originally file their suits on the federal admiralty side "without demand for jury trial." Sullivan defied the clause and filed her passenger-injury suit against the carrier as a diversity case on the federal law side and demanded a jury trial. Of course, the cruise line moved to strike the jury trial demand. However, a U.S. district court denied the carrier's motion, saying that the right to a jury trial is guaranteed by the seventh amendment to the United States Constitution. The seventh amendment generally affords no right to a jury for claims that are filed within the court's admiralty jurisdiction, but there are two exceptions. The first exception where Congress provides the right to a jury trial involves the Jones Act, which grants a negligence action against the seaman's employer. The other exception is when a claim falls within the "Saving-to-Suitors" clause when there is diversity jurisdiction.

In Nunez v. American Seafoods, 52 P.3d 720 (Alaska 2002), the Supreme Court of Alaska invalidated a maritime federal-forum clause, which conflicted with the concurrent jurisdiction provisions of the Saving-to-Suitors Clause. In Nunez, the seaman/plaintiff's employment contract required that "any legal action . . . involving this contract or any incident or injury occurring aboard the vessel . . . may be brought only in the Federal District Court for the Western District of Washington at Seattle." Nunez nevertheless filed his maritime injury suit against his employer in Alaska state court under the federal Saving-to-Suitors clause and the Jones Act. The employer successfully moved to dismiss based on its federal forum clause.

The Alaska Supreme Court reversed the decision because the "Saving-to-Suitors" clause generally means that a suitor asserting an in personam admiralty claim may elect to sue in a "common law" state court through an ordinary civil action. In such actions, the state courts must apply the same substantive law as would be applied had the suit been instituted in admiralty in a federal court. The Alaska Supreme Court concluded that the Saving-to-Suitors clause gave Nunez the right to select a state or federal forum and that any contractual provision attempting to limit it must be deemed void.

An arbitration agreement in a shoreside commercial setting can validly operate to waive a jury trial of right. Then, why can't a maritime contract of adhesion accomplish the same result for nondiversity passenger/suitors who are thereby diverted from a state court jury action into nonjury federal admiralty court? One reason is a maritime nonwaiver statute (46 U.S.C. §183c(a)) which precludes arbitration agreements in marine passenger tickets for "U.S.-touching" voyages.

Title 46 U.S.C. §183c(a) was originally enacted in 1936 to promote uniformity of rights and remedies among all passengers embarking on voyages from or between U.S. ports. Under federal court provisions in a cruise ticket, however, one subgroup of passengers (whose claims satisfy all federal-diversity requirements) retains its constitutional right to a jury trial associated with a common-law remedy. The other subgroup (whose claims fail one or more diversity requirements) does not retain that constitutionality. In my opinion, all passengers should have the right to a jury trial if they want one, regardless of whether or not federal diversity requirements are met.

Although cruise ships pay no U.S. federal taxes, the U.S. Coastguard spends millions of dollars rescuing crippled ships. This is very unfair to all U.S. taxpayers because the cruise lines make billions every year. Why are all the major cruise lines so lax when it comes to safety precautions? Why don't cruise passengers demand accountability and sweeping industry-wide change when people get hurt on cruise ships? The answer has to do with the fact that the International Council of Cruise Lines, the lobbying arm of the cruise industry, has enormous political clout. It donates a lot of money to congressmen and senators to encourage them to pass laws that are favorable to cruise-ship owners. Because of the lobbying money, legislative steps are not being taken to bring the cruise industry under control.

The cruise industry wants us to believe that taking a cruise is safe, but nothing could be further from the truth. During the 1994 sinking of the cruiseship Estonia in the Baltic Sea, more than 850 perished when that ship sunk within 30 minutes of taking on water during a storm. Since 2000, there have been more than 100 incidents in which ships have gone adrift, lost power, experienced severe lists (when a ship tilts and nearly tips), or had other events that posed a safety risk to passengers. Many passengers have been seriously injured, killed, sickened by contagious infections, or sexually assaulted on cruise ships. If you or a loved one is on or plans to go on a cruise ship, it is critical that you understand both your legal rights, as well as the best ways to stay safe while onboard.

The Rights of Injured Seafarers

The Jones Act is a federal law passed in 1920 that protects seafarers (also called crew members) by allowing them to recover money if they are injured on the job. The basic premise of the Jones Act is that seafarers are wards of the court and are entitled to special protection, which involves an increased standard of liability and a decreased level of required proof. This act applies to U.S. seafarers as well as foreign seafarers. If the base of operations of the employer or shipping company is in the U.S., foreign seafarers can claim the protection of the Jones Act. A Jones Act remedy is against the employer in personam only. Seamen have no remedy against the ship for personal injuries caused by negligence attributable to the vessel.

The Jones Act was an important piece of U.S. legislation that supported the American Merchant Marine, while also providing additional protection for seafarers and sailors. Officially titled the Merchant Marine Act of 1920, this legislation came to be best known for its sponsor, Senator Wesley Jones. Prior to its passage, seafarers who were injured on the job had very few options for recovering damages or getting assistance. Traced back to the Medieval Sea Codes, the doctrine evolved over the centuries out of a concern that hard-working crew members should not be abandoned in distant ports.

Seafarers who are injured at sea are entitled to *maintenance and cure* from their employers. To be considered a seafarer, a worker must spend 30 percent or more of his or her working hours onboard either a specific vessel or a fleet of vessels under common ownership or control. *Maintenance* is a seafarer's day-to-day living expenses. *Cure* is a seafarer's medical costs. Employers are only obligated to pay maintenance and cure until the seafarer is fit for duty, or until he or she has reached a point where additional medical treatment will not help him or her (maximum medical cure). All seafarers working on a ship that sails from a U.S. port are entitled to maintenance and cure, regardless of their nationality. Shipowners *must* provide maintenance and cure regardless of whether or not they were negligent in causing the seafarer's injuries. It is completely different for passengers, who must prove negligence to recover money if they are injured during a cruise.

The concept of "maximum medical cure" is more extensive than the concept of "maximum medical improvement." The obligation to "cure" a seafarer includes the providing him with medications and medical devices that improve his or her ability to function, even if they don't "improve" his actual condition. Included may be long-term treatments that permit him or her to continue functioning well. Examples include prostheses, wheelchairs, and pain medications. A seafarer who is required to sue a shipowner to recover maintenance and cure may also recover his or her attorney's fees. If a shipowner's breach of his or her obligation to provide maintenance and cure is willful and wanton, the shipowner might be subject to punitive damages.

The definition of a seafarer includes deckhands, officers, cooks, waiters, engineers, cruise shop concessionaires and other workers in the cruise or shipping industry. Seafarers do not have to pay for shelter, food, water, or utilities. Work contracts vary in length based on the class of employment. Officers usually work approximately 4 months and then take 2 months off. Seafarers who work in the dining room, kitchen, or cleaning passenger cabins work approximately nine or 10 months followed by a 2-month vacation. Some seafarers work 12 months without any vacation or days off, especially if they are from nonindustrialized nations and are desperate for the income.

Wet decks, unsecured and shifting cargo or objects, line breaks, or other unsafe work conditions can quickly cause accidents resulting in:

- Slip-and-fall injuries, such as broken bones
- Lifting injuries, such as a serious back injury
- Leg and knee injuries
- Head and neck injuries

These injuries can severely limit or prevent a seafarer from performing his or her normal responsibilities. Shipowners will often try to trick seafarers into giving a recorded statement after an accident because they might be able to use such a statement to limit the amount of medical costs they have to pay. A seafarer should never give a recorded statement to the shipowner before getting advice from a maritime lawyer. Shipowners will also try to get seafarers to sign medical paperwork after seeing the ship's doctor. A seafarer should always see his or her own doctor and should not sign away any of his or her legal rights.

Another way shipowners try to limit what they owe their employees is by putting an arbitration clause in the seafarer's contract. Arbitration clauses can have dire consequences for seafarers, since a foreign cruise-ship seafarer on a U.S.-based ship has very limited rights to sue his or her employer in a U.S. court. This is because the ship and the company operating the ship are both foreign-registered. The desire to circumvent the Jones Act gives cruise lines a very strong disincentive to hire American workers. In addition, the arbitration clauses in seafarer contracts are job killers for Americans because U.S. workers are protected under U.S. labor law, protections *not* held by non-U.S. workers. Foreign seafarers should not work for ships that require them to sign a contract with an arbitration clause that forces them to give up their Jones Act rights.

Although the U.S. minimum wage was extended to ships registered in the U.S. in 1961, Congress left intact the exemption for foreign ships. A 1963 Supreme Court decision extended this exception by ruling that U.S. labor laws, including the right to organize, do not apply to foreign vessels engaged in American commerce, even if the owners of these ships are from the U.S. Seafarers usually work 12-hour days, 7 days a week for much less than the U.S. minimum wage.

The International Transport Workers' Federation

The International Transport Workers' Federation (ITF) is an international trade union organization that influences the wages and conditions of seafarers working on ships that fly flags of convenience, that provide a means of avoiding labor regulation in the country of ownership, and that enable shipowners to pay very low wages and force employees to work very long hours. Since flag-of-convenience ships have no real nationality, they are beyond the reach of any single national seafarers' trade union. The ITF has, therefore, been obliged to take on internationally the role usually exercised by national trade unions, to organize and negotiate on behalf of flag-of-convenience crews. The ITF has been waging a vigorous campaign against shipowners who abandon the flag of their own country in search of the cheapest possible crews and the lowest possible training and safety standards for their ships. In 1974, the ITF defined a flag-of-convenience as: "Where beneficial ownership and control of a vessel is found to lie elsewhere than in the country of the flag the vessel is flying, the vessel is considered as sailing under a flag-of-convenience." The ITF campaign against flags of convenience, which was formally launched at the 1948 World Congress in Oslo in Norway, has two elements:

- A political campaign designed to establish by international governmental agreement a genuine link between the flag a ship flies and the nationality or residence of its owners, managers and seafarers, and so eliminate the flag-of-convenience system entirely;

- An industrial campaign designed to ensure that seafarers who serve on flag-of-convenience ships, whatever their nationality, are protected from exploitation by shipowners.

The ITF's maritime affiliates have developed a set of policies to establish minimum acceptable standards for seafarers serving on flag-of-convenience vessels. The policies form the basis of an ITF Standard Collective Agreement, which sets the wages and working conditions for all crew on flag-of-convenience vessels irrespective of nationality. All flag-of-convenience vessels covered by an ITF-acceptable agreement are issued an ITF Blue Certificate by the ITF Secretariat, which signifies the ITF's acceptance of the wages and working conditions onboard. About 25 percent of all flag-of-convenience vessels are currently covered by ITF agreements.

Compliance with ITF-recognized agreements is monitored by a network of more than 130 ITF inspectors in ports throughout the world. ITF Inspectors are union officials who work directly with the ITF. By inspecting flag-of-convenience ships, they monitor the payment of wages and other social and employment conditions and take action when necessary. The ITF tries to help exploited and mistreated seafarers throughout the world. Every year, millions of dollars are recovered by the ITF and its affiliated unions in back pay and compensation for death or injury on behalf of seafarers who have nowhere else to turn.

Following are several stories about injured seafarers. Many of them have been exploited by either the cruise line or the laws of another country.

An Injured Seafarer's Tragic Story

Doran McDonald was a seafarer responsible for wiping every surface from counters to walls, cleaning the daily residue of bacon grease and chicken fat, and sweeping up shreds of lettuce and other salad vegetables. McDonald, like many cruise-line employees, is from a very poor country. Large cruise ships provide an appealing economic opportunity for people from Third World nations in Eastern Europe, the South Pacific, and the Caribbean.

McDonald was no stranger to shipboard living. Even for $500 a month, doing janitorial duty onboard a cruise ship was more remunerative than harvesting bananas in St. Vincent. McDonald had gone to work for Premier Cruise Line in 1998, and he advanced from galley worker to waiter. He made more than $1,000 a month and sent most of it home. In 2000, Premier went bankrupt. McDonald had to start at the bottom again at Royal Caribbean in 2002.

McDonald was severely burned in an accident while working for Royal Caribbean

International. McDonald picked up a pot full of oil from a fryer that had just been switched off. The pot was heavy and hot and he attempted to carry it to a sink where he could dump the oil and scour it. Halfway to the sink, McDonald slipped. The scalding liquid got inside the rubber boot on his right leg and the oil burned his leg and the top of his foot. His right leg had literally been boiled, and the odor of decay oozed from his burned flesh. The top of his foot was a huge blister, the stretched skin was tight and shiny. He was unable to elevate his leg and the swelling and pressure were extremely painful.

When McDonald called home and told his mother, Pearlie Hector, about his injury, she was irate. She thought her son should have remained in the Juneau, Alaska, hospital where he had received preliminary medical care the day before rather than being flown to a different hospital outside the United States. Royal Caribbean tried to transfer McDonald outside of the United States to the Caribbean from Alaska even though the cruise lines are based in Miami. Besides, their cruise ships regularly call on ports in Florida where appropriate medical care is readily available.

Royal Caribbean has a history of keeping its crew members out of the U.S. whenever they are injured or become sick to avoid having to pay for the crew member to receive state-of-the-art medical treatment at a decent hospital. Royal Caribbean is based in Miami, which is a good place to manage its crew members' medical needs. However, the cruise line often abandons its sick crew members in Third World countries, especially the Dominican Republic. McDonald decided to retain a lawyer, which prompted Royal Caribbean to set in motion the federal government's immigration policy machinery so that McDonald would probably soon be held at a detention center.

Miami-based Royal Caribbean Cruises is the second largest cruise line in the world. Like other U.S.-based cruise lines, Royal Caribbean registered its business overseas in Liberia and flagged its cruise ships in foreign countries (Liberia and the Bahamas) in order to avoid paying U.S. taxes. Although Royal Caribbean collects between $5 and $6 billion a year from U.S. tax-paying citizens, Royal Caribbean does not pay U.S. taxes by virtue of its foreign-corporate citizenship. Its crew members are 99 percent non-U.S. citizens. Royal Caribbean has a net worth of around $15 billion dollars, but it pays its hardest working crew members $1.50 an hour. It is sad that some people are so desperate for income that they are willing to work 84-hours a week cleaning cabins for only $1.50 an hour. However, the lobbying arm of the cruise industry fights hard to keep current legislation in place that allows shipowners to exploit people from nonindustrialized countries.

A Senior Engine Fitter's Tragic Story

Filipino crew member Lito Asignacion worked as a senior engine fitter for Global Management Limited on a vessel flagged in the Marshall Islands. In October 2010, while the ship was in the port of New Orleans alongside 7th Street Wharf, crew member Asignacion sustained serious burns on his abdomen and legs when scalding water overflowed a tank. The crew member underwent extensive and painful medical treatment in the burn units of West Jefferson Medical Center and Baton Rouge General Medical Center in Louisiana. Asignacion was treated and underwent skin grafting because of burns covering 35 percent of his body. He was then returned to the Philippines where he continued undergoing medical treatment at several hospitals. Several different doctors performed plastic surgery on Asignacion. He is now disabled and scarred for life.

Asignacion filed suit in state court in Jefferson Parish where the accident occurred, but his case was dismissed and he was ordered to proceed with arbitration in the Philippines. The shipping company argued that the case was completely controlled by Philippine law and Asignacion had no rights under U.S. law. The company argued that under the Philippines Overseas Employment Agreement (POEA), the crew member suffered a grade-14 disability, which would entitle him to only 3.74 percent of $50,000 or a total award of $1,870. The Filipino Labor Board agreed and awarded Asignacion just $1,870, even though his disability meant he was unable to work for the rest of his life.

Chief Mate Wins Lawsuit Against Maersk Lines, Limited

William Skye, a 57-year old seafarer from New Jersey, worked for Maersk Lines Limited as a Chief Mate aboard a Maersk container vessel called the Sealand Pride. Mr. Skye's lawyer alleged that Skye was assigned and required to perform so many duties in connection with his job as a Chief Mate for Maersk that, over a 4-year period, he was required to violate the work/rest hour laws that comprise the STCW (Standards of Training, Certification and Watchkeeping).

The STCW provides, in part, in 46 USC 8104(d), that "A licensed individual or seafarer in the deck or engine department may not be required to work more than 8 hours in one day."; and 46 CFR 15.1111 states:

> (a) Each person assigned duty as officer in charge of a navigational or engineering watch, or duty as a rating forming part of a navigational or engineering watch, onboard any vessel that operates beyond the Boundary Line shall receive a minimum of 10 hours of rest in any 24-hour period.

The rest received may not be less than 70 hours in any 7-day period. Further, a seafarer must receive at least a 6-hour uninterrupted rest period daily. As part of his required job duties, Skye alleged that he was required to stand two 4-hour watches a day, and then perform additional tasks associated with his position as Chief Mate. Skye's lawyer alleged that, on average, Skye was required to work approximately 15.75 hours a day, violating both 46 USC 8104(d) and 46 CFR 15.1111.

As a result of his long hours and inability to receive enough uninterrupted rest, Skye's lawyer alleged that Skye was diagnosed with left ventricular hypertrophy by his cardiologist, Dr. Joseph Wachspress, in June 2008. This condition is a physical thickening of the left ventricular portion of the heart, making it difficult for the heart to pump blood and significantly increasing the chance of a heart attack. In addition, Skye was diagnosed with an adjustment disorder by his psychiatrist, Dr. Arnold Goldman, in 2008. Both his cardiologist and psychiatrist related his injuries to his working conditions aboard the Sealand Pride and recommended that he retire early, at age 54, from working aboard ships. During his last year of work, he earned approximately $171,000 and received approximately $36,000 in fringe benefits (food, shelter, medical care, etc.)

Skye was also a licensed attorney. He went to law school in the 1980s and practiced for a short period of time before deciding to return to a life at sea. Although his doctors did not restrict his ability to earn a living as a lawyer, because he had not practiced law since the 1980s, he found it very difficult to earn a significant amount of money as a lawyer. Nevertheless, Skye's vocational rehabilitation expert, Dr. Robert Lessne, testified that if he were able to find a job as a lawyer, he could expect to earn approximately $69,000 based on his current level of expertise. Dr. Lessne further testified that Skye's working life expectancy, from the point that he retired in 2008, was approximately 17 more years.

During trial, two former Maersk employees, Michael McCright and Steven Krupa, testified on Skye's behalf. McCright was a former relief Chief Mate aboard Maersk ships and he testified that it was impossible to do the job without working a significant amount of overtime, which was exhausting. Steven Krupa was a former Fleet Manager for Maersk, and he testified that ultimately Maersk was responsible for complying with the STCW laws. According to Krupa, Maersk did not affirmatively do anything to check that its crew members were able to complete their job duties and comply with the STCW work/rest hours. In addition, one of Skye's Maersk captains, Captain James Brennan, testified that Skye was a competent Chief Mate who told him that complying with the STCW work/rest hours was very difficult.

Skye's lawyer also introduced evidence showing that Maersk actually budgeted 185 percent of the Chief Mate's base salary to overtime. This was far more than the overtime budget for any other position on the ship. By comparison Maersk's overtime budget for the Captain was 26 percent of his base salary. Maersk's attorneys presented arguments that it was primarily Skye's responsibility as Chief Mate to make sure that he complied with the work/rest hours law. Further, they argued that

Skye failed to delegate tasks which would have made it feasible for him to comply with the work/rest hours and allow him to obtain uninterrupted rest. Maersk's attorneys also argued that Skye's injury was caused by a cardiac condition that he began complaining about in 2000. Therefore, his filing a lawsuit in May 2011 violated the applicable three-year statute of limitations.

In addition, Maersk's attorneys presented testimony from cardiologist, Dr. Theodore Feldman, who said the left ventricular hypertrophy did not preclude him from working aboard ships and was easily controlled with medication. Maersk's attorneys also presented testimony from maritime safety expert, Captain Douglas Torborg, who went through three and a half years of work-hour logs regarding Skye. Torborg testified that, based on the exceptions to the work/rest hours of the STCW, the working hours did not constitute a violation of the laws.

At the end of the trial, the jury did not find there were statutory violations of the STCW laws. However, they found that Maersk was negligent and its negligence was a legal cause of Skye's injuries. As a result of such injuries, which were first discovered by Skye in 2008, he was forced to retire 10 years earlier than he had planned. The jury found

Maersk 25 percent negligent and Skye 75 percent comparatively negligent. They awarded $2,088,549 (present value) for 10 years of lost wages. The jury also found that Skye's non-economic damages totaled $273,750.

An Injured Female Seafarer's Story

An arbitration panel in Miami, Florida, has ordered Royal Caribbean Cruises to pay $1,250,000 to a crew member following an injury aboard the Jewel of the Seas cruise ship. The crew member, a woman from Serbia, sustained a serious back injury in June 2008 when a crew member slammed a door into her back while she was walking down a narrow hallway. She sustained a large herniated disc. She reported to the ship's infirmary and the ship doctor found her unfit for duty. However, her supervisor instructed her to continue working. The ship doctor listened to her supervisor and decided not to take her medical condition seriously. At the next port of call, an X-ray was not taken and an MRI was not ordered because the supervisor disagreed with the ship's doctor. After seven weeks of continuous work, her medical condition deteriorated. She collapsed and had to be taken from the cruise ship on a stretcher with an IV morphine drip to manage her pain.

How did Royal Caribbean respond? The inconsiderate cruise line sent her back to Serbia and refused to arrange for any medical treatment. Also, Royal Caribbean paid her only $12 a day for lodging and food, which is not nearly enough to live on. It took Royal Caribbean more than five months to finally authorize back surgery in January 2009. The doctor then performed surgery at the wrong level. Royal Caribbean then refused to pay for her rehabilitation or arrange for follow-up X-rays or an MRI.

She wisely decided to hire a Florida maritime attorney to represent her because Royal Caribbean's home port is in Miami even though it flies a Liberian flag and is incorporated in Liberia. When her attorney complained to Royal Caribbean's attorney that she was not being provided with the rehabilitation and medical treatment she needed, Royal Caribbean terminated her living expenses! One of the in-house lawyers overseeing Royal Caribbean's medical department, Tony Faso, decided to abandon her. Faso sent an email to her attorney stating that he was sure any arbitrator would agree that Royal Caribbean was not responsible for paying for her rehabilitation and medical treatment. Her attorney then flew her to Miami and arranged for her to see a U.S. board-certified orthopedist who determined that the surgery performed on her was a complete failure. Royal Caribbean nonetheless refused to reinstate her benefits or provide her with the medical care that she needed.

The three-member U.S. arbitration panel found Royal Caribbean's refusal to pay maintenance and cure benefits to be unreasonable and awarded her $1,250,000. Royal Caribbean was also found responsible for $11,650 for the administrative costs of the International Center for Dispute Resolution (ICDR) as well as $48,970 to compensate the arbitrators. The award demonstrates the consequences of a cruise line unlawfully abandoning an ill seafarer and terminating her necessary medical benefits.

Duarte vs. Royal Caribbean Cruises, Ltd.

In Duarte vs. Royal Caribbean Cruises, Ltd. 761 So. 2d 367; (Fla. App. 3rd 2000), the appellant was a seafarer who was receiving maintenance and cure for several months when she was injured in an automobile accident. The cruise line refused to pay the appellant maintenance and cure for expenses arising from the accident, and the appellant filed suit. The trial court granted summary judgment in favor of the cruise line. The appellate court reversed, holding that the appellant was receiving maintenance and cure at the time of the accident because she had yet to obtain maximum medical recovery. In this situation, the appellant was still in the service of the ship and was therefore entitled to maintenance and cure for the additional injuries incurred. Because the appellant had not yet obtained maximum medical recovery at the time she sustained injuries in a car accident, Royal Caribbean's refusal to pay for maintenance and cure for such injuries was improper.

A seafarer may bring a negligence suit if the accident was not his or her fault, which may entitle him or her to future medical care beyond maximum medical improvement, past and future lost wages, as well as pain, suffering, and/or mental anguish. However, the damages can be reduced if the shipowner successfully proves that the seafarer was negligent and contributed to his or her own injuries. An experienced attorney handling a seafarer's case will recognize the distinction between assumption of risk and contributory negligence. This is a very critical distinction which must be recognized by the seafarer's maritime attorney so he or she can refute the defenses of the shipowner's attorney.

Passenger Accidents and Injuries

Maritime personal injury actions are governed by a set of rules that are separate and distinct from the general body of tort law applicable in nonmaritime cases. Cruise ships have a duty to provide care for all of their passengers, to protect all passengers from physical harm, and to make sure they arrive at port safely. In a suit for negligence, a plaintiff's attorney must prove that the defendant failed to fulfill his or her duties and that the failure, in turn, caused the plaintiff's injuries.

The ticket contract always includes the requirements for bringing a lawsuit. Most cruise lines try to limit their liability by requiring passengers to take certain steps before filing a lawsuit, including: providing written notice of the injury within a certain period of time after it occurs (usually 6 months), bringing a claim within a certain period of time (usually one year), and suing in a specific court in a specific state. Awards for damages in maritime personal injury cases are reduced in the proportion of any negligence of the plaintiff relative to the fault of the defendant in causing the personal injury.

General maritime law does not recognize loss of consortium (the material services, happiness, companionship, financial support, and sexual relationship with a spouse, which has been deprived and is reasonably certain to be deprived in the future) claims on the high seas. Maritime rules may apply to damages for personal injuries supplemented by state rules allowing non-pecuniary (not related to money) losses such as compensation for emotional distress, loss of consortium, loss of society (the mutual benefits that each family member receives from the other's continued existence, including love, affection, care, attention, companionship, comfort, guidance, and protection), if:

1. The injured person was not a seafarer,

2. The injury occurred in the territorial waters of a state, and

3. The casualty did not involve a commercial vessel.

Disaster on the M/V Horizon Leading to Numerous Lawsuits

In July 1994, cruise passengers aboard the *M/V Horizon* contracted Legionnaires' disease, a potentially fatal form of pneumonia, as the vessel was sailing between New York and Bermuda. A class action suit against *Celebrity Cruises, Inc.* and *Fantasia Cruising, Inc.* was filed. *Essef Corporation, Pac-Fab, Inc.* and *Structural Europe N.V.* were also sued because these companies were responsible for the manufacture and distribution of the filter used in the whirlpool spa system on the *M/V Horizon* where the disease originated.[1] In order for admiralty jurisdiction to apply, a tort has to take place on navigable waters and be related to a traditional maritime activity. In this case, the court decided that admiralty jurisdiction applied because the plaintiffs got the disease on a cruise ship on navigable waters, and maritime commerce was significantly disrupted when the passengers had to disembark in Bermuda and fly to New York so the vessel could be decontaminated before the next cruise.

The attorney for the plaintiffs sued for negligence, strict products liability, and breach of warranty. *Celebrity Cruises, Inc.* then filed a complaint and cross-claims against the companies responsible for manufacturing and distributing the whirlpool spa filter. Some plaintiffs included in their complaint a demand for punitive damages against both *Celebrity Cruises* and *Essef*. Some plaintiffs did not include a demand for punitive damages and later decided that they wanted their attorneys to file motions to amend their complaints pursuant to Rule 15(a) of the Federal Rules of Civil Procedure and add claims for punitive damages.

The Essef defendants opposed these motions on the grounds that they were untimely and that punitive damages are unavailable under admiralty law, but this is not always true. Punitive damages are available under maritime law in many cases. The earliest reported case in which punitive damages were awarded took place in 1823. The damages were awarded by an American court in Chamberlain v. Chandler, 5 F. Cas. 413 (C.C.D.Mass.1823) (No. 2,575), in which the passengers sued the master of a vessel for his conduct toward them. Numerous other maritime cases either granted punitive damages to passengers, or at least indicated that they were available, if the defendant's intentional or wanton and reckless conduct amounted to a conscientious disregard of the rights of others.

Although it is true that the plaintiffs' attorneys who wanted to amend the complaints were slow in doing so, the court determined that delay alone without bad faith or prejudice is not a sufficient basis for denying permission to amend. The main reason for the delay was that the principal facts on which the claim for punitive damages was based did not come to light until depositions took place in 1998. The court denied the motion of the Essef defendants to strike the claims for punitive damages and the motions to amend were granted.

Following are stories of passengers who were injured on cruise ships or other types of vessels.

Boat Skipper Charged with Vehicular Homicide and Vehicular Assault in Tragic Hudson River Boat Crash in New York

On July 26, 2013, a moonlit pleasure cruise on the Hudson River ended in tragedy when the intoxicated skipper steered the boat into a construction barge, killing a bride-to-be and best man, who were thrown from the boat. Seriously injured was the groom-to-be, Brian Bond, and the other members of the wedding party. It was supposed to be a short boat ride up the Hudson River from the village of Piermont in Rockland County to Tarrytown. At about 10:30 p.m., the 21-foot roofless *Stingray* suddenly smashed into a construction barge under the Tappan Zee Bridge. Despite suffering serious head injuries, Bond called 911 from the boat at 10:41 p.m. and reported that the boat had struck an object south of the bridge.

The skipper, Jojo K. John, was charged with first degree vehicular manslaughter and second-degree vehicular assault after allegedly boating while he was drunk, according to Rockland County

Undersheriff Robert Van Cura. John was arraigned in his hospital bed and was ordered held on $250,000 bond. The bodies of bride-to-be Lindsey Stewart and best man Mark Lennon were recovered from the water and taken to the medical examiner's office.

Bond was taken to Westchester Medical Center. In addition to head injuries, he had a fractured eye socket and a puncture wound to his elbow. John and the other victims were treated for head trauma. Some of the injured passengers were able to provide information to investigators, but Bond was unable to speak due to his injuries.

Brian Conybeare, special advisor to the governor, stated:

> [w]hile the Rockland County Sheriff, New York State Police and U.S. Coast Guard continue to investigate this tragic incident, the New York State Thruway Authority is conducting its own review of safety procedures on the Hudson River as part of a New York Bridge Project. Tappan Zee Constructors, LLC, has reported to the Thruway Authority that all Coast Guard lighting requirements were met and that the barges were properly lit on the night of the accident. All lighting was checked

Saturday morning and was fully operational at all barge locations associated with the project.

Intoxicated Passenger Falls Overboard and Sues Carnival

On Oct. 21, 2012, Sarah Alexandra Badley Kirby was a passenger on Carnival's *Destiny* with her fiancé and her friend Rebecca. Kirby described the *Destiny* as "a floating dram shop." A dram shop is a bar or tavern where alcoholic beverages are sold by the dram, a small unit of liquid. After drinking too much alcohol and falling overboard, she hired a lawyer to sue Carnival Corporation in federal court because of how poorly the accident had been handled. When eyewitnesses reported that they saw Kirby fall overboard, the captain insisted on searching the ship for 90 minutes to look for her onboard, rather than believing the eyewitnesses immediately. When the captain finally stopped the ship and Kirby was found in the water, the captain then refused to airlift her to a hospital to treat her fractured bones and other injuries, even though they were unable to properly treat her injuries onboard.

Kirby claimed that a bartender had encouraged her to drink too many Long Island iced teas after she was clearly intoxicated. The bartender offered her and her companions free $5 coupons for the ship's casino with every drink purchase. At approximately 12:10 a.m., Kirby stepped out to the cabin balcony to get some air. As she was holding on to the balcony's wooden banister, Kirby lost her grip and balance, slipped off the ground, and fell overboard into the ocean. As she fell from the balcony, which was seven stories high (approximately 100 feet), she fell onto a life raft. After hitting the life raft, she fell five more stories into the water.

Kirby said she swam with exhaustion towards the ship, then floated face up, swallowing and coughing up water from the waves that crashed into her face. She thought she would either drown or be eaten by a shark. Kirby's complaint stated that not only her fiancé and Rebecca immediately noticed that she had fallen overboard, but other passengers also had seen her fall. The indicent was reported to several Carnival staff members. Rebecca and Ms. Kirby's fiancé repeatedly demanded the cruise ship staff to stop the ship, but their requests were denied. Instead, the cruise ship staff explained that they were not going to stop the vessel. It was their standard procedure to first search the ship.

Rebecca and Kirby's fiancé were then escorted to the Captain's quarters. Over the next 90 minutes (while the ship was still moving) they were questioned by the ship's security staff and the ship's officers regarding the incident. Rebecca and Kirby's fiancé repeated their account of the incident several times, and they again demanded that the ship be stopped immediately. Once again, however, their request was denied. At approximately 1:45 a.m., while the ship was still moving and Ms. Kirby had been in the water for more than an hour and a half, the ship's officers finally notified all passengers via intercom that they were going to turn around to search for a passenger who had fallen overboard.

The crew finally found Kirby after she had spent nearly two hours in the ocean. She had suffered severe injuries, including fractured orbital bones, lung contusions, hypothermia, fractured ribs, dissection of the carotid artery, heart arrhythmia, broken optical shelves, and blood clots in her eyes, arms, and legs. She also had extreme hematomas all over her body. The ship's doctor gave her pain medication but was unable to properly treat her injuries with the equipment on the ship. Kirby's lawyer asserted that Carnival personnel had refused to airlift her to a hospital despite her broken bones. When she got home from the cruise, she was hospitalized for three weeks. Kirby's lawyer claimed the captain intentionally and recklessly decided to search the ship even though witnesses had made it clear that she had fallen overboard. Carnival was sued for punitive damages for negligence and intentional infliction of emotional distress, because Kirby had been intentionally abandoned in the middle of the ocean for an unreasonable period of time.

Cruise ships are not the only place where passengers frequently suffer injuries. There are also many serious or fatal accidents on smaller boats. According to the Florida Fish and Wildlife Conservation Commission, there were 704 reportable boating accidents in 2012, with 386 injuries and 55 boating-related fatalities. Monroe County reported the highest number of accidents and injuries (100 total accidents with 5 fatalities and 61 injuries). Seventy-one percent of the operators involved in fatal accidents had no formal boater education.

New York Powerboat Accident

In July 2011, a powerboat struck a concrete abutment along the Hudson River and sank before sunrise, killing four occupants and seriously injuring two others, all New Yorkers. Six people were aboard the 19-foot boat when it rammed into a concrete footing not far from the shoreline near Red Hook, New York, about 45 miles south of

Albany, according to Lt. John Watterson of the Dutchess County Sheriff's office.

The body of 26-year-old John J. Uvino of Saugerties was found in the water, and it appeared he was thrown from the boat on impact. Divers recovered the bodies of three other boaters: Robert P. Macarthur, 27, of Kingston; Deena C. Cordero, 26, of Kingston; and Jay J. Bins, 41, of Kingston. Two boaters, 23-year-old Joseph J. Vehnick of Kingston and 27-year-old Jessica K. Hotaling of Hyde Park, made it to shore. Vehnick, who was badly injured, found a telephone in a barn near the crash site and called 911 just before 6:30 a.m., about two hours after investigators believed the crash occurred. Vehnick and Hotaling both suffered multiple fractures and were treated at local hospitals.

Watterson stated that it wasn't immediately clear who had been driving the boat. The boat's bow and underside were heavily damaged, leading authorities to believe the driver had been speeding. The medical examiner conducted autopsies to determine the cause of death of the four people who drowned. Authorities found beer bottles inside the boat and believed the occupants might have been intoxicated.

The powerboat, which has a single deck with no quarters below, is known as a bow rider because its passengers generally ride up front while the driver sits behind them. Part of the boat was still sticking out of the water when rescuers arrived. Its bow had smashed into the concrete, which may have been part of a dock or other previous shoreline structure. Watterson was not sure if it was marked off by a buoy. The boat was pulled from the water and brought to an impound lot.

New York Ferry Debacle

In January 2013, a high-speed ferry loaded with commuters from New Jersey crashed into a dock in lower Manhattan during the morning rush hour. Eleven people were seriously injured, including one who suffered a severe head wound after falling down a stairwell. Many people, who had been standing and waiting to disembark, were hurled to the deck or launched into the walls by the impact. The crash occurred after the catamaran, *Seastreak Wall Street,* slowed following a routine trip across New York Bay. When the boat hit the dock, passengers tumbled on top of one another. "People were hysterical," said Ellen Foran, of Neptune City, New Jersey, and a passenger. Some passengers were bloodied when they banged into walls and toppled to the floor.

The crash, which ripped open a small part of the hull like an aluminum can, happened at 8:45 a.m. at a pier near the South Street Seaport, at Manhattan's southern tip. Approximately 70 people suffered minor injuries, and for nearly two hours paramedics treated bruised and dazed passengers on the pier. Firefighters carried several patients on flat-board stretchers as a precaution. Other patients left in wheelchairs. The cause of the crash was investigated. The ferry, built in 2003, had recently undergone a major overhaul, resulting in new engines and a new propulsion system. Officials were not sure if anything from the overhaul played any role in the accident.

Dee Wertz, who was on shore waiting for the ferry, saw the impact. She said just moments before the ferry hit, she had been having a conversation with a ferry employee about how the boat's captains had been complaining about its maneuverability. "He was telling me that none of these guys like this boat," Wertz said. "It was coming in a little wobbly. It hit the right side of the boat on the dock hard, like a bomb."

James Barker, the chairman of the ferry's owner, Seastreak LLC, said he was shocked by what had happened. He also stated the company would work with investigators from the National Transportation Safety Board to determine what went wrong. About 330 passengers and crew members were aboard the ferry, which had arrived from Atlantic Highlands, a part of the Jersey Shore still struggling to recover from Superstorm Sandy that hit in October. Passenger Frank McLaughlin, said he was thrown forward on the ferry and wrenched his knee.

New York City's transportation commissioner, Janette Sadik-Khan, said the ferry was coming in at 10 to 12 knots, or about 12 to 14 mph, when it struck one slip and then hit a second. After the impact, the boat was able to dock normally. Wertz, who saw the crash from the dock, said passengers raced off once the ramp was down.

Police said the boat's crew passed alcohol breath tests given after the crash. Officials identified the captain as Jason Reimer, an experienced seaman. In a 2004 profile in Newsday, Reimer said he had joined Seastreak as a deckhand in 1997 and became a captain three years later at age 23. The *Seastreak Wall Street* had previously been in minor accidents. Coast Guard records revealed the ferry hit a cluster of fender piles while docking in 2010, punching a small hole in the ship's skin. In 2009, it suffered another tear on the bow after another minor docking collision. No one was injured in either of those mishaps.

The naval architectural firm that designed the reconfiguration was Incat Crowther. The ferry's water-jet propulsion system had been replaced with a new system of propellers and rudders to save fuel costs and cut carbon dioxide pollution in half. Barker said the overhaul made it "the greenest ferry in America." The hull had been reworked, and the boat was made 15 metric tons lighter. At top speed, the ferry traveled at approximately 35 knots or 40 mph.

Ferry accidents happen every few years in New York. In 2003, 11 people were killed when a Staten Island Ferry crashed into a pier on Staten Island after its pilot passed out at the wheel. Three people were badly hurt and about forty were injured when the same ferry hit the same pier in 2010 because of a mechanical problem.

Suski Siblings Fishing Trip Nightmare

On April 21, 2013, Dan Suski, a 30-year-old business owner and information technology expert from San Francisco, had been wrestling a 200-pound marlin in rough seas with help from his sister, Kate Suski, a 39-year-old architect from Seattle. They were in San Juan, Puerto Rico, off the rugged north coast of St. Lucia, when the boat's electrical system suddenly crackled and popped. Dan was still trying to reel in the fish when water rushed into the cabin and flooded the engine room, prompting the captain to radio for help as he yelled out their coordinates.

As the waves pounded the boat they had chartered from Reel Irie Company, more water flooded in. The captain threw life preservers to the Suskis and told them to jump out. The Suskis obeyed and jumped into the water, along with the captain and first mate. Less than five minutes later, the boat sank. The group was at least 8 miles from shore, and waves more than twice their size tossed them back and forth. The captain told them to stay together and wait for help. The group waited for about an hour, but no one came.

Kate decided it would be better to swim than to wait. As they began to swim, the Suskis lost sight of the captain and first mate. Then, they lost sight of land when it began to rain. A plane and a helicopter appeared in the distance and hovered over the area, but no one spotted the siblings. They continued to swim for approximately 12 to 14 hours, talking and shivering as they swam in the ocean. Dan tried to ignore images of the movie "Open Water" that kept running through his mind. The movie was about a scuba-diving couple left behind by their group and attacked by sharks. Kate was so scared of being bitten by a shark that she felt nauseous and thought she would vomit.

When the siblings finally came within 30 feet of land, they realized they couldn't get out of the water because they saw cliffs rising into the ocean. Kate was afraid of being crushed by the cliffs, but Dan thought they should try to reach the rocks anyway. They swam until they noticed a spot of sand nearby. When they got to land, they collapsed, barely able to walk. It was past midnight, and they didn't notice any homes in the area.

"Dan said the first priority was to stay warm," Kate recalled. They hiked inland and lay side by side, pulling up grass and brush to cover them. Kate was only wearing her bikini, having shed her dress to swim better. Dan had shed his shorts to make it easier for him to swim. They heard a stream running nearby but decided to wait until daylight to determine whether or not the water was safe to drink.

As the sun rose, they began to hike through thick brush, picking up bitter mangoes along the way and stopping to eat green bananas. Approximately three hours later, they spotted a young farmworker walking with his dog. He gave them crackers and water and called the police. The

Suskis were hospitalized and received IV fluids because both were very dehydrated. They were informed that the captain and first mate had been rescued after spending nearly 23 hours in the water and were in the care of relatives.

St. Lucia's tourism minister called it a miracle that all four survived the freak accident, and the island's maritime affairs unit began to investigate exactly what caused the ship to sink. Marine Police Sgt. Finley Leonce said they had already interviewed the Captain, and police did not suspect foul play or any criminal activity in the sinking of the ship. A man at the Reel Irie Company declined to comment except to say he was happy that everyone was safe. Although Dan and Kate could have sued Reel Irie Company for negligence since the boat's electrical system malfunctioned, they were so happy to be alive they decided not to sue. Upon returning to their hotel in St. Lucia, Dan and Kate were upgraded to a suite, where they began to recover from cuts on their feet, severe tendonitis in their ankles, and abrasions from the lifejackets.

Major Disasters on Cruise Ships

On Feb. 10, 2013, the 14-story Carnival Cruise Line *Triumph* was disabled following a fire in the ship's engine room. This caused the vessel to lose power and become stranded in the Gulf of Mexico. Two tiny tugboats had to pull the ship to the nearest port. More than 4,000 people were stuck onboard a "floating toilet" for five long days as the ship made its way to land. Sewage and waste overflowed from deck to deck, creating a breeding ground for many diseases, including lung infections, urinary tract infections, norovirus, and hepatitis.

When the nightmare was over and the passengers finally returned home, Carnival Cruise Lines provided each passenger with a complete refund, a free future cruise credit, plus an additional $500 per person as compensation for their suffering. However, many passengers and maritime attorneys believed that $500 was not nearly enough compensation for their emotional suffering and illnesses. It is important to note that this is *not* the first disaster for Carnival Cruises. Three other Carnival cruise ships—the *Elation*, the *Dream* and the *Legend*—all became disabled following mechanical malfunctions because of generator problems.

In March 2013, passengers on Carnival's *Dream* headed to the airport instead of sailing home after an on-board generator problem halted their trip. The *Dream* was on a seven-day cruise of the Caribbean with 3,646 passengers. The *Dream* was in St. Maarten on the final stop of a Caribbean cruise when the crew announced it would not be sailing home to Port Canaveral, Florida, because of a mechanical issue with a backup emergency diesel generator. Carnival officials decided to fly all its guests either to Orlando or to their hometown and offered its guests a refund for three days of travel and a 50 percent discount on a future cruise.

The Centers for Disease Control and Prevention (CDC) run a unique Vessel Sanitation Program, in which its agents randomly inspect cruise ships twice a year to determine their level of hygiene and sanitation. Any cruise ship that carries 13 or more passengers and features a foreign itinerary with U.S. ports is subject to these inspections. Following the inspection, the CDC grades the vessel on a 100-point scale. Anything equal to and below an 85 is considered failing, and the ship will be responsible for correcting any problems and will be subject to reinspection. If the CDC believes conditions onboard the ship pose an immediate public health risk, the ship will be ordered to remain at port and cancel itineraries until the issue has been corrected.

Carnival's *Fascination* failed a CDC inspection in February 2013. In a detailed report, CDC inspectors documented many problems with the food areas. The inspectors found food items on the top shelf of a buffet area that were not protected by a sneeze guard. A pulper in a food preparation room was heavily soiled with food waste. The drain below a juice dispenser in the room service prep room was inaccessible for cleaning, and when it was opened several small flies and a roach nymph were near the drain.

CDC inspectors also discovered one crewmember on the *Fascination* had reported for a partial day of work after the onset of acute gastroenteritis symptoms. The crew member had not been isolated in a cabin after these symptoms began. The CDC recommendation is employees with acute gastroenteritis symptoms should report to the medical center as soon as the first symptoms appear. These employees should be restricted from work and isolated in a cabin, or designated restricted area, until thay are symptom free for at least 24 hours. Additional violations were cited for several instances of corroded equipment, loose piping in the galley, and missing or cracked tiles.

Personell of all cruise lines are expected to exercise reasonable care to furnish aid and assistance that ordinarily prudent persons would render under similar circumstances. They are responsible for the health, safety, and well-being of the passengers and crew. As part of maintaining onboard safety, cruise operators are required to uphold sanitary conditions throughout their vessels, regularly test equipment to prevent malfunctions, fully train crew members regarding emergency operations, and respond to medical emergencies as quickly as possible.

In addition to providing a safe environment onboard, employees of the cruise lines are also responsible for ensuring that passengers and crew members obtain adequate food, water, and shelter. Carnival *Triumph* passengers had limited food; not enough clean water to drink; and, because of the lack of electricity onboard, cabins were dark, hot, and contaminated with sewage waste. The Coast Guard spent nearly $780,000 of its own funds responding to the *Triumph* incident.

Carnival representatives responded to an inquiry by U.S. Senator Jay Rockefeller, a West Virginia Democrat who chairs the Senate Commerce Committee, about the *Triumph* stranding and the cruise line's overall safety record. One of Rockefeller's questions was whether Carnival would repay the government $780,000 for Coast Guard costs in the *Triumph* case. Another questionis asked if Carnival would repay $3.4 million to both the Coast Guard and Navy from the 2010 stranding of the Carnival *Splendor* in the Pacific Ocean. Rockefeller believed that it was unfair that these costs must ultimately be borne by federal taxpayers.

In response, a Carnival representative said its policy is to "honor maritime tradition that holds that the duty to render assistance at sea to those in need is a universal obligation of the entire maritime community." It was noted that Carnival's ships frequently participate in rescues at the Coast Guard's request, including 11 times in the past year in Florida and Caribbean waters. Carnival officials stated there was no intention of repaying any money to the U.S. government, Coast Guard, or Navy. Senator Rockefeller called Carnival's response "shameful" and stated he is considering "all options to hold the industry to higher passenger safety standards."

Rockefeller's letter asked Carnival's CEO whether the money the cruise line pays in taxes covers the costs of various federal benefits it receives. The question was not answered. Rockefeller asked for details about 90 incidents aboard Carnival's ships that were filed with the Coast Guard in the past five years. The response was that 83 were not considered serious under federal regulations. Three were the *Triumph* and *Splendor* mishaps and the capsizing of the Costa *Concordia* off Italy's coast, which killed 32 people in January 2012. According to Carnival records, the other incidents were minor ship collisions, illnesses, and one passenger who jumped off a ship.

The issue of Carnival management's avoidance of paying taxes for U.S. services has been brewing for years. The International Cruise Victims (ICV) organization, a non-profit organization focused on crimes and disappearances of passengers on cruise ships, has addressed the issue of cruise tax avoidance. ICV CEO Ken Carver sent a Freedom of Information Act (FOIA) request for the costs associated with the U.S. Navy and U.S. Coast Guard responding to the disabled Carnival Splendor in November 2010. Carver's investigation led to a response from the Navy that revealed the Navy incurred $1,884,376.75 in responding to the disabled Splendor. Expenses included sending a U.S. aircraft carrier and helicopters to the fire-stricken cruise ship.

Many news sources published articles highly critical of Carnival. Carnival has been the butt of "poop ship" jokes. All the bad publicity caused Carnival executives to have a change of heart regarding helping to repay the government agencies it relied on whenever there is a problem with its ships. On April 15, 2013, Carnival released a statement saying, "Although no agencies have requested remuneration, the company has made the decision to voluntarily provide reimbursement to the federal government."

Senator Rockefeller responded by saying "I'm glad to see that Carnival owned up to the bare minimum of corporate responsibility by reimbursing federal taxpayers for the Triumph and Splendor incidents. I am still committed to making sure the cruise industry as a whole pays its fair share in taxes, complies with strict safety standards, and holds the safety of its passengers above profits."

Cassie Terry of Brazoria County, Texas, hired a lawyer to file a lawsuit in Miami federal court following her cruise on the *Triumph*. Terry's lawyer stated that his client was forced to endure unbearable and horrendous odors on the filthy, disabled vessel. She had to wade through human feces in order to reach food lines where the wait was very long, only to receive rations of spoiled food. During her horrifying journey back to the U.S., the ship tilted several times causing human waste to spill out of non-functioning toilets, flood across the vessel's floors and halls, and drip down the vessel's walls.

Terry's lawyer sued for breach of maritime contract, negligence, negligent misrepresentation and fraud as a result of the "unseaworthy, unsafe, unsanitary, and generally despicable conditions" on the crippled cruise ship. Terry worried constantly about contracting a serious infection or illness from the raw sewage that filled the vessel. Terry's lawyer proved that the cruise line was negligent in letting the ship sail, despite past engine problems and that Terry's mental suffering was so severe that she had to seek psychological counseling.

Another lawsuit was filed by passengers Matt and Melissa Crusan of Oklahoma who said they were fearful for their lives aboard the *Triumph*. They said they and other passengers suffered nausea, headaches, insomnia, and nightmares, made worse by the decision to tow the *Triumph* to Mobile, Alabama rather than go to a closer port in Mexico. In addition to individual lawsuits, a class action suit representing hundreds of passengers was filed for gross negligence. This is because Carnival employees should have known about the engine problem (fire in the engine room).

After five days of squalor, the Triumph finally docked in Mobile on Feb. 14, 2013. Taking the ship's position into consideration, Carnival executives made the decision to have the disabled Triumph towed to Mobile, instead of Progreso, Mexico. Carnival officials stated the ship was essentially equal distance to both ports, but some maritime attorneys believe this is not true. The fact that the ship was not taken to Progreso, which was only 105 miles away instead of Mobile, which was much further, warrants legal action if it can be proved that Carnival officials intentionally made decisions for financial reasons. Carnival executives claim tugging the disabled ship to Galveston avoided delays with Mexican and U.S. immigration and customs authorities. Also pointed out was the logistical nightmare of disembarking, housing, and transporting more than 4,000 people to Mexico and flying them back to Houston on charter flights, instead of busing them to Galveston that would have added another two or three days to the trip home for all of Triumph's passengers and crew. However, wouldn't this have been better than spending five days on a floating toilet?

The fine print on Carnival's cruise tickets does not allow claims for emotional distress. Believing there is limited liability because of the disclaimer printed on its tickets, Carnival cruise line will likely be held liable for punitive damages. This is because of the wanton and reckless conduct toward more than 4,000 passengers. Carnival executives will most likely try to settle the lawsuits for as little money as possible if it cannot get the lawsuits dismissed based on its ticket restrictions.

Two months after it was towed to shore, the Carnival *Triumph* broke away from its moorings again after a storm blew through Mobile, Alabama. Winds exceeding 70 miles per hour sent the ship adrift. The powerful winds blew two people into the water during the storm. Steve Hoffman of the Mobile Fire-Rescue stated that wind knocked over a guard shack, blowing it and the two occupants into the water. One person was rescued from the water, but the Coast Guard did not find the other person. The missing occupant is an employee of BAE Systems, the company that was repairing the disabled ship. Mobile Fire-Rescue brought in search dogs to help find the missing employee, but they were not successful. A week later, his corpse was discovered and identified.

Cruise ship disasters prompted Senator Charles Schumer of New York to propose a "Cruise Ship Passenger Bill of Rights." Schumer asked the cruise industry to voluntarily agree to a list of guidelines, including the right to backup power if generators fail and the right to disembark a docked ship "if basic provisions cannot adequately be provided onboard." The senator also asked the International Maritime Organization to investigate whether cruise lines are following existing guidelines, and whether existing standards are being enforced by countries where cruise ships that serve U.S. passengers are based. Schumer's Bill of Rights is meant to ensure that passengers are not forced to live in Third World conditions or put their lives at risk when they go on vacation. While there are international maritime regulations, unless an accident occurs that results in an investigation, the breach of international maritime regulations often go unpunished. This is because no one is onboard or out in the open ocean inspecting or enforcing maritime regulations.

In April 2013, Carnival executives announced that it would spend up to $700 million to upgrade its fleet of 101 ships. As a first step, each Carnival Cruise Line ship received an additional emergency generator to power stateroom and public toilets and keep fresh water and elevators running in case of a power outage. A second permanent backup power system was then installed to keep cooking facilities and cold-food storage operating, as well as provide Internet and telephone access during a power outage. In addition, there were plans to invest in new fire prevention, detection and suppression systems, and make changes that would reduce the chance of losing propulsion or primary power. A comprehensive fleet-wide review of vessel operation systems and training was executed in an attempt to improve safety regulations across all Carnival ships.

Despite all these upgrades, the Carnival Triumph failed an inspection after all repairs were completed, and it was briefly detained by the U.S. Coast Guard in June 2013. Rear Admiral Joseph Servidio, assistant commandant for prevention policy for the U.S. Coast Guard, testified before the U.S. Senate Committee on Commerce, Science and Transportation on July 24, 2013. Servidio explained that inspectors found "three serious deficiencies" related to fire detection and lifeboat drills during the Triumph's first examination in Galveston, Texas, after the completion of $115 million in repairs. The Coast Guard, which uncovered a total of 28 deficiencies, found problems with the fire detectors and sprinkler systems in many areas of the Triumph. Passengers were barred from boarding the ship until all violations were fixed. Asked about the circumstances of the failed inspection, Carnival spokesperson Jennifer de la Cruz stated: "The U.S. Coast Guard inspected the Carnival Triumph for two days and identified some items for corrective action that were addressed. The Coast Guard approved the vessel to sail on June 13, 2013 and the vessel sailed at its scheduled departure time."

Senator Jay Rockefeller castigated Carnival's Gerald Cahill for narrating a video posted on June 12, 2013, ensuring the public that the Carnival Triumph had been fully repaired. That was approximately the same time when the ship was failing the Coast Guard inspection! Rockefeller asked Cahill why anyone should believe him about anything related to passenger safety. Cahill insisted that Carnival created a fire safety task force after the 2010 Carnival Splendor fire, conducted a fleet-wide operational review after the Carnival Triumph incident, is in the process of investing $300 million in emergency generator upgrades, fire safety improvements, and other changes. Also, Cahill said a safety review board had been formed with outside experts. Coast Guard Rear Admiral Joseph Servidio said that the Carnival Triumph would be subject to quarterly examinations for the next three years.

Carnival cruise line had a much worse tragic event than the *Triumph* debacle on Jan. 13, 2011, when the Costa *Concordia*, owned and operated by a subsidiary of Carnival Corporation, capsized after hitting a rock near the Italian island of Giglio. The vessel's captain, Francesco Schettino, was charged with several counts of abandoning ship and manslaughter. Schettino chose to alter the *Concordia*'s course in order to perform a maneuver known as a "salute," which brought the ship too close to land. The crash tore a hole in the hull of the ship, causing the vessel to partially sink. Passengers recounted how crew members were unable to communicate with each other, and the entire evacuation process was chaotic and traumatic. A total of 32 people died as a result of the captain's actions.

Ian and Janice Donoff were nearly killed as a result of the Costa Concordia disaster when the vessel ran aground. Telling about their harrowing escape, the London couple explained they were on their honeymoon when the accident took place. Although they survived, the experience has forever changed them. Janice, who broke several bones in her hands and feet during the evacuation off the vessel, now suffers from post-traumatic stress disorder and feels uncomfortable when around large crowds.

Costa Cruises owners accepted a $1.31 million fine to settle potential criminal charges concerning the deadly accident off the coast of Italy. Costa Cruises had been under investigation as the employer of the *Concordia* crew when it hit a rock.

According to reporters, the prosecution is satisfied with the ruling by the preliminary court judge, Valeria Montesarchio, and will not appeal. The fine was close to the maximum allowed by law. The settlement means that Costa owners will not face a criminal trial, and the potential liability with Italy is ended. However, private lawsuits could be filed by passengers or crew members.

Another major problem for cruise ships is norovirus outbreaks. A norovirus is any of various single-stranded RNA viruses including the Norwalk virus and closely related viruses. In December 2012, many passengers and crew members aboard the luxury cruise ship *Queen Mary 2* were sickened and suffered from vomiting and diarrhea. In 2012, including the *Queen Mary 2* incident, a total of 16 outbreaks on cruise ships was reported to the U.S. Centers for Disease Control, up from 14 in 2011. Vessels are required to notify the CDC when 2 percent of those onboard develop a gastrointestinal illness.

In March 2013, 108 people became ill with a gastrointestinal illness believed to be a norovirus on the Royal Caribbean Cruises' *Vision of the Seas*. The ship docked in Port Everglades, Florida, at the end of an 11-day trip. The 915-foot-long *Vision of the Seas* was ending a Caribbean cruise that departed from Port Everglades on Feb. 25, 2013. A

Royal Caribbean spokesperson told reporters those sickened had responded well to the over-the-counter medicine they were given. The ship and the cruise terminal had been thoroughly sanitized to prevent another outbreak.

Norovirus causes an inflammation of the stomach or intestines called acute gastroenteritis, producing stomach pain, nausea, and diarrhea. It is the most common cause of acute gastroenteritis in the United States. Each year, norovirus causes approximately 21 million illnesses, of which 70,000 require hospitalization. It kills about 800 people a year, according to the CDC. Noroviruses are found in the feces or vomit of infected people, who can become infected with the virus in several ways, including:

- Eating food or drinking liquids that are contaminated with norovirus
- Touching surfaces (such as doorknobs) or objects (such as eating utensils) contaminated with norovirus
- Having direct contact with a person who is infected and showing symptoms

Norovirus is very contagious and often spreads rapidly on cruise ships. Like the common cold, norovirus has many different strains, which makes it difficult for a person's body to develop long-lasting immunity. Therefore, norovirus illness can recur throughout a person's lifetime. In addition, some people due to genetic factors are more likely to become infected and develop a more severe illness than others.

Symptoms of norovirus illness usually begin about 24 to 48 hours after exposure to the virus, but they can appear as early as 12 hours after becoming infected. People infected with norovirus are contagious from the moment they begin feeling ill until at least three days after recovery. Some people may be contagious for as long as two weeks. Therefore, it is particularly important for people to use good hand-washing practices after they have recently recovered from the virus.

Since norovirus is not bacterial, antibiotics are ineffective in treating the illness. Unfortunately, like the common cold, there is no antiviral medication that works against the virus, and there is no vaccine to prevent infection. Anyone vomiting or having diarrhea, should try to drink plenty of fluids to prevent dehydration, which is the most serious health effect that can result from the norovirus infection.

Chances of coming in contact with the norovirus on a cruise ship are decreased by following these preventive steps:

- Frequently wash hands, especially after using the toilet, changing diapers, and before eating or preparing food.

- Immediately remove and wash clothing or linens (with hot water and soap) that may be contaminated with virus after an illness episode.

- Flush or discard any vomitus and/or stool in the toilet and make sure that the surrounding area is kept clean.

Anyone deciding to take a cruise, despite the risk, should buy third-party travel insurance that covers medical evacuation rather than buying travel insurance offered by the cruise lines. Travel insurance plans from cruise lines are meant to protect the ship from liability and have limited protection for the travelers. The major difference between third-party insurance policies and cruise-line insurance policies is that third-party insurance providers can't hide behind the ticket contract after a major disaster.

Medical Malpractice on Cruise Ships

Even though international maritime law does not require cruise ships to provide medical services to passengers, most ships have an infirmary onboard that offers basic medical services 24 hours a day, 7 days a week. The doctor on a cruise ship is a revenue generator for the cruise line. A visit seeking an aspirin or a Tylenol is going to cost a lot, and if passengers get sick onboard, their medical insurance probably will not cover what the cruise ship is going to charge. This is true especially if anyone needs to leave the ship for treatment or hospitalization.

Before buying a cruise ticket, it is important to realize that most cruise ships do not have full trauma units or an intensive care unit. If anyone has a heart attack or other serious illness, the on-board doctor can only stabilize that person until the nearest port is reached, or transportation can be made to a medical facility. It is wise to purchase special medical evacuation and repatriation insurance, in addition to traditional travel insurance. Also, make sure the policy chosen allows for evacuation to the medical facility of choice – not just the hospital at the closest port of call. No one wants to have open heart surgery in a Third World country.

The vast majority of doctors on cruise ships do not have the credentials to work in any

U.S. hospital. No legislation has ever been passed to establish minimum standards for medical care on cruise ships. The primary reason is because the International Council of Cruise Lines is far more powerful than the American Medical Association. Under maritime law, cruise lines are not responsible for the actions of the doctors they hire, because the doctors are independent contractors. As long as cruise lines are not liable for bad medical care, there is no financial incentive for the ships to hire more qualified and experienced doctors and nurses.

In Barbetta v. S/S Bermuda Star, 848 F.2d 1364 (5th Cir. 1998), the Fifth Circuit held that "when a carrier undertakes to employ a doctor aboard ship for its passengers' convenience, the carrier has a duty to employ a doctor who is competent and duly qualified. If the carrier breaches its duty, it is responsible for its own negligence. If the doctor is negligent in treating a passenger, however, that negligence will not be imputed to the carrier." *Barbetta*, 848 F.2d at 1369. Cruise lines should be forced to employ doctors who are licensed in the U.S. regardless of what flag the ship flies, because passengers have no alternative for medical care when the vessel is at sea and a passenger gets sick or injured. Even when the ship is at or near port, the port is often in a developing world country with developing medical care.

The following story about Elizabeth Carlisle describes how one appellate court tried to hold Carnival Cruises vicariously liable for the poor performance of one ship's doctors in 2003. Although the appellate court won, the verdict was eventually overturned by the Florida Supreme Court a few years later. Elizabeth's parents appealed to the U.S. Supreme Court, which refused to hear the case, so the Florida Supreme Court's decision was binding.

Elizabeth Carlisle's Story

In 2003, 14-year-old Elizabeth Carlisle and her family was on a Caribbean cruise on Carnival's *Destiny*. On the second night out of Miami, Elizabeth developed severe abdominal pain. Her mother took her to the ship's physician, Dr. Mauro Neri, who had finished medical school in Italy in 1981. He held nine medical jobs in Italy, Africa, and England in the 15 years before joining Carnival Cruise Lines, and he was earning $1,057 a month from the cruise line.

When Elizabeth saw Neri and complained of abdominal pain, Dr. Neri advised Elizabeth's mother that Elizabeth was suffering from the flu and sent them back to their cabin. However, he was wrong and Elizabeth's pain soon became much worse. Elizabeth visited the doctor a second time and was told the same thing. On the third visit to the infirmary, after Elizabeth's parents specifically asked whether the problem could be appendicitis, Neri told Elizabeth's parents that he was sure the problem was not the girl's appendix. Elizabeth's parents did not believe that this was a correct diagnosis and they called their family physician in Michigan, who advised them to return home.

The family took the advice and shortly after arriving home, Elizabeth underwent emergency surgery to remove her ruptured appendix. The infection had rendered the 14-year-old sterile and caused lifelong medical problems. Elizabeth's parents sued Carnival Cruise Line in Florida state court, a case lost on Carnival's lawyers motion for summary judgment. The cruise line lawyers claimed it was not responsible for the medical negligence of the doctor onboard and pointed to the fine print in the passenger cruise contract to support its position.

The family appealed the circuit court's decision to Florida's Third District Court of Appeal, where the parents argued the cruise line should be held vicariously liable for the doctor's negligence. Judge Joseph Nesbitt agreed and reversed the lower court's decision. The judge believed the cruise line had control over the doctor's medical services for agency law purposes, and the doctor was hired to provide medical services to passengers and crew in accordance with the cruise line's guidelines. The judge also believed it was foreseeable that some passengers at sea would develop medical problems (and that the only realistic alternative for such passengers was treatment by the ship's doctor), the cruise line had an element of control over the doctor-patient relationship, and the cruise line's duty to exercise reasonable care under the circumstances extended to the actions of a ship's doctor hired by the cruise line.

Nesbitt held that the doctor was an agent of the cruise line whose negligence was imputed to the cruise line. Therefore, this invalidated the cruise ticket's purported limitation of the cruise-line's liability for the negligence of its agents. Nesbitt's decision was groundbreaking, because it was the first case where a cruise line was held vicariously responsible for the care provided to a passenger by the ship's physician. Unfortunately, Carnival lawyers appealed the case to the Florida Supreme Court, which ruled in favor of Carnival. The case was then appealed by Elizabeth's parents to the U.S. Supreme Court and the court refused to hear it. The Florida Supreme Court's decision was the final verdict.

The Florida Supreme Court made a significant ruling regarding the liability of cruise-line companies for the medical malpractice committed by cruise-ship doctors. The court ruled that cruise lines are *not* legally responsible for the negligent acts committed by ship doctors who harm cruise-line passengers during treatment. The doctors who committed malpractice could be sued and the cruise line could be sued for its direct negligence in hiring an incompetent physician. However, the Florida Supreme Court's ruling meant a cruise line could not be held vicariously liable (that is, indirectly and without any culpability on its part) for the harm caused by its onboard physicians. Because of this Florida Supreme Court decision, all cruise-ship doctors are now considered to be independent contractors and, therefore, the cruise line is not responsible for the medical negligence of the doctor or the nursing staff who treats its passengers.

If the Carlisles family wanted to pursue the case further, they would have had to sue the physician directly. That would have been very difficult in their case (and in most cases involving medical malpractice on cruise ships) since that they would have to locate Neri in his present home. Malpractice cases involving treatment in international waters must be filed in the court of the physician's country of origin, which is both difficult and expensive. The biggest problem with suing cruise-ship doctors directly, however, is the very difficult burden of acquiring jurisdiction in U.S. courts, since most cruise-ship doctors are foreign residents. In addition, even if jurisdiction can be obtained, most cruise-ship doctors do not carry malpractice insurance and they usually do not have assets that can legally be seized in the U.S.

The Florida Supreme Court decision applies only to cruise-ship passengers, since pursuant to U.S. labor law, the same doctor who is considered to be an independent contractor when treating passengers is considered to be an employee when treating crew members. Cruise lines are vicariously liable for medical malpractice committed on crew members. A cruise line has a duty to the crew members and seafarers it employs to provide prompt, adequate, and appropriate medical care. The cruise line is also liable for injuries resulting from medical negligence that occurs off the ship if the cruise line refers the crew member to a land-based doctor or medical facility for treatment. The following story describes a medical malpractice law suit in which a crew member was awarded one million dollars.

Celebrity Cruises Held Vicariously Liable for Bad Medical Treatment of Chef

In November 2011, a jury in Miami returned a $1,000,000 verdict against a Miami-based cruise line whose ship employee underwent an unnecessary surgery to insert a pacemaker that he did not need. The case involved a Celebrity Cruises' chef, Shalesh Buttoo, who experienced headaches and pain to his face while working on the cruise ship. Although only 31 years old and apparently in good health, a doctor in Santo Domingo inserted a pacemaker into Buttoo's chest. The issues at trial focused on whether Buttoo needed this surgery and, assuming he did, whether or not the surgery was performed correctly.

In 2009, the cruise line had flown Buttoo from Europe, where the Celebrity cruises' ship was based, to Santo Domingo, which is in the Dominican Republic. Buttoo testified at trial that the pacemaker caused him debilitating injuries and forced him to use a walker. The pacemaker not only was medically unnecessary but was improperly placed and caused inflammation. Buttoo eventually traveled to Miami for follow-up medical care where cardiac surgeons removed the pacemaker. The jury found the cruise line negligent in its care and treatment of its crew member. Buttoo's trial lawyer argued that Celebrity Cruises sent the ship employee to Santo Domingo to save money because the doctors in the Dominican Republic are much cheaper than in Miami where Celebrity Cruises is based. The jury believed that the lawyer was telling the truth.

The next story is about a passenger who received bad medical treatment on Holland America cruise ship and died and all his wife got was a bill for the abysmal medical services. CBC News in Canada published a story in early December 2011 about cruise passenger Bernie Hamilton, age 66, who died following a Holland America Line cruise. His death was attributed to many errors by the ship's medical personnel. Heather and Bernie Hamilton booked a holiday ocean tour to celebrate their retirement and 38 years of marriage. It was supposed to be a risk-free adventure; but, when Bernie collapsed on the cabin floor, their dream holiday became a medical nightmare. In Bernie's case, the ship's doctor thought that Bernie had either a common cold or asthma. The doctor prescribed Ventolin, which accelerates a patient's heart rate.

After Bernie collapsed on the floor of his cabin, Heather watched in horror as the medical personnel tried to decipher the instructions for the automatic defibrillator. It was clear to Heather that the medical personnel were not familiar with the equipment and were struggling. After the medical team on the ship inserted an intravenous line and intubation tube and finally "stabilized" Bernie, the ship put Bernie ashore in Spain. The shore-side doctors declared him brain dead. Heather Hamilton received no apologies from Holland America. All that she received from Holland America was a bill for $2,000.

Wrongful Death on the High Seas

Wrongful death cases, where a death occurs on the water, involve multiple and overlapping laws, jurisdictions, and possible remedies. This area of law is further complicated because rights and remedies vary, depending on the location of the death. The cruise-ship industry is usually protected by an unjust and archaic U.S. law that was enacted in 1920 called the Death on High Seas Act (DOHSA). This Act was meant to provide a legal remedy for the families of passengers who had fatal accidents at sea. DOHSA is a federal statute which is found at 46 U.S.C. §§ 30301-30308.

When DOHSA was originally passed, Congress never envisioned it would bar all recovery for any of the millions of retired passengers and children who cruise annually. The Cruise Line International Association (CLIA) doesn't inform its 14 million customers that it lobbies every year to make certain DOHSA remains in place. A cruise line is the only business in the world where a child or retired passenger's life has no monetary value in the eyes of the law.

With help from a powerful lobby, Congress, and the U.S. Supreme Court, DOHSA has become an impenetrable shield that protects wealthy cruise-ship companies from those who are grieving the death of a family member for which a cruise line is responsible. DOHSA does provide for compensation to survivors of someone who has suffered death "caused by wrongful act, neglect, or default occurring on the high seas beyond a marine league (three nautical miles) from the shore of any state, or the territories or dependencies of the United States."

Damages that are compensable, according to DOHSA, are limited to the pecuniary loss of the person for whose benefit the suit is brought (46 U.S.C. § 30303). This includes loss of financial support, loss of nurturing and guidance, medical expenses, and burial costs. DOHSA does not allow nonpecuniary or punitive damages to families of someone who has died at sea. When an unemployed, retired, elderly, or minor passenger fatally dies at sea, cruise-ship companies have to pay only for funeral expenses–if the body is found. If the body is not found, and there are no burial expenses, the family receives nothing.

For wrongful deaths that occur on land, most states have wrongful death statutes to compensate surviving family members for both the economic and emotional loss of a loved one. Florida's Wrongful Death Act §768.21, as with most states, recognizes that humans are more than just economic assets and provides noneconomic compensatory damage elements that DOHSA does not include, provides no recovery for loss of society, loss of love and affection, loss of companionship, loss of consortium, or mental anguish sustained by grieving families who have lost a loved one on a cruise ship or other type of boat in international waters. This essentially means there is no legal liability for the loss of a human life, other than the deceased passenger's lost wages and burial expenses. All cruise lines are insulated from liability, as long as no one dies within the three-mile limit, which is considered to be territorial waters rather than the high seas. Within the three-mile limit, recovery is possible for predeath pain and suffering, loss of love and affection, and loss of society.

Wrongful death on the high seas can result from collisions between pleasure yachts, speeding boats, reckless jet ski operators, defective cranes, defective forklifts, or substandard or delayed medical care on a cruise ship. Understanding the differences between a wrongful death and a survival action requires identifying on whose behalf the suit is being brought and for what type of damages. A wrongful death action recognizes the right of a victim's dependents to recover for their losses, resulting from a loved one's death. This claim typically allows for the recovery of loss of support, the value of services which would have been rendered by the deceased if that person had not died, and the value of parental guidance. A survival action recognizes the right of the personal representative of a victim's estate to recover damages for the decedent's personal injuries prior to death. This includes: the decedent's pain and suffering before death, medical expenses, future lost wages or loss of accumulated earnings, and funeral expenses.

DOHSA usually does not allow recovery under survival causes of action. No matter how serious was the negligence that caused the death, punitive damages are never recoverable if DOHSA applies. Cruise lines love DOHSA because, unlike companies ashore, cruise lines face virtually no financial exposure when their guests are killed or disappear. Cruise lines and their insurance companies profit greatly from this ancient law, and it is unlikely that DOHSA will be repealed in the near future because of the political climate in this country.

The International Cruise Victims organization (ICV) has been trying to amend DOHSA to permit the recovery of fair compensation when passengers die during cruises. A cruise safety bill reviewed by Congress originally contained a provision to amend DOHSA so there is no difference if an American citizen dies ashore or at sea. The cruise industry spent millions of dollars lobbying Congress to eliminate the amendment and they got what it wanted. According to Jamie Barnet, president of ICV and whose daughter was killed on a cruise ship, some politicians would never do anything that displeases the wealthy cruise-ship companies. Historically, DOHSA was applied to aviation disasters when airplanes crashed in international waters. The families of dead children or elderly, retired parents were excluded from any recovery by virtue of DOHSA. Following the crash in the Atlantic ocean of a jet full of U.S. citizens, TWA flight 800, the American public became outraged by this injustice. In response, Congress excluded air travel from DOHSA.

After the Deepwater Horizon floating-oil platform exploded more than 200 miles offshore of the United States, killing 11 workers on April 20, 2010, members of the U.S. House of Representatives voted to amend DOHSA and passed H.R. 5503. It retroactively expanded DOHSA damages. In July 2010, U.S. senators debated amending DOHSA to permit the families of the oil workers killed in the BP Deepwater Horizon explosion to recover compensation for their emotional suffering. The bill was killed in the Senate at the end of July 2010, after the Cruise Line International Association (CLIA) paid millions of dollars to the lobbying firm Alcalde & Fay to ensure DOHSA stays in place. Morover, CLIA did not want to be exposed to lawsuits that could be unpredictable and expensive, and that would likely happen if DOHSA were repealed. CLIA was joined in its campaign by the U.S. Chamber of Commerce, which is always opposed to any law that might make it easier for an individual to sue a big corporation.

Below are several stories of wrongful deaths that have occurred on cruise ships and other types of boats.

Two Wrongful Deaths on a *Ride the Ducks* Tour Boat

A wrongful death lawsuit filed in the aftermath of a boat accident questions the safety of amphibious tour vessels. On July 7, 2010 a 250-foot sludge barge pushed by a tugboat overran a disabled 33-foot *Ride the Ducks* tour boat, plunging the amphibious vessel with its 35 passengers and 2 crew members under the surface of the Delaware River in Philadelphia, Pennsylvania. Two student tourists from Hungary, Dora Schwendtner, 16, and Szabolcs Prem, 20, drowned. Several other passengers suffered minor injuries, according to a National Transportation Safety Board initial report released September 10, 2010. In a statement released to the media, Herschend pointed to the tugboat's failure to heed repeated radio calls alerting it to the disabled vessel in its path.

Since starting operations in 2003, *Ride the Ducks* has safely transported more than 1 million passengers on more than 42,000 tours in the Pennsylvania city. *Ride the Ducks* is a subsidiary of Herschend Family Entertainment of Norcross, Georgia. The original duck boat, with a standard

Army six-wheel truck frame and a propeller, was designed to ferry troops and materiel from warships to land during World War II. General Motors Corp. built 21,000 of the vessels, officially called DUKWs, between 1942 and 1945. Most were scrapped after the war, but entrepreneurs converted a few dozen for tourist excursions across land and water.

Herschend's boats were designed to look like the WWII workhorses. Today, 128 duck-style boats have certificates to remain in service with several companies, according to the U.S. Coast Guard. Only one other fatal accident involving a DUKW has been documented. In 1999, the *Miss Majestic*, owned by a now-defunct company, sank in Lake Hamilton near Hot Springs, Arkansas and 13 passengers drowned.

The National Transportation Safety Board (NTSB), an independent federal agency charged by Congress with determining the probable cause of an accident and issuing safety recommendations aimed at preventing future accidents, investigated the accident and recommended several changes to the design and operation standards, but the Coast Guard did not concur. Citing "an unacceptable level of risk to passenger safety," the NTSB recommended in May 2002 that duck operators and refurbishers "provide reserve buoyancy through passive means, such as installing watertight compartments or buoyant foam in the hull." Most modern boats include these features. The NTSB also found that several of the *Miss Majestic* victims were trapped under the vessel's canopy as it rapidly sank and recommended that duck canopies be removed or modified to come off easily in an emergency. In a September 2002 response, the Coast Guard said existing regulations and standards, if followed, were sufficient to ensure passenger safety.

"When you follow the navigation rules, everything usually goes fine. The Coast Guard doesn't certificate inherently unsafe vessels" stated Capt. Eric Christensen, chief of the Office of Vessel Activity at Coast Guard headquarters in Washington. The attorney representing the Philadelphia victims' families, stated, "If they had canopies that were retractable and foldable, like we've had on convertible cars for about 100 years, they wouldn't have the problem of trapping passengers underwater. Coast Guard regulations do not require duck passengers to wear personal flotation devices, which puts them in danger of drowning, but the devices could pin their wearers against the vessel's canopy, which is what happened to several victims in the Arkansas accident, according to the NTSB.

Jury Awards $35M in WaveRunner® Collision that Killed a Teenaged Girl

On June 11, 2011, Daniel Perez heard a court clerk begin reading a jury verdict, holding Yamaha responsible for a 2005 WaveRunner® accident that killed his 14-year-old daughter, Jaysell. By the time the clerk announced that he and his wife would share roughly $35 million with their late daughter's best friend, who was horribly injured in the crash, it was clear the couple was having a hard time stifling sobs.

The amazing verdict—$19 million for the Cooper City, Florida couple and $16 million for now 21-year-old Samantha Archer—was the culmination of a six-week trial, accusing Yamaha Motor Corp. USA of failing to correct steering problems with the water scooter and then failing to warn people of the hazards posed. DOHSA did not apply in this case, because Yamaha is a land-based corporation with a negligent product. When a consumer is harmed as a result of a defective product, the manufacturer can be held liable, regardless of whether the party acted negligently or not. Because the teenager was using the Wave Runner as it was meant to be used at the time of her injury, her family was able to recover substantial punitive damages. In this case, the state's wrongful death statute applied.

Archer, whose doctors testified will need multiple hip and knee replacements and will be haunted by a host of physical, mental and psychological problems, was also dumbstruck by the verdict. Her mother, Nicolette Archer, said the verdict will give her daughter the required resources to deal with the gruesome injuries she sustained when the WaveRunner® she and Jaysell borrowed from a friend at an Easter party collided with a boat.

The jurors said Yamaha had years to figure out how to make sure operators could steer WaveRunners® when the throttle was released. They didn't do so until 2003. The young girls were riding a 2001 model. Archer testified that she took her hand off the throttle to turn. Instead of turning, the scooter plowed into the boat.

"They put sales against lives," said juror Josephine Williams.

"They delayed taking action and they knew there was a problem," said another juror, agreeing.

The jurors did not find Yamaha totally responsible for the crash. They found Yamaha's distributor and manufacturer 88 percent responsible. They assigned one percent blame to both Samantha and retired neurosurgeon Dr. Eugene Holly, who let the girls use his WaveRunner®. Nicolette Archer, who took the girls to the party and gave them permission to ride, was held 10 percent responsible.

Royal Caribbean Fails to Rescue Cruise Ship Passenger

In October 2012, several weeks after the disappearance of her daughter from Bahamas-bound cruise ship *Allure of the Seas*, a grief-stricken mother retained legal counsel to gather facts and ask tough questions of *Royal Caribbean International*, the ship's owner. Shortly after the ship left Port Everglades on Sept. 16, 2012, Vera Marion's daughter, Ariel, fell overboard under undetermined circumstances. A U.S. Coast Guard effort to find her was discontinued on Sept. 18. According to an Oct. 3, 2012, report in the Sun Sentinel, when Ariel joined her mother on the cruise, from which she would never return, Ariel was happily anticipating the start of a new modeling job.

Vera Marion believes if the cruise ship personnel had acted promptly on the initial report of Ariel's fall, Ariel could have been rescued. According to reports, Royal Caribbean International owners have, in fact, admitted some fault. After ship officials received an urgent call from a passenger who witnessed the fall, instead of undertaking rescue efforts, ship's security personnel proceeded to take over an hour to review surveillance videos for evidence of what had already been reliably reported. Making matters worse, according to the U.S. Coast Guard, it was not notified of the incident until more than two hours after Ariel was seen tumbling into the ocean. During this time, the *Allure of the Seas* was sailing full-steam ahead, away from the location of Ariel's disappearance. Eventually, the *Allure of the Seas* was stopped and turned around, and the Coast Guard and three nearby ships undertook a search, but it was too late.

Attempting to defend its conduct in this case, *Royal Caribbean* representatives told the Sun Sentinel that it was obliged to be very sure that a passenger was not still onboard before it the Coast Guard was asked to dedicate assets to a search operation. An urgent call from a witness should have been sufficient for the cruise line to turn around immediately to find the passenger who fell. However, cruise ship personnel always waste time searching the ship while the passenger remains in the water. Perhaps the cruise ship owners don't really care if a young person with no income dies because they are not liable financially when this happens. If cruise ship operators find an overboard passenger who has been injured, the cruise line would likely be liable for the injuries and would face a lawsuit. Coast Guard regulations and International Maritime Organization guidelines require immediate action in the event of a report of an overboard passenger. Such requirements include measures such as promptly reducing travel speed, directing the ship back to the reported location of the overboard fall, and making preparations to dispatch life craft.

The duty to undertake adequate rescue operations is not the only responsibility of cruise-ship staff in relation to preventing drowning deaths. Cruise-ship owners have a duty to correct defects in handrails that could cause passengers to topple overboard. Ship officials have a duty to warn passengers of rough sea conditions that increase the risk that they may be swept overboard. Unfortunately, all this is usually ignored.

American passengers are not the only ones being unjustly harmed when there is a wrongful death. Seafarers from other countries, who work on cruise ships, also find recovery difficult or impossible—not by DOHSA, but by their arbitration contracts. Several years ago, U.S.-based cruise-line owners began insisting that injured crew members seeking compensation for their injuries must pursue their claims through arbitration in foreign countries. Carnival, NCL, and Royal Caribbean started moving to dismiss lawsuits filed in Miami, arguing that seriously injured crew members are not entitled to jury trials in the U.S. Rather, arbitration claims must be filed in either home countries or where the cruise ships are flagged. The cruise industry's lawyers understood perfectly well that many of these foreign countries—like the Philippines, Bermuda or Panama—had virtually no laws that provided compensation to their employees, or the existing compensation scheme was a pittance.

In 2003, the NCL Norway blew up at the port of Miami. Eight Filipino crew members were scalded to death. In addition, many other crew members were seriously burned in the explosion. NCL responded to lawsuits, filed by the dead men's surviving wives and children, by moving to dismiss the cases. Lawyers for NCL argued that the grieving family members could not file suit in Miami, where the explosion took place. Instead, the only claims permitted were through a non-jury arbitration process in Manila.

The arbitration process is extremely unfair. NCL paid very small amounts to the families for these wrongful deaths. Since then, lawyers for most of the cruise lines have drafted onerous terms and conditions for the crew members' employment contracts. Included are prohibiting lawsuits to be filed in the U.S. and limiting recovery to the smallest imaginable amounts for serious injuries, even in cases where the cruise-line personnel is grossly negligent.

Cruise Ship Crime

Most people don't realize that when they go on a cruise and sail out of U.S. territorial waters, countries like Panama, Bermuda, Liberia, or the Bahamas are overseeing the cruise ship's operation. When the shore slowly fades into the horizon, so do most legal rights for U.S. citizens. All cruise-line personnel are supposed to report crimes committed against a U.S. citizen to the Federal Bureau of Investigation (FBI), even if the crime was committed in international waters. However, cruise-lines owners don't like to report crimes because they want to avoid bad publicity. They also know they have the legal right to divert responsibility for investigating a crime to the flagged-country's authorities. Cruise-line owners often exercise this right because it is usually in their best interest to do so. Panama, Bermuda, Liberia, and the Bahamas are usually very lax about investigating crimes committed on cruise ships.

In 2010, the Cruise Vessel Security and Safety Act was passed. This Act provides minimal regulation of crimes committed on cruise ships. The cruise-line owners and their lobbying group, the Cruise Line International Association (CLIA), were allowed to provide significant input into the process of creating this legislation. These groups have a lot of money to contribute to legislators, which gives them a lot of power. The Act does not define or even come close to a baseline or minimum effort with which the cruise-line owners must comply. In other words, just because a cruise-line owner complies with the Act does not mean that it has acted reasonably to prevent cruise-ship sexual assaults or any other crimes.

The Cruise Vessel Security and Safety Act of 2010 was first proposed by a group of people who had suffered from the negligence of the cruise-lines' personnel in failing to prevent crimes onboard their ships. Ultimately, the bill was a series of compromises by members of Congress based on pressure from the cruise-lines' lawyers and CLIA. The Act has requirements for vessel design, equipment, construction, retrofitting and it requires the rails on the vessel be located not less than 42 inches above the cabin deck. The Act also requires that all cabins be equipped with entry doors that include peepholes or other means of visual identification. Any vessels, the construction of which was started after commencement of the act, are required to have security latches and time sensitive key technology on all cabins.

The Act also requires to the extent that technology is available that vessels use technology to capture images of passengers who have fallen overboard. However, most cruise-line owners are unwilling to pay for man overboard (MOB) systems that accurately detect an individual falling overboard because these MOB systems are very expensive. The Act requires vessels to have available for each passenger a guide describing medical and security personnel designated onboard to prevent and respond to criminal and medical situations. The guide must also describe which admiralty jurisdiction is applicable.

The Act requires that vessels maintain supplies of anti-retroviral medications designed to prevent STDs and maintain equipment and materials for performing medical examinations in sexual-assault cases (rape kits). It also requires the ship to evaluate the patient for trauma, provide medical care, preserve relevant medical evidence, and make available on the vessel at all times medical staff who have specific credentials. The cruise-line owner is supposed to verify that the medical personnel possess a current physician's or registered nurse's license. They also must have at least three years of post-graduate or post-registration clinical practice in general and emergency medicine or hold board certification in emergency medicine, family practice, or internal medicine. These standards have been in place through the Cruise Ship Committee of the American College of Emergency Room Physicians for a number of years.

Under the sexual-assault provision, the Cruise Vessel Security and Safety Act requires that every patient be given free and immediate access to contact information for law enforcement, the FBI, the United States Coast Guard, and other authorities. Means of access include private telephone line and Internet connectivity access through a computer terminal. The Act provides that crew members access to passenger cabins be limited; or, the owner of a vessel shall establish and implement procedures restricting which crew members' have access to cabins. The Act does not, however, clarify what those procedures and restrictions should be. The Act requires the vessel owner to maintain a logbook and have reporting requirements for all complaints of crimes committed on any voyage that embarks or disembarks passengers in the U.S. The logbook has to be made available upon request to any agent of the FBI, any member of the United States Coast Guard, and any law enforcement officer performing official duties in the course and scope of an investigation.

The Act requires that the Department of Transportation:

> maintain a statistical compilation of all incidents described in paragraph (3)(A)(i) on an internet site that provides a numerical accounting of the missing persons and alleged crimes recorded in each report filed under paragraph (3)(A)(i) that are no longer under investigation by the FBI. The data shall be updated no less frequently than quarterly, aggregated by cruise line. Each cruise line shall be identified by name, and each crime shall be identified as to whether it was committed by a passenger or a crew member.

This excludes reporting of crimes which are not homicide, suspicious death, a missing U.S. national, kidnapping, assault with serious bodily injury, firing or tampering with the vessel, or theft of money or property in excess of $10,000.

Before members of Congress enacted the Cruise Vessel Security and Safety Act of 2010, the cruise industry was unregulated and cruise-line owners did not have policies in place to protect rape victims. The Act mandated that serious crimes and missing persons be reported to the FBI if a U.S. citizen is involved. Those statistics would then, for the first time, be made public on a website that would allow consumers to see which cruise lines had which types of crimes.

Unfortunately, the Cruise Vessel Security and Safety Act of 2010 has *not* made it safe for women and children to take cruises, nor have the crime statistics been made public on the Internet. The problem centers on language that FBI lawyers quietly inserted, stating that crimes would be reported "that are no longer under investigation by the Federal Bureau of Investigation." International Cruise Victims (ICV), a victims' advocacy organization, began to notice a precipitous drop in the number of cruise crimes being reported under the new system. In the third quarter of 2011, zero crimes were reported, even though the FBI admitted that alleged crimes had occurred.

In a 2011 letter to the FBI, ICV President Jaime Barnett, whose daughter died on a Carnival Cruise ship, complained about the criminal reporting statistics listed on the Coast Guard website. "We believe and firmly assert that the FBI reports, which are published by the U.S. Coast Guard, are not in compliance with the reporting requirements as outlined in the Cruise Vessel Security and Safety Act of 2010, which clearly indicates that all alleged crimes that are not under investigation by the FBI, be reflected," she wrote. At the time she wrote this, Barnett had no idea those in the FBI were behind the change. Not once did the FBI director or the representatives sent to four meetings with the ICV, beginning in April 2011, admit they were responsible for changing the crime-reporting provision. That acknowledgement came on May 30, 2011, when the ICV learned from Sen. John Kerry's office that the FBI director had requested additional language be added to the criminal-reporting requirement when the bill was updated by the Commerce Committee.

Kendall Carver, who founded the ICV after his daughter disappeared from a Royal Caribbean Celebrity Cruise in 2004, says after he was made aware of the change in language, he asked lawyers to look at it. The lawyers concluded the language change was nothing to worry about, but they did not realize how the FBI officials would interpret this particular sentence. The language was also approved by the bill's sponsors, Sen. Kerry and Rep. Doris Matsui from California. But, they did not realize the FBI lawyers would interpret the "no longer under investigation" part of the language to mean that a case would be reported *when the FBI had opened and closed a case.*

Since FBI cases are only opened for approximately 10-20 percent of the crimes that are reported on cruise ships, this method leads to a misleadingly low-crime rate. In addition, even for the crimes for which cases are opened, it can often take a long time for them to be declared closed, because they remain open while appeals are processed. Therefore, the crimes would not show up in the statistics until years after they'd actually happened! Reporting crime in this manner destroys the bill's original intent to give American consumers timely crime statistics so they can decide what cruise provider is the safest, or whether cruising is too risky for them and their families. The insertion of a seemingly innocuous sentence by the FBI lawyers turned out to be the root of the entire crime reporting problem!

In an interview about the reporting provision, Supervisory Special Agent Kurt Schmidt of the FBI's Violent Crimes Unit explained how crimes committed today would not be reported in the near future. "We have to take into consideration not only the verdict and sentencing of the individual, but also potential appeals, so the case may remain open until all appeals are exhausted," Schmidt said. The cruise-line owners want potential passengers to believe that sexual crimes rarely occur on their vessels, despite the fact that this is not true. The truth is not good for the cruise lines' profit margin, so they try their best to keep sexual crimes a secret.

The FBI's decision is somewhat suspicious because the way the Bureau reports crimes that take place on cruise ships is completely different from how it reports crimes within the United States. Each year under the Uniform Crime Reporting system, the FBI director releases nationwide crime statistics based on the number of criminal complaints and reports received from local and state law enforcement officers. The system essentially gives the benefit of the doubt to reported crimes since surveys underreported crimes, says Professor Michael Walker, a former police chief and adjunct faculty member in the Department of Law and Police Science at John Jay College of Criminal Justice in New York City. Walker believes reporting only crimes that have been closed and/or prosecuted is a complete misrepresentation of how many crimes were reported, which is exactly what owners in the cruise industry want.

Why did FBI lawyers go out of their way to sneakily put an entirely new and faulty crime-reporting system in place specifically for cruise ships? Advocates of stronger regulations and reporting requirements, such as the ICV, allege an improper relationship between those in the FBI and the cruise line industry. Royal Caribbean, the industry's second largest cruise line, was particularly mentioned. When former executive assistant director for the National Security Branch Gary Bald retired from the FBI in 2006, Royal Caribbean created a new position for him as vice president of global security. A year later, Eleni P. Kalisch, assistant director of congressional affairs for the FBI, became Royal Caribbean's vice president for federal government relations. Carver, the ICV founder, noted every two months, the cruise industry's trade association, CLIA, hosts a closed-dinner meeting with representatives from the FBI and the Coast Guard to discuss security issues. All these ICV requests were completely ignored.

Despite the Cruise Vessel Security and Safety Act of 2010, the public will probably never see reports of all alleged crimes on cruise ships. On a website updated quarterly by the Coast Guard, only cases *closed* by the FBI are made public. According to critics, those in the cruise industry have too much influence over law enforcement, primarily because they have enough money and power to significantly influence legislative decisions.

When a crime occurs on a cruise ship, cruise-line lawyers first try to settle the case and a confidentiality agreement is required. This means the victim agrees to drop a lawsuit in exchange for a specific sum of money. If that does not work, the cruise line personnel usually delay reporting the crime to the FBI, because if the cabin is cleaned, the crime scene evidence disappears before it can be investigated. Sometimes, cruise line personnel try to bribe the victim to keep quiet with champagne or a cabin upgrade.

Unlike airplanes with Federal Marshals, cruise ships have no police authorities aboard. The security guards on the ships are loyal to their employers who pay their salaries, not to the passengers. When a crime occurs, the cruise-line owner immediately notifies its risk managements department and defense lawyers. If the closed circuit television (CCTV) tapes exculpate the cruise-line owner, the cruise-line owner keeps the tapes. Otherwise, the CCTV images are invariably taped over, "lost," or the cruise line will claim the CCTV system was not working.

In 1999, the Royal Caribbean and celebrity owner hired two top notch firms to study the problem of sexual assaults on the Royal Caribbean and Celebrity fleet of cruise ships. A consulting firm called Sheridan Swailes was retained to study the ship' security systems. The Royal Caribbean and Celebrity owner also retained a nationally recognized expert on sexual harassment issues, Dr. Kay Krohne, who previously was a commanding officer at the Naval Training Station in San Diego. After conducting an extensive analysis of the Royal Caribbean/Celebrity fleet, these experts concluded sexual misconduct occurred "frequently" during cruises. The experts attributed this problem to the fact that most crew members were not afraid of being arrested, much less convicted. Most crew members know that nothing will happen to them if they commit a sexual crime on a cruise ship. Krohne reported the worst thing that could happen to a crew member who committed a crime on a Royal Caribbean or Celebrity cruise ship was to be sent on a one-way flight home, a flight usually paid for by the cruise-ship owner.

Krohne also concluded that most crimes occur in a passenger's cabin. She recommended many improvements, such as placing CCTV cameras in the passenger hallways, deactivating passenger cabin key cards after working hours used by crew members, and implementing steps to collect and preserve evidence to be used against the crew members at trial. Without having a system in place that will result in crew members being arrested, Krohne concluded that the crimes would continue. Unfortunately, when the executives at Royal Caribbean and Celebrity received the reports, they did not implement any of the recommended improvements.

In an article entitled "Crime Rocks the Boats," TIME Magazine (March 2006) reported on cases involving Janet Kelly, who was drugged and raped during a cruise from Los Angeles to Mexico, and Jennifer Hagel, whose husband, George Smith IV, "disappeared" from a Royal Caribbean cruise ship during their honeymoon. In both cases, the cruise-lines' executives called their defense lawyers to the cruise ships and quickly began compromising the passengers' potential criminal and civil cases. The article described how the cruise-line executives purposely failed to preserve evidence.

In the case of Janet Kelly, a cruise line flew her attacker from the cruise ship in Los Angeles back to Jamaica after he drugged and raped her. He then applied for a job with Princess Cruises, which accepted him into its fleet of cruise ships. No one was aware of his criminal past. The current system of flying rapist crew members back to their home countries with no criminal accountability, only to be rehired by another cruise line, is exactly the problem that Krohne warned about.

Senate Commerce Committee Tries To Make Cruising Safer

On July 24, 2013, the U.S. Senate Committee on Commerce, Science, and Transportation held a hearing titled, "Cruise Industry Oversight: Recent Incidents Show Need for Stronger Focus on Consumer Protection." At the hearing, Chairman Jay Rockefeller reviewed the current state of consumer protection in the cruise industry. Focus was on many safety and security incidents that endangered thousands of Americans and "The Cruise Passenger Protection Act of 2013," was introduced to make cruising safer for U.S. passengers. This legislation compels cruise-ship owners to provide better consumer protection for passengers and significantly broadens the federal government's role in cruise industry oversight. Senator Richard Blumenthal from Connecticut co-sponsored this legislation to close gaps in crime reporting, because the cruise industry is far more concerned with profit than passenger safety. Owners in the cruise industry have no valid excuse for accidents resulting from overlooked mechanical problems; lack of sufficient security onboard vessels; overworked, exhausted crew members; and a failure of cruise-line owners to maintain a sanitary environment.

Rockefeller's legislation builds on the senator's ongoing oversight of the cruise industry. The Cruise Passenger Protection Act of 2013:

- Gives consumers a clear summary of the restrictive terms and conditions in cruise contracts pertaining to personal injuries. Consumers can read a plain language summary of the key rights and limitations they have before they buy tickets.

- Makes the Department of Transportation (DOT) the lead federal agency for cruise-ship consumer protection, similar to the role it has in aviation-consumer protection. Passengers also have additional protections in the event of a problem because the DOT has the authority to investigate consumer complaints. The DOT also sets standards for summarizing key terms of cruise-lines' contracts of carriage, including, style, formatting, and terminology.

- Helps passengers who encounter problems on cruise ships by having the DOT establish a toll-free hotline for consumer complaints.

- Makes all crimes alleged on cruise ships publicly available information and require ships to have video cameras in public areas where there is no expectation of privacy.

- Mandates that people will be able to access all video surveillance records for civil action purposes.

- Directs the Coast Guard to make widely known final standards within one year detailing requirements for the retention of video surveillance records.

- Ensures that if an alleged crime occurs while the vessel is still in a U.S. port, the FBI will be notified before that vessel leaves the port.

- Requires vessel owners to report an alleged offense to the U.S. Consulate in the next port of call, if the alleged offense is by or against a U.S. national.

- Transfers authority for maintaining the Internet website of alleged crimes on cruise ships from the Coast Guard to the DOT. Requires that the website break out the crimes that are reported against minors and alleged "man overboard" incidents.

- Forces cruise lines to include the consumer complaint number on their websites, on electronic confirmation and on promotional literature and advertising "through any medium," as determined by DOT.

- Authorizes DOT and other federal agencies to investigate consumer complaints regarding cancellations, delays and port-skipping; lost, damaged and delayed baggage; onboard conditions; problems with fares, refunds or fare adjustments, and deceptive advertising.

- Authorizes DOT to impose civil penalties of up to $25,000 per violation or up to $50,000 for continuing violations, and to refer criminal matters to the Justice Department for prosecution, with criminal penalties of up to $250,000 or up to one year in prison.

- Creates a DOT consumer advisory committee with representatives of cruise lines, cruise-industry associations, state and local governments, and nonprofit groups dedicated to consumer protection and victim assistance.

- Imposes additional requirements for crime reporting and crime-scene preservation training.

- Creates a federal Director of Victim Support Services.

Kendall Carver, the president of International Cruise Victims, sent a Freedom of Information Act request to the FBI and found out more than 400 crimes were alleged on cruise ships in 2012. The FBI posted only 15 crimes on the Coast Guard Internet site. The new legislation will not allow the cruise industry to continue to cover up sexual crimes. Below are stories from many different victims of crimes on cruise ships. Not surprisingly, the cruise industry and its lobbying groups will use all means to try to influence this legislation to protect its image and profits.

Laurie Dishman's Story

When Laurie Dishman was brutally raped by a crew member on a Royal Caribbean cruise, she had no idea that sexual assaults were a common occurrence onboard cruise ships. To make matters worse, FBI lawyers declined to prosecute her assailant because they determined it was a "she said, he said" case, despite physical evidence of ligature marks around her neck and an impacted tampon. Dishman and her friend, Michelle, were in the lounge of a cruise ship on February 21, 2006, and they were approached by a crew member whose badge indicated that he was a "security guard." He demanded to see their IDs and asked whether they were old enough to be drinking in the bar. He also asked for their cabin number.

As the night continued, Michelle and Laurie talked and danced with other passengers. When Laurie decided to go up and request a song, that same crew member approached her, held her wrist and forcibly kissed her, while trying to whisper something in her ear. She said, "no, get away" and went back to her cabin. Later, there was a knock at the door. Thinking it was Michelle, Laurie opened the door halfway, but it was the security guard. He forced his way into her cabin and pushed her onto the bed. She tried to resist, but he raped her and left ligature marks around her neck.

When Laurie woke up, she did not know who to call, because her rapist was supposedly "security." Laurie told Michelle what had happened, and they decided to call the Purser's desk, which prompted two officers to come to their cabin. An officer told Michelle and Laurie to collect the sheets and clothing from the incident and to place the items in plastic bags, which the officers had provided.

Laurie was never told to see the ship's doctor for a rape kit to later be used as evidence. Instead, she was told to go home.

Laurie and Michelle flew to Los Angeles, where FBI agents interviewed them. The women were informed that FBI officials were was taking this matter very seriously. On March 3, 2006, Laurie received a call from someone in the FBI, who informed her that the Department of Justice was not going to prosecute her case. She was told it was a clear "he said/she said" case. The Department of Justice declined the case for prosecution and the FBI agents closed the "investigation" on the same day the cruise ship returned to port and before anyone began to investigate the crime.

Royal Caribbean Cruise Line officials refused to provide Laurie with the name, address, nationality, or current whereabouts of her rapist. She also was refused access to her medical records and her statement from the ship. Laurie was not told if her rapist had HIV/AIDS or any other sexually-transmitted disease. The only thing Laurie received from the cruise-line officials was a promotional letter from the president stating, "Thank you for sailing with us and giving us the opportunity to send you home with an experience to remember." A discount coupon for another cruise was included with the letter. A good maritime attorney could successfully sue a cruise-line owner in civil court for covering up a crime, if there was proof on a ship surveillance tape.

The following section describes how Disney Cruise line clearly knew about a crime and paid to send the criminal back to his native country as soon as possible. The crew member got away with his crime, but Disney did not succeed in avoiding bad publicity.

Disney Cruise Line Covers Up a Crime and Sends Crew Member Back to India

On May 20, 2013, WKMG-TV (Channel 6 in Orlando, FL) reported that a Disney Cruise Line crew member was captured on a ship surveillance video molesting an 11-year-old girl in an elevator. An investigation revealed the incident was not reported until the next day, long after the ship had left Port Canaveral. The delay enabled the 33-year-old suspect to evade investigation and prosecution by Florida authorities. At first, Disney Cruise Line representatives lied to reporters and stated the crime had been reported while the ship was still in port on Aug. 5, 2012. Then, after being told by a Local 6 newsreporter and Port Canaveral police that this was not true, the cruise-line officials changed their story. They then claimed employees did not know until the next day that a crime had been committed—another lie!

Disney Cruise Line security personnel began its investigation of the molestation, which it called an "inappropriate sexual act," at 3:22 p.m. on Aug. 5, 2012. Eight minutes after the molestation, and two hours before the ship departed, the victim and her grandmother emerged from the elevator at 3:03 p.m. and headed toward the guest services counter, where they reported the incident. The child stated that a man had repeatedly grabbed her breasts through her clothes and forcibly kissed her on the mouth as he cornered her in an elevator on the *Disney Dream*. Security personnel were contacted and initiated the investigation at 3:22 p.m., followed by the child relaying the criminal allegations to a cruise security officer.

At 3:57 p.m., the 11-year-old from Brazil led the officer to the spot where she encountered the suspect. The girl "appeared to be uncomfortable when she walked to the elevator where the crew member touched and kissed her," the security officer wrote in her report. The officer then retrieved and reviewed the video from the elevator lobby outside the elevator where the attack occurred. The footage confirmed the actions of a uniformed crew member, a dining-room server from India, were consistent with the

11-year-old's retelling of the story. Such an attack, even through clothing, is a lewd or lascivious molestation of a child under 12, a felony punishable by 25 years to life in prison under Florida law.

The suspect was called to the security office at 7:50 p.m. and he denied molesting the girl, according to the Disney Cruise Line report. He was then removed and kept away from children. The suspect was questioned again by Bahamian authorities after the ship arrived in Nassau on Aug. 7, 2012. Jurisdiction of the investigation was assumed in the Bahamas because the *Disney Dream* flies a Bahamian flag. In a statement to Bahamian Police, the suspect, Milton Braganza, finally admitted, "I touched her on her right breast with my left hand." By then, the victim's grandmother decided that she did not want the crime investigated.

If Floridian law enforcement officers had been informed immediately by the Disney Cruise Line owner (The Walt Disney Company) of the crime and found probable cause, Port Canaveral Police Chief Joseph Hellebrand stated the suspect would have been arrested, regardless of the victim's grandmother's wishes. Hellebrand said his department can investigate and refer for prosecution crimes on ships that occur within

1,000 feet of its shoreline, as this incident did, with the *Disney Dream* tied to dock. The Disney Cruise Line owner had a confidential incident report they did not want anyone to know about. A minor being sexually assaulted on a Disney ship would have been very bad publicity.

If Disney Cruise Line representatives had reported the incident as soon as they found out about it, a Florida Law Enforcement officer could have been sent aboard the ship, notified the on-call detective, interviewed the family and the victim, and arrested the suspect. The Disney Cruise Line owner flew the crew member home to India, at the cruise line's expense, rather than arranging for him to return to Florida to be arrested. Police officials in Brevard County are furious that the Disney Cruise Line owner helped a child molester get away with his crime and go home to India.

Brevard State Attorney Phil Archer is tired of cruise-ship owners covering up crimes, and said he is willing to exercise the State of Florida's jurisdiction to crimes that occur on ships when they are in waters beyond Florida's three-mile limit. The video of the cruise-ship molestation of the 11-year-old passenger sent shock waves through the maritime community. Archer, relying on a Florida Supreme Court ruling, said he wants to file charges for crimes occurring anywhere on the sea, as long as the ships sail from Brevard County and federal authorities decline to investigate or prosecute. It is unlikely that Florida's cruise-ship owners will cooperate by reporting crimes promptly.

Young Canadian Girl Allegedly Molested by Japanese Passenger

Crew members are not the only people on cruise ships accused of groping a child. On July 12, 2013, Leila Kheiry from KRBD-FM radio station in Ketchikan, Alaska, reported that a suspected sexual assault (molestation) of a 12-year-old girl by a 30-year-old Japanese passenger onboard a cruise ship on June 28, 2013, had been forwarded to the Ketchikan District Attorney for review. According to Alaskan State Troopers, the alleged incident occurred onboard the *Celebrity Century* cruise ship while still in Alaskan waters. The girl and her friend were walking near the ship's pool.

The incident was reported to ship security personnel who decided not to detain the man. Instead, the incident was reported to the Vancouver Police Department. Authorities began an investigation and should have arrested the man since the victim was Canadian, but they decided to turn the matter over to FBI agents. This was foolish because FBI agents did not have jurisdiction since the incident occurred in the state territorial waters of Alaska. So, the case was referred to Alaskan State Troopers, who then referred the case to the district attorney in Ketchikan for review.

Trooper Megan Peters explained, "In cases where charges are referred to the district attorney, the allegations have been documented, and whatever evidence affiliated with the case is given to the DA's office and the DA's office will review it and they'll make a determination if charges should move forward into the court system." Unfortunately, by the time the Alaskan State Troopers became involved, the Japanese man was long gone. The local district attorney in Ketchikan had no idea how to prosecute a Japanese cruise passenger, who allegedly molested a young Canadian girl, and who probably would never return to the U.S. from Japan.

Casey Dickerson Convicted of Raping Girl on Carnival Sensation

On Aug. 22, 2012, the Orlando Sentinel reported that a 31-year-old male passenger on the Carnival *Sensation* was arrested on a federal sex charge a day after allegedly participating in the gang rape of a 15-year-old female passenger. The story received international coverage with news stations across the U.S. and the U.K. According to a criminal complaint filed by FBI agents and the United States Attorney's Office, Casey Dickerson invited the victim, her 15-year-old female friend, and four teenage boys back to his cabin, where he supplied them with lots of liquor. Dickerson and the four teenage boys took turns raping the victim, while her female friend was locked in the bathroom. After the two girls were released, the victim proceeded to the onboard medical center, where she received medical treatment and a rape test was administered. According to the complaint, Dickerson denied the charges, saying that "he was drunk and that he did not know when anything got sexual."

Dickerson, who is married, admitted to FBI agents that he had sex with women other than his wife on the cruise. A judge found Dickerson to be a danger to the community and ordered that he be jailed until trial. Carnival officials released a statement saying they would fully cooperate with law enforcement officials. Upon learning of the incident, Carnival officials immediately contacted all appropriate authorities, including those in the FBI. Dickerson was taken into custody when the ship arrived at its homeport. On Dec. 14, 2012, a jury convicted Casey Dickerson of the rape. If Dickerson had been a crew member, rather than a passenger, Carnival officials probably would have prevented this rapist from being convicted using their usual tactics.

Conclusion

Sexual assault is the number one crime on the high seas. Women sailing on a cruise ship should not drink too much. Bartenders earn their living on tips and the food and beverage employees are under pressure to meet drink quotas. Women have to be on the lookout for men who try to lure them with a charming personality to a secluded area on the ship, where assault or rape may occur without the cruise operator's knowledge.

If a woman is raped while on a cruise, she should immediately report it to the security officer onboard the ship (unless, as in Laurie Dishman's case, the security officer is the one who committed the rape). The FBI agents should be contacted by satellite phone and give instructions on how to proceed. A rape victim should not eat, drink, shower, or even change her clothing before being examined by the ship's doctor. The ship's physician should give a blood test, do a complete rape test, and give antibiotics to prevent sexually-transmitted diseases. A victim should ask if she can hold the rape kit as evidence so ship crew members can't accidentally lose it. All evidence must be reported and properly logged. The security officer on the ship should be asked to preserve the crime scene until law enforcement officers can examine the area. If possible, pictures should be taken of the crime scene, in addition to any physical injuries or bruises resulting from the assault. If there were any witnesses, their names, addresses, and telephone numbers should be kept. When a rape victim arrives home, 800-656-HOPE can be called to find out where psychological counseling can be received. A law firm that handles these types of cases should be contacted as soon as possible.

Will the Law of the High Seas Ever Change?

According to a survey conducted by global market research company J.D. Power and Associates in June 2013, approximately 18 percent of people who went on cruises reported experiencing a problem on their trip–and reported being unsatisfied.[2] According to a CNN article dated June 29, 2013, *Disney Cruise Line, Royal Caribbean International*, and *Holland America* ranked first, second, and third, respectively, in customer satisfaction. *Carnival* ranked last in the report of eight cruise lines. The survey measured seven factors that affect a customer's experience, as follows:

- service
- state of the room
- quality of food
- efficiency of boarding and departing on the ship
- entertainment
- cost
- excursions

As long as 82 percent of cruise passengers remain satisfied with their cruising experience, it is very unlikely that cruise owners will change anything in the near future. However, if the kinds of problems discussed in this chapter continue, satisfaction will gradually decrease and more people will flock to social media sites and organizations like International Cruise Victims to voice their complaints. When more complaints are voiced online, fewer people will buy tickets for cruises. When cruise owners begin to lose profit, they might change the way they treat passengers.

In the U.S., it is clear that a tiny minority of people exert a massive influence regarding politics by virtue of how much money is in their bank accounts. Clearly, the owners in cruise-ship industry will not give up laws that limit their liability, whether the laws are fair to the passengers and crew members or not. Unless the political climate changes, it is unlikely that we can count on legislators changing the laws so cruise line owners will be held liable for the harm they cause. However, although we cannot force the cruise-ship industry to treat their passengers and crew members better, you can fight back against the cruise industry in other ways, such as:

- Read the small print on the cruise ticket very carefully before deciding whether or not to buy a ticket. Also, check the CDC website (http://www.cdc.gov/nceh/vsp/default.htm) and make sure the cruise ship of interest receives a 90 or above from the Vessel Sanitation Program.

- Passengers who are injured or become ill due to cruise ship negligence, should hire a lawyer immediately and discuss pursuing a lawsuit. For cruise lines with ports of call in the United Stated, there is a one-year suit limitation in all passenger-carriage contracts for claims of bodily injury, subject to a 6-month notice period to the carrier. 46 U.S.C. § 30508(b). Despite the ticket contract, punitive damages are available in many admiralty cases.

- Anyone raped while on a cruise ship should get a rape test done by the ship's doctor. A lawyer should be hired, even if cruise-ship personnel cleaned up the crime scene. Ship owners are responsible for providing adequate security to keep passengers safe, and lawsuits can be filed, suing for breach of contract (such as a sexual assault by a crew member). Florida law recognizes a breach-of-contract action against cruise line owners when the cause of action is predicated upon a wrongful intentional act. This includes a physical assault or a sexual battery battery on passengers by a member or members of the ship's crew.[3] All of these cases establish that passenger contracts contain implied duties of reasonable care owed to passengers.

We might not be able to change the laws so cruise-ship companies pay U.S. taxes and fly a U.S. flag, but we can use U.S. maritime law to hold cruise-ship owners accountable for all the evil things they do to increase their profit.

[1]In re Horizon Cruises Litigation Nos., 94 Civ. 5270(BSJ)(JCF), 94 Civ. 6147(BSJ)(JCF), 95 Civ.

0374 (BSJ)(JCF), 96 Civ. 3135(BSJ)(JCF) 101 F.Supp.2d 204 (S.D.N.Y. 2000)

[2]Alisha, Ebrahimji (June 29, 2013) <u>Nearly 20 percent report problems on cruises</u>, *CNN*, (Retrieved from http://www.cnn.com/2013/06/28/travel/cruise-customer-satisfaction-survey/index.html?iref=allsearch).

[3]<u>Nadeau v. Costley</u>, 634 So. 2d 649 (Fla. 4th DCA 1994); <u>Commodore Cruise Line, Ltd. v. Kormendi</u>, 344 So.2d 896 (Fla. 3rd DCA 1977), cert. denied, 352 So.2d 172 (Fla.1977).

Chapter 6: Conclusion: Is there Hope for a Better World?

"Horses live on dry land, eat grass and drink water. When pleased, they rub their necks together. When angry, they turn round and kick up their heels at each other. Thus far only do their natural dispositions carry them. But bridled and bitted, with a plate of metal on their foreheads, they learn to cast vicious looks, to turn the head to bite, to resist, to get the bit out of the mouth or the bridle into it. And thus their natures become depraved."
    Zhuangzi

"Boys you got your weapons pointed in the wrong direction
Better turn them the other way
Right toward all the generals and the mighty corporations
Who have sent you to die while they get paid
If you look around you'll see who's your enemy
It's the one you're working for I am afraid
If you gotta go and fight, then you better get it right
It's not your leaders but yourself you must obey

Is it really patriotic or simply idiotic
To be fodder for the corporate war machine?"
Turn Your Guns Around - Kate Boverman and Ethan Miller

Researchers recently concluded that U.S. governmental policies rarely align with the preferences of most Americans, but instead they favor special interests and lobbying organizations. When a majority of citizens disagree with economic elites and/or with organized interests, they usually lose. In addition, because of the strong status-quo bias built into the U.S. political system, even when fairly large majorities of Americans favor policy change, they rarely get what they want. The main point that emerges from the research is the economic elites and organized groups representing business interests have substantial independent impacts on U.S. governmental policy. At the same time, mass-based interest groups and average citizens have little or no independent influence.[1] That only happens in oligarchies, not republics.

The theory of "biased pluralism" is what some Princeton and Northwestern researchers believe applies to the U.S. system. "Biased pluralism" holds that policy outcomes "tend to tilt towards the wishes of corporations and business and professional associations." This theory was introduced after McCutchen v. Federal Election Commission, a controversial piece of legislation heard by the Supreme Court justices, that abolished campaign contribution limits.[2] The justices found how many candidates or causes a donor may support can no longer be restricted. That means the rich make the rules for all citizens. We now have what Americans fought against back in 1776, taxation without any real representation.

Can anything be done to stop all the corruption that created an oligarchy in America? Those who abhor government but love capitalism believe there should only be laws that prohibit initiatory force and fraud and define how violators will be punished. They call this the Non-Aggression Principle (NAP). The NAP is a guiding principle many people may choose to apply in their lives to better themselves or their communities. According to those who call themselves anarcho-capitalists, when one person or group initiates force against another person or group, a victim is created, consequentially the thief or killer should be labeled a criminal, rather than being allowed to control society. They also are against the state demanding property taxes but have no problem with property owners demanding rent. Anarcho-capitalists do not want a monopoly within the judiciary and they advocate for private competing courts, a model for justice used for hundreds of years in England. The Irish did not think much of English justice. The courts that seemed fairest to the citizens got more business.

Capitalism is about control. Those with the most capital get the most control over the lower class. There are no poor without rich, there are no rich without poor. What I'd like to see is equality in access, opportunity, and outcome. I believe horizontal, bottom-up organizing would result in less inequality. The current state is the result of capital-buying privilege. Profits are all that matter to capitalists, and ensuring high profits justifies using any means necessary. Ultimately, it is a game of monopoly that we were born into mid-game with all assets already owned. As capital builds, the entrepreneur is able to procure more state protection. His wealth is then grown exponentially through state enforcement of private property. It's a rigged game with a few winners and many losers.

Anarcho-capitalists believe the U.S. would be better off without any national government. Is a small government better for humans than a big powerful government? Will everyone have access to healthcare if those in governmental positions do not provide it for all its citizens? What if governments are just natural functions of the market? What anarcho-capitalists do not understand is when the demand for power and influence arises, people representing different governments naturally arise in an open market to meet that demand. Anarchy might be achievable, but it would definitely be a temporary state.

Anarcho-capitalists cherish freedom far more than I do. They are like little birds that love to fly. They find their own food and protect themselves from the hawks that want to eat them. I would prefer to live in a little cage where food and water is provided for me by my loving owner. Nobody can harm me inside the cage. I can no longer fly, but I don't mind because all the danger is gone. I would sing loudly from my cage because I am happy to be safe. Anarcho-capitalists do not cherish safety and think they can defend themselves from everyone who wants to harm them. To them, morality is nothing more than an appropriate code of social conduct. They are convinced people should be allowed to enjoy their lives and keep all their money to pay for what they need with a completely free market and no governmental regulations.

Anarcho-capitalists insist they do not want any help from people working in governmental agencies no matter what happens to them. According to anarcho-capitalists, when government officials take money the people earned, this "enslaves" them by forcing them to help others against their will. They want to help only their friends, not strangers they never met. Anarcho-capitalists think if the rich were not forced to help the poor they would do so voluntarily (they tend to be overly optimistic and delusional). They claim they did not consent to be governed and see authority as illegitimate and corrupt.

Anarcho-capitalists think people who believe they are entitled to what others have earned are ungrateful and arrogant to expect other people to provide for them. They believe extreme inequality is completely fair because people are only entitled to what they can earn, plus what people are willing to give them when they ask for help. They like living in an oligarchy. If you can't earn, you are stuck begging from strangers and writing letters to charities to get help in their world. That is not the kind of world I want to live in, certainly not the kind of world that would please our Creator. Because I am certain that God exists even though there is no proof, I have difficulty believing there is any virtue in selfishness, as their heroine Ayn Rand claimed. There is virtue in helping others, in forgiving others for their mistakes, in showing kindness, empathy and compassion.

Anarcho-capitalists preach how great it is to own your own labor, but what good does it do to own your own labor if you can't earn enough to live above the poverty level? The number of unemployed people is a bargaining tool for all big companies who own the labor power to leverage interests in their favor, which makes capitalism exploitive. Those who own the capital have all the power, and the workers must sell their labor to people they despise simply because they have the money and power. Anyone who gets sick and cannot work is out of luck unless somebody wants to voluntarily help that person. Anarcho-capitalists speak with incendiary language about how taxation is theft and slavery. The main reason I don't want to live in their world is they try (much like conservatives) to shove personal responsibility down everyone's throats. Is it my fault if I get a horrific disease? Is it my fault if a car or truck puts me in the hospital, making it impossible for me to earn money until I am well? Of course not—but it is not their responsibility either, because they are not their brothers' keepers. Many of them claim they don't believe

God exists and even if He does, they don't like the way God behaves in the King James Bible. Therefore, He must not exist if He does not behave the way some people want Him to. It never occurred to these idiots that God may exist even though He did not write the Bible). Anarcho-capitalists consider stealing food or medicine initiatory force and think that should be punishable by natural law, meaning you might get shot for the theft without a trial or jury. Anarcho-capitalists because force, coercion, threat of force, or fraud initiated against any individual for any reason by any individual, groups of individuals, societies, or any government is morally wrong.

I want to live in a world where people collectively help one another and try to ease the suffering of their neighbors, a place without exploitation. A capitalist society constrains workers by forcing them into a position of mutual antagonism among themselves as they compete for a living wage. Capitalists advocate for systemic injustice because the only important thing to them is to secure a position on the side of exploitation and oppression. They don't understand how evil capitalism is and, no matter what you say to them, they do not want to understand why it is exploitive. They will probably call you a communist if you disagree with their delusional ideology.

With nobody in government to create a regulation for you there will definitely be members of a mafia who make sure things go your way. With anarcho-capitalism, I could easily imagine owners of a large business enslaving a population of workers in order to save money on wages to provide cheaper products and undercut the competition of ethically produced goods. This happens today with a profit motive. The most ruthless business owners win, and those who act more ethically will lose money and fall in the market rankings. Therefore, market forces incentivize more slavery, not less, in order to stay competitive. Anarcho-capitalists are right that the capital owners will have far more freedom in their society, but they will be the only winners. It will not benefit the working class at all.

In addition, for private courts to work, there must have a degree of force to support rulings. In a completely voluntary society, what if business owners do not show up to court? After all, you can't force them because that would violate the Non-Aggression Principle they worship, and wouldn't business owners this controversial have well-trained private security personnel to protect their bosses? In other words, you can only punish individuals if they voluntarily go to court, and most won't. The profit motive destroys the idea of people with private courts bringing justice into an unfair world. If I were the CEO of a large immoral company, would I pay more money in making the company ethical. Or, would I pay less money to bribe those who are involved with the largest private courts so they will always rule in my favor? They will gain from letting me get away with slavery; it's a win-win situation for me and for the private court system. The oligarchs rule the workers, as usual. It isn't much different from the status quo.

Anarcho-capitalists believe the only possible way to make the best uses of resources is by the many combined inputs of each marginal person acting. This means being willing to pay the price for a product, which they say coordinates industries and balances their consumption against each other in line with their respective value to society. This is difficult for central planners, because all real evidence about human value is eliminated by the centralization process. A centrally-planned industry is cut off from market prices. Therefore, it becomes impossible to compare the value to society of the inputs versus the outputs to know if the state officials are wasting resources or doing something productive. Owners of private companies know automatically because of profits or losses.

Anarcho-capitalists are tired of violence and force that are endorsed by state officials and paid for by citizens because they never consented to being governed. They believe even though those with state-government positions are professedly dedicated to the good of all citizens, there will eventually be a collapse due to other government officials destroying the market. They claim the freer the market, the higher the competition between businesses both for customers and for employees. This results in all the more power with which an individual has to bargain, both as consumer and employee, resulting in lower prices and higher wages. They think those holding jobs in the government retard the ability of more efficient innovators to replace them and relieving entrenched corporation CEOs of their need to continually innovate and become more efficient to maintain their market share.

What they do not understand is the highly unequal prior distributions of wealth, which characterize capitalist society, contributes to the vulnerability of workers. Employers are able to achieve profitability because they are able to control the workplace. Employers obtain this control through the terms of the employment contract. The problem for all employees is that if someone else can do what you do for less money, you don't get the job unless you sell your skills for far less than what you deserve.

The disparity in wealth ownership is the root of most of our social problems. Those working for the United States Department of Agriculture are part of one of the greatest forces of destruction in the world. Its policies promote the degradation of the earth's arable soils, and the devaluation of healthful food, all in the name of transferring the wealth of the commons to the pockets of the few. There is no moral balance in the actions of our elected government officials; it is biased to the benefit of the wealthy class only. Until this changes, we will continue to see America decline as a nation.

It isn't just inequality that is the problem. Under capitalism, the kindest spiritually evolved people on earth are the most tragic victims of brutality. The most beautiful, rewarding, and beneficial to all cultures and bodies of knowledge are being systematically erased. Vast potentials for innovation, for knowledge, for understanding, for life improvement–are suppressed, strangled, and completely extinguished. This is because of the subjection of billions of minds in meaningless jobs, by the removal and debilitation of colossal amounts of value and energy simply because of the trillions locked away in offshore tax havens.

When most people say "capitalism," they mean "the prevailing economic system in the West" and imperialism is usually part of the definition. Capitalism is an economic process by which capital goods of various types accumulate, lengthening structures of production, diversifying the economy, increasing productivity and making more and varied goods available to more people. Capitalism without people in government jobs is impossible despite what the delusional anarcho-capitalists believe. Today's policies slow the accumulation of capital, while increasing consumption by manipulating interest rates. The system will inevitably crash if we continue to consume more than we produce.

Capitalism is organized around the private accumulation of profit and economic competition. Selfishness, greed, and individualism are rewarded by the workings of capitalism and promoted by the institutions of capitalist society. They are not hardwired into our genes. People's thinking, behavior, values, and our conceptions of "human nature," are shaped by the economic structure and corresponding institutions and culture of a given society. There is no such thing as innate human nature, because human nature is based on how people are treated, which is based on the societal systems in place. If you want to create competitive, sneaky, selfish, greedy people, then capitalism, imperialism, and oligarchy are for you.

Because of these terrible systems, people who are the most vile, selfish, violent and despicable grow stronger every day. They proliferate, expand, multiply, and infect every corner of the earth. Instead of freedom from toil, self-actualization, the pursuit of higher objectives, and comfort for all, we are constantly looking at destitution, misery, genocide, and war. We are living on a dying planet full of dangerous destructive storms caused on by human behavior and the "winners" of this diseased system aren't happy because they constantly want more. Their greed will destroy the planet for all human beings.

Increased production will likely generate more wealth, but I doubt the producers will give their extra stuff to the needy. If people can't afford to pay, stockpiles will go to waste instead of being donated, and the capitalists will want to minimize how much they pay workers and maximize shareholder dividends. That is why many believe capitalism to be an exploitive system. It always creates a permanent precariat class, because without paupers there can be no aristocrats and I doubt the aristocrats. I doubt the aristocrats and plutocrats want a stateless, classless society.

Capitalism will always lead to oligarchy and will never lead to an egalitarian society. It will also never meet the needs of all those who can't produce and rely on charity, because most people care more about their own kids than other people's kids who live in Third World countries. Wasting the mental energy of our brightest people is exactly what the ruling class wants. The plutocrats do not want citizens to focus on limiting their power and empowering ourselves to protect us from their exploitation. No matter how "evil" or "immoral" government officials are, the alternative is always worse. It is also extremely naive to not understand that those in governmental positions are there to defend others like them who are trying to exploit those in power. We have fought for centuries to reach to the point where we have some protections, and it is utterly foolish to remove those hard-earned protections for which our ancestors fought and died.[3]

"But people won't buy from unethical companies!" insist the anarcho-capitalists! This is another common argument for suggesting that people will suddenly be aware of all their options and, therefore, they will pay more for a product made under ethical conditions. Not only does this not happen today, it won't change if those holding government positions do not change and if we keep the profit motive. Poorer people have a budget, and to keep within this budget, they will have to purchase less expensive goods made under terrible working conditions. Private-company owners will see it as more profitable to build and maintain roads toward city centers from middle-class neighborhoods with much more purchasing power than spending money to help poor people who can't buy much. This would lead to more class segregation than we already have.

Voluntary contracts can still be coercive, exploitative, and oppressive if there is no other way to survive except to agree with the terms. With anarcho-capitalism, there is nothing standing in the way of the "haves" effectively enslaving the "have-nots" in this "voluntary" fashion. Private ownership, and its inevitable concentrations of capital, ultimately consolidates power and freedom around a select few and always will.

There will always be people who are willing to exploit others, as well as those wanting to enforce their ideas on those who do not agree with them. Inevitably, some of these people will be able to accumulate enough wealth to do it. When voluntaryists claim that landlordism and capitalism are voluntary and therefore benign, they are omitting the facts of landlordism and capitalist exploitation as well as omitting the coercion embodied by those within these institutions. The fact that an action is voluntary is not a sufficient criterion for calling it moral or ethical.

Anarchy cannot work unless everyone in the entire world is onboard with the idea. That will never happen simply because there will always be those who would prefer to subject themselves to an external authority. Anarchists are very unhappy with the way a statist society operates. They tend to feel various behaviors are logically or morally inconsistent and violate their consent, and they wish to remove themselves from such a society. Freedom of association means giving people the right to "enslave" themselves. Anarchists have no more right to force acceptance of a stateless society than they have to force others to accept a statist one. Whether through cowardice or apathy, or inability, or simply the division of labor, there will always be those who prefer to outsource the defense of their liberties to others.

Anarchy is a logical contradiction, an impractical strategy, a romantic fantasy, a utopian ideal, and I live in the real world. Anarchy won't save our republic. I advocate a constitutional government, a government that protects the citizens instead of the plutocrats. Just as natural laws for individuals have been discovered by philosophers, so too have natural laws for groups. This is sometimes referred to as the "Law of Nations," which has been codified in our Western legal tradition. It also is expressly referenced in the U.S. Constitution.

The greatest roadblock to maintaining anarchism is authoritarians who are ready to use violence as a means to return to the status-quo. Historically, anarchist societies were dismantled through murderous invasions waged by fascists, statists, and other reactionary forces. The failures of anarchism throughout history says much more about the dangers of authoritarianism, and why it must be stopped, than it does about the perceived impracticality of anarchism. To succeed, socialism cannot exist within the context of a single country or a few communities. Socialists must normalize themselves throughout the whole world, just as capitalists have in order to work. Getting everyone in the whole world to agree to a classless society is probably not possible. It isn't what everyone wants and there cannot be rich people without poor people to take jobs cleaning their homes, doing their gardening, and taking care of their children.

An anarchist society must exist in the whole world for it to work. Otherwise, it has to be protected against those in control of foreign states that will likely invade and exploit the anarchist society. It also has to be protected from people representing internal factions that could impose their will by force. History has shown that leaders of foreign states are likely to invade. Fighting wars demands things that are not amenable to voluntarism, including consensus-decision seeking, decentralized structures, and open flow of information. A military force must maintain secrecy to avoid giving the invader the advantage. It must have a centralized and co-ordinated command for efficiency and fast decision-making during the urgent, confusing conditions of an invasion. It must have a hierarchical structure with a chain of command, including whose orders are not questioned when enemy ships armed with dangerous weapons are coming at us.

The profit motive has been corrosive to social cohesion and civil society in its amplification of individualist materialism and rewarding of psychopathic egotism. It is not a good idea to rely on the profit motive to sustain civil society. Some very rich people donate most of their money, but there are not enough of these generous individuals to meet the needs of all citizens. The only way to meet those needs is to get all the hidden money out of offshore accounts. Also raise taxes on those who earn a considerable amount of money and can afford to pay more even if they don't wish to do so. People are definitely not willingly going to take care of those people who are unproductive—it always will require coercion backed by a threat of force. An estimated $8.7 trillion, 11.5 percent of the world's Gross Domestic Product (GDP), is held offshore by people in very wealthy households in a handful of tax shelters. Most of this money isn't being reported to the relevant tax authorities. A register of financial wealth would have enormous benefits, because these comprehensive registries would make it possible to not only reduce tax evasion, but also curb money laundering, monitor international capital flows, fight the financing of terrorism, and better measure inequality.[4]

Those controlling the giant multinational corrupt corporations have their fangs on every continent, extracting the resources and labor from exploited areas to move and sell the commodities on markets that can afford them. This imperialist relationship is a natural stage in the course of capitalism's development. The exploited nations are also capitalist. In the imperialist-exploited nations in Asia, South America, and Africa, what personal freedom is enjoyed by a sweatshop worker who cannot afford education or healthcare? What liberties does a miner have who is paid very little for the metal he collects? If an individual worker requests better working conditions, it will result in the loss of his employment that he needs to survive. Is selling your labor to the capitalists who own everything really voluntary if it is necessary for survival? American freedom is nothing more than the freedom of capital owners to dominate the working class, and individual liberty refers only to the liberty of the ruling class. How much upward mobility do the poor have when a proper education, healthcare, housing, and proper nutrition are out of reach?

Private property is a problem because land is easily monopolized and is it possible for one individual or corporation to own all the land? The land simply has to be purchased, making other humans rent slaves because all land has been "claimed" long ago. In the past we called this feudalism. Today it's called private-land ownership. A piece of unoccupied land is claimed to be owned by individuals who paid a fee to state agencies, to other individuals, or whose ancestors "claimed" large extensions of land long ago. Under that system, every person doesn't have the right to provide for himself food nor shelter nor become independent because one must pay others for using land. Eventually all the land in a region has been claimed and is legally owned, even if there are hundreds of thousands of unoccupied/free acres. Whether it is in the city or in the middle of a forest, every square acre of land has been claimed or at some point in time will be. Freedom is impossible without access to land.

Property that is used to generate profit was created through with coercion and the threat of violence and can only be maintained under the same conditions. Claiming property as yours does not work without enforcing those borders with the threat and ability to cause bodily harm and kill. Capitalism is based on not only the ownership and maintenance of private property, the collection of rent, and paying workers in privately owned factories a fraction of the value they create. The rest of the money is pocketed and reinvested with the business in order to grow. This compulsion to grow is built into capitalism, and it tends to lead to environmental degradation and impending climate catastrophes.

How many buildings sit empty while people who can't afford the rent sleep in the streets? Capitalism always creates concentrations of wealth and leads to oligarchy. That is why we cannot get our Republic back now that the plutocrats have taken over the world.

Violence is built into capitalism and its unjust property relations. The dynamic of domination, exploitation, colonialism, extraction, and coercion is part of it. Destroying countless democratically-elected socialist leaders around the world, as well as violent repression of domestic movements in the U.S., we are forced to endure an endless list of horror, torture, and death. This is because the rich people wanted to keep their unjustifiable and exponentially disproportionate wealth, land, and property holdings. All of this was amassed from genocide of indigenous populations, colonialism, and transatlantic chattel slavery. Imperialist economic violence in the form of sanctions and blockades and political violence in the form of forced isolationism were the main reason for deprivation and underdevelopment in poor countries. John Perkins, who worked for the National Security Agency (NSA), explains how American leaders exploit other countries and make it clear that their goal is not a classless society at all. As long as greed and racism exist, there can be no classless society.

The New Confessions of an Economic Hit Man is an autobiographical book first published in 2004 and republished in 2016. It provides Perkins' account of his career with engineering consulting firm Chas. T. Main in Boston. Chas. T. Main Inc. was an engineering company of the United States that specialized in power generation—mainly hydroelectric power. Perkins' job was to convince leaders of underdeveloped countries to accept substantial development loans for large construction and engineering projects. This would primarily help the richest families and local elites, rather than the poor, while making sure these projects were contracted to U.S. companies. Later these loans would give the U.S. political influence and access to natural resources for U.S. companies. That is why he calls himself an "economic hitman." Perkins describes what he calls a system of "corporatocracy" and greed as the driving force behind establishing the U.S. as a global empire, in which he played a role to expand its influence. He states he was "under tremendous pressure to produce highly inflated economic forecasts, or that much of my job revolved around arranging huge loans that countries like Indonesia and Panama could never repay."[5]

Perkins' book heavily criticizes U.S. foreign policy and the widely-accepted idea that all economic growth benefits humankind. He questions "the greater the growth, the more widespread the benefits" because in many cases only a small portion of the population benefits at the expense of the rest. Perkins writes about increasing income inequality where owners of large U.S. companies exploit cheap labor and oil-company executives destroy the local environment by ignoring regulations to save money. Economic hitmen are highly paid professionals who cheat people in other countries around the globe out of trillions of dollars. They funnel money from the World Bank, the U.S. Agency for International Development (USAID), and other foreign "aid" organizations into the coffers of huge corporations and the pockets of a few wealthy families who control the planet's natural resources. Their tools include fraudulent financial reports, rigged elections, payoffs, extortion, and murder. They play a terrifying game and exploit many countries.

Perkins believes that imperialism has been and continues to be the cause of most wars, pollution, starvation, and genocides. Perkins writes ". . . in many cases helping an economy grow only makes those few people who sit atop the pyramid even richer, while it does nothing for those at the bottom except to push them even lower. Indeed, promoting capitalism often results in a system that resembles medieval feudal societies."[6]

Perkins' job was to convince the political and financial leadership of underdeveloped countries to accept enormous development loans from institutions like the World Bank and USAID. Saddled with debts they could not hope to pay, government leaders in those countries were forced to acquiesce to political pressure from governmental leaders of the U.S. on a variety of issues. Perkins argues in his book that developing nations were effectively neutralized politically, had their wealth gaps driven wider, and economies crippled in the long run. Isn't imperialism great? I guess it depends where you live.

What was great for Americans was not so great for the rest of the world.

According to Paul Krugman, who writes columns for the New York Times, the Republicans are engaging in

> "class warfare aimed at perpetuating inequality into the next generation. Taken together, the elements of both the House and the Senate bills amount to a more or less systematic attempt to lavish benefits on the children of the ultra-wealthy while making it harder for less fortunate young people to achieve upward social mobility. Or to put it differently, the tax legislation Republicans are trying to ram through Congress with indecent haste, without hearings or time for any kind of serious study, looks an awful lot like an attempt not simply to reinforce plutocracy, but to entrench a hereditary plutocracy."[7]

Who can stop members of Congress from doing this to Americans? The citizens - especially Marines, Navy SEALS, Air Force Personnel and Coastguard Personnel, and all governmental employees who are used to following orders. They must all unite and disobey or accept top-down warfare. They must, as Ethan Miller's song suggests, "turn their guns the other way" to stop the powerful leaders in government and corporations from allowing the plutocrats to enslave us and force us to live in a hereditary oligarchy.

For many years, progress has meant retarding working-class wages to increase competition, then eliminating work (closing or moving plants), and now shrinking safety nets for the weakest members of society. Today we have a mature economy, we face diminishing returns, difficulty in increasing aggregate demand (for more cars, phones, clothing, computers, etc.). In addition, capital no longer depends on labor or production; its excesses now create waste, and that waste created a gig culture full of part time jobs with no benefits or guaranteed hours. Either we subject the ruling-class oppressors to our collective authority, or we face continuously ever more brutal enslavement as monopoly capitalism and imperialism consumes all it can in pursuit of individual profits for a privileged few. Only by uniting do the world's workers have power against their exploiters.

There is currently a war going on regarding the foreign debt. It is a war that has as its main weapon interest, which is a weapon more deadly than a bomb. Governmental debt is a way to "legitimately" take money from all of us, transfer it to the government, and then transfer it into the pockets of the ultra-wealthy. Will the central bankers ever forgive the debt? Will the corruption ever end? There is evil in the world and it will not be destroyed with mere words. It will require force. Niccolo Machiavelli wrote, "It is just as difficult and dangerous to try to free a people that want to remain servile as it is to enslave a people that wants to remain free." That is the choice you as an American have to make: Do you want to live in an oligarchy controlled by plutocrats, or do you want to fight for freedom?

References

[1]Boren, Zachary Davies (April 16, 2014) Major Study Finds The U.S. Is An Oligarchy. The Telegraph. (Retrieved from http://www.businessinsider.com/major-study-finds-that-the-us-is-an-oligarchy-2014-4)

[2]Boren, Zachary Davies (April 16, 2014) Major Study Finds The U.S. Is An Oligarchy. The Telegraph. (Retrieved from http://www.businessinsider.com/major-study-finds-that-the-us-is-an-oligarchy-2014-4)

[3]Anarcho-capitalism is a Utopian Delusion (July 2017) Steemit. (Retrieved from https://steemit.com/politics/@ozzz169/anarcho-capitalism-a-utopian-delusion)

[4]Zucman, Gabriel (November 10, 2017) How Corporations and the Wealthy Avoid Taxes (and How to Stop Them). New York Times. (Retrieved from https://www.nytimes.com/interactive/2017/11/10/opinion/gabriel-zucman-paradise-papers-tax-evasion.html?rref=collection%2Fsectioncollection%2Fopinion&action=click&contentCollection=opinion&region=rank&module=package&version=highlights&contentPlacement=5&pgtype=sectionfront&_r=0)

[5]Perkins, John, p. 145. The New Confessions of an Economic Hit Man. Berrett-Koehler Publishers, Inc. a Bk Currents book. Co. 2016. Second Edition.

[6]Perkins, John, p. 38. The New Confessions of an Economic Hit Man. Berrett-Koehler Publishers, Inc. a Bk Currents book. Co. 2016. Second Edition.

[7]Krugman, Paul (November 13, 2017) Republican Class Warfare: The Next Generation. New York Times. (Retrieved from https://www.nytimes.com/2017/11/13/opinion/republican-taxes-next-generation.html)

Comments

Dr. Joyce H. Winfield, Writing Resources, Chief Editor

To be informed is to be empowered. Through well-documented research, this book by Sheldon and Associates provides information needed for readers to feel empowered. Each chapter should cause readers to pause and reflect, make decisions, and take action.

Joy Louison, R.N

In this remarkable book, the big pharmaceutical companies are exposed for the criminals they are. **They pay fines and never go to jail for the evil things they do, while millions suffer and often die.** The EPA is slammed for not keeping our water safe to drink. The cruise ship industry is slammed for mistreating both passengers and crew members. This was clearly written by an intelligent group of attorneys who know their subjects well.

Liehventz Jean Gilles, Insurance consultant

This book is a must read because of how well it depicts the state of the economic affairs in America and the rest of the world. The

Federal Reserve is exempt from being audited. The kleptocratic elite has been empowered as too big to fail and corporations have not been held accountable for the crimes committed against humanity. The Associates reveal the truth about the federal reserve, which is engaged in financial warfare that may lead to a worldwide financial meltdown.

Shakhizada Suleimenova of The L.N Gumilyov Eurasian National University

This remarkable, exciting book by Sheldon & Associates exposes America's corrupt fractional reserve banking system and urges citizens to fight back against corrupt legislation made by the ruling class that hurts most citizens. These legal associates explain in detail many of the controversial cases regarding tobacco companies, pharmaceutical companies, and food companies that produce toxic processed food. A maritime lawyer also explains the corruption taking place on the high seas, revealing the evil secrets of many big cruise ship corporations. The writers did a scrupulous job presenting the legal cases, making them easy to follow and comprehend for those without a legal background.

Cristina Salcedo Co, R.N, B.S.N
Sheldon and Associates book gives

awareness of the large threat American society faces in a clear yet eye-opening writing style. Very in-depth and thought-provoking work.

Peter Hines, Author

This most informative book written by Sheldon and Associates describes in detail how the big banks have taken control over the average citizen's life.

Vicki L. Weatherman, Realtor and time share specialist

Chapter 2 is spot on. The federal government allows us to consume neurotoxins in our food while forbidding us to consume cannabis, which has a patent as a neuroprotectant. How dare they tell us cannabis has no medical use!